Communication Between the Sexes: Sex Differences and Sex-Role Stereotypes

Lea P. Stewart
Rutgers University

Pamela J. Cooper
Northwestern University

Sheryl A. Friedley
George Mason University

Gorsuch Scarisbrick, Publishers
Scottsdale, Arizona

Gorsuch Scarisbrick, Publishers
8233 Via Paseo Del Norte, Suite E-400
Scottsdale, AZ 85258

10 9 8 7 6 5 4 3 2

ISBN 0-89787-325-4

Printed in the United States of America.

Communication Between the Sexes: Sex Differences and Sex-Role Stereotypes

Contents

Preface

As the title suggests, this book is about the influence of sex differences and sex-role stereotypes on communication. There are major differences between our sometimes stereotyped image of how men and women are supposed to behave and how men and women actually communicate. This book is designed to introduce you to these differences and explain how they influence our communication with each other. In each chapter, we identify significant sex differences and sex-role stereotypes, explain the implications and consequences of these differences and stereotypes, and suggest some strategies you might use to change either your own communication behavior or some of the images that are presented to you.

Throughout this book, we have chosen to use the terms *sex differences* in communication and *sex-role stereotypes*. As you may know, some other authors refer to concepts such as these with the term "gender"; however, we have found this usage somewhat confusing. Some authors use the word "gender" to refer to biological differences between men and women. These authors, for example, refer to gender differences between men and women when they are writing about how men and women respond to an item on a questionnaire. Other authors use the term "gender" to refer to psychological sex differences. These differences depend on whether people identify with characteristics that traditionally have been identified as feminine (such as shyness and friendliness) or with characteristics that traditionally have been identified as masculine (such as aggressiveness and forcefulness). To avoid confusion, we will use the term "sex differences" when we are discussing actual behavioral differences between women and men. We will use the term "sex-role stereotype" when discussing communication behaviors that have been ascribed to men and women based on beliefs about the proper way a member of a particular sex should act.

We hope our choice of terms will help you understand that, in some ways, men and women do communicate differently. But these communication differences do not mean that women communicate better than men or vice versa. In addition, people often have expectations regarding how men and women should or will communicate in a given situation, and thus react to each other according to these sex-role stereotypes. Individuals may either conform to or violate these sex-role stereotypes. In later chapters of this book we will examine the roles of both people who conform to and people who violate certain sex-role stereotypes.

There are, of course, many similarities in the communication behaviors of men and women, and a great deal of research has been conducted on this behavior. In fact, most books on interpersonal, organizational, and mass communication focus on these similarities. Though in this book we focus on the differences, we do not intend to imply that these important similarities do not exist.

Many people helped in the preparation of this book. In fact, this book would not have been completed without the guidance of two very special people—Ralph Webb and John Gorsuch. Ralph Webb guided all three of us in our graduate education and taught us a deep respect for learning and enabled us to see beyond the stereotypes. John Gorsuch, our publisher, was more patient with us than we had any right to expect. He helped us take this book from a vague idea and turn it into a completed project.

Sue Klaren provided the activities that accompany each chapter, developing excellent experiential exercises to supplement the material presented in each chapter. Try to participate in at least one activity for each chapter. We believe that these activities will help you to become aware of the sex differences and sex-role stereotypes that affect your communication with others.

Dwayne Ferguson read the manuscript for this book and turned our words into the illustrations you will find in each chapter. His drawings are more than just cartoons. Each has a deeper message that should provide you with material to discuss in class or think about on your own.

Our reviewers, Sonja Foss from the University of Denver and Virginia Eman Wheeless from West Virginia University, provided us with helpful comments and insights.

A number of students in the Department of Communication at Rutgers University helped in various stages of manuscript preparation. Our thanks to Clary Fernandez, Alison Bremner, Maris Feldman, Trisha Tayan, Patrick McHale, Sue Cottrell, and Beryle Chandler.

And finally, our thanks to our families and friends who loved and supported us during power failures, computer breakdowns, missed deadlines, and the thousand other things that happen during the course of a project like this. We couldn't have done it without all of you.

Introduction

1

In our daily lives we encounter an ever-changing variety of communication situations. From walking down the street to delivering a public speech in a classroom, we face an almost uncountable number of opportunities to communicate with others. These situations involve both the intentional messages we communicate (such as asking a question in class) and the unintentional messages we communicate (such as a woman being perceived by a garage mechanic as unknowledgeable about cars because, after all, she's a woman; or a man being expected to understand how an engine works because, after all, he's a man). As you probably have observed, in many of these situations men and women communicate differently, and people communicate differently to men and women.

Have any of the following situations happened to you?

You are jogging down the street on a bright spring day. The birds are chirping and all seems right with the world. You've completed half a mile and the ankle that had been bothering you feels pretty good. You start to get a little nervous, though, because you're coming up to that construction site. You really don't like to run there, but there's no way to get from your apartment to the park without passing it. As you start to run by, it happens again. One of the construction workers starts yelling: "Hey there, cutie. Nice shorts. What's the matter—too stuck up to talk to us? Wanna come home with me, babe?" Your mood turns sour, and you continue your run dreading the run back. Maybe tomorrow that guy will be someplace else when you go by. Maybe you should run at a different time . . . .

Remember when you went to see your computer science instructor because you weren't doing very well on the tests? You felt stupid and frustrated, but you decided you'd better see him before your grades got even worse. You couldn't make it during his office hours so you asked him after class for an appointment. He seemed a little rushed, but told you to come Tuesday at 3:00. On Tuesday, you walked over to his office with copies of all your tests so he could look at them. When you got there, a male graduate student was talking to the professor about his master's thesis. The professor looked up and said, "Oh, right, we had an appointment. Well, I don't have time to talk now. Why don't you just see the teaching assistant?"

What about the time you were working on that group project? Remember the first meeting? You decided to make some popcorn because you wanted the group to be friends, not just people who got stuck together and had to do a project. Everybody seemed to like the popcorn, but no one seemed to like your ideas. It's hard to pin down, but something was wrong. Every time you said something, Joe interrupted, and then Fred told Joe what a great idea he had. You really didn't want to do the typing, but everybody voted on the idea so fast that you couldn't say no. Now that you think about it, the guys kept leaning forward and blocking your view. And, of course, whenever Fred wanted to say something his voice just got louder and louder until everyone else stopped to listen to him.

Do any of these situations sound familiar to you? Can you remember similar situations happening in your life? If you are a woman, you are probably nodding in agreement. Although you may not have experienced situations exactly like these, you can probably remember situations that are similar—situations in which you were harassed, situations in which you were ignored in favor of a man, situations in which you were subtly discouraged from participating in a group. If you are a man, you may not be able to identify as strongly with these situations. You probably have not been harassed on the street by a group of male workers. Groups probably listen to you. If you are interested in chemistry or computer science, you probably were encouraged to pursue those interests. But how would you react if these types of situations did happen to you?

This book is designed, in part, to help you explore why you may not be able to identify with the situations presented above. These situations, and thousands of situations we experience every day, are instances of communicative experiences that have helped shape our identities as men and women. As human beings, we are born either *male* or *female*. The way we communicate (and the way other people communicate with us) is determined, in part, by whether we are male or female. For example, in general, men have deeper voices than women because of the structure of their vocal cords. Regardless of the shape of their vocal cords, though, men often talk louder than women and interrupt women more often than women interrupt them. These are sex differences in communication. You can probably think of many more examples of situations in which people interact differently on the basis of their sex. In this book, when we are discussing the differences between the communication behavior of men

Some men are adopting typical women's roles.

and women, we will refer to these differences as *sex differences in communication behavior*.

Sex differences in communication behavior are actual differences in the ways men and women behave. People also may communicate with others differently because of perceived *sex-role differences*. Sex roles are behaviors that traditionally are labeled *masculine* or *feminine*. These behaviors are stereotypically associated with males and females, but such associations are not necessarily accurate. For example, women are viewed stereotypically as less assertive than men. Of course, we all know many women who are more assertive than some men, but the stereotype still exists. It is "masculine" to fix cars, but there are many men who have neither the desire nor the skill to tune an engine or change an oil filter. Nevertheless, these *sex-role stereotypes* affect our perceptions and, consequently, our communication. For example, a male nurse may be communicated with differently because he is filling a role traditionally occupied by women. He is filling a role that is seen, by traditional stereotypes, as inappropriate for his sex role.

You may be asking yourself, when are sex differences important, or when do sex-role stereotypes affect our interactions? Although these concepts will be explained in more detail in Chapter 2, there are three critical questions to remember when examining communication:

Which sex differences and sex-role stereotypes are important factors affecting our communication?

What are the implications and consequences of these sex differences and sex-role stereotypes?

What can be done to change the sex-role stereotypes that have negative consequences for individuals?

Throughout this book we will examine what we know about sex differences and sex-role stereotypes in communication, and we will attempt to answer these three questions. One way to answer these questions is to examine the various contexts in which communication occurs.

Communication Contexts

Sex differences and sex-role stereotypes are important influences in many communication contexts. Being categorized as male and female is one of the most important social groupings. We are all either *male* or *female*. In the majority of instances, when we interact with others they are aware of our sex. In some instances, our behaviors are different based on our sex. For example, in nonverbal communication, women tend to touch each other more while talking than men do. Men stand farther apart, while women stand closer together.

In some situations, we are categorized or we categorize others as *masculine* and *feminine*. This social grouping is based on stereotypical perceptions of qualities belonging to males and females, or *sex-role stereotyping*. For example, a teacher may criticize a male student more harshly than a female student because "he can take it and she might cry." The teacher is grouping male and female students into masculine or feminine categories and modifying the communication behavior based on this grouping.

These categorizations occur in the various contexts we encounter in our lives. Our first experience with social categorization occurs in the family. The degree to which your parents adapted their communication behavior based on your sex influenced your developing self-concept. As a child, were you encouraged to do the dishes, play with toy soldiers, wear pretty dresses, or learn to defend yourself? Were you told how pretty you were or what a tough little man you were? If adults communicated with you differently based on their perception of appropriate behavior for your sex, this behavior affected your self-concept and, consequently, your communication behavior.

The educational context provides another situation in which people react to others on the basis of sex-role stereotypes. Teachers treat male students differently than they treat female students. Textbooks portray boys and girls or men and women differently. Perhaps you can remember those elementary school readers in which Mom stayed home and Dad went to work. These early experiences helped to mold your view of appropriate communication behavior for men and women.

The media also portray men and women according to stereotypical images. Although it is becoming more common, until recently it was difficult to find a television situation comedy in which a woman worked outside the home. Even today most of the employed women characters on TV hold traditionally female jobs, such as secretary, housekeeper, or nurse. For every police sergeant, doctor, and lawyer, there are several teachers, maids, and housewives. And a number of men on TV spend most of their time hitting people with their fists and driving very expensive cars very fast.

The occupational context is another area in which people are categorized based on sex-role stereotypes. Males and females may find it difficult to gain access to certain occupations or to move up within the organizational hierarchy. Employees communicate differently with male and female supervisors, and supervisors communicate differently with male and female employees.

Thus, we believe that sex differences and sex-role stereotypes affect communication in different contexts. The four primary contexts in which sex differences and sex-role stereotypes have a major impact on our communication are in intimate relationships, in the educational setting, in the media, and in the workplace.

Men and women communicate differently in *intimate relationships* like friendship and marriage. Women share more intimate details of their personal lives, such as how they feel about relationships, than men do. In addition, when talking to men, women are more likely to provide conversational support by asking questions and generally keeping the conversation going.

In the *educational setting,* students are faced with numerous sex-role stereotypes. Children read about stereotyped examples in textbooks written in sexist language. In classroom interaction, teachers call on male students more often than on female students and expect male students to be smarter. Overall, males dominate classroom talk and space. Consequently, both males and females are hesitant to take courses they believe belong to the domain of the other sex.

Sex-role stereotypes are communicated through various popular *media,* such as films, television, cartoons, music, and even literature. Generally, in the media, males are portrayed as active, independent professionals; women are portrayed as passive, dependent wives and mothers. Such portrayals serve to perpetuate these sex-role stereotypes in society.

In the *workplace,* men and women face a different environment. Men are rewarded for using an assertive communication style, yet women using the same communication style are perceived as less attractive and friendly. In general, women populate organizations, but men run them and establish the norms for effective communication behavior.

Each of these contexts influences communication behavior and is dealt with in more detail in later chapters. By examining the various contexts in which communication occurs, we can determine which sex differences and sex-role stereotypes are important factors affecting our communication. In addition, after examining the implications and consequences of these differences and stereotypes, we may be able to change the sex-role stereotypes that have negative consequences for people interacting in these contexts.

Our Perspective

As you can see from this discussion, we are concerned with sex differences and sex-role stereotypes that affect communication in various contexts. You probably can think of a great deal of evidence from your own experience that suggests how men and women communicate differently or how their communication is stereotyped in various situations. Many of the differences you may have observed are supported by evidence from research. In the chapters that follow, we discuss the results of a great deal of this research.

Given our experiences and the research we have examined, we believe that there are three important areas to consider when discussing sex differences and sex-role stereotypes that affect communication in various contexts. First, we must know what these *differences* and *stereotypes* are. To understand the communication process more fully, we need to know what sex differences exist (that is, how men and women communicate differently) and what types of sex-role stereotyping occur (that is, how people communicate differently based on their expectations of stereotypically "masculine" or "feminine" communication behavior).

In addition to knowing which sex differences and sex-role stereotypes affect communication, we need to know the *implications* and *consequences* of these behaviors. In other words, how are men and women affected by the actual or perceived differences in their communication behaviors? We know, for example, that women who use more "feminine" speech (such as starting sentences with "I think" or "perhaps") are perceived as less certain of their ideas. Men who use these same speech forms are considered polite. In another communication context, employees are more satisfied with supervisors who use the communication patterns associated with their sex roles. Male supervisors are expected to be assertive, and female supervisors are expected to be friendly. Employees are not as willing to respect friendly male supervisors and assertive female supervisors. Thus, sex differences and sex-role stereotypes have certain consequences that need to be understood.

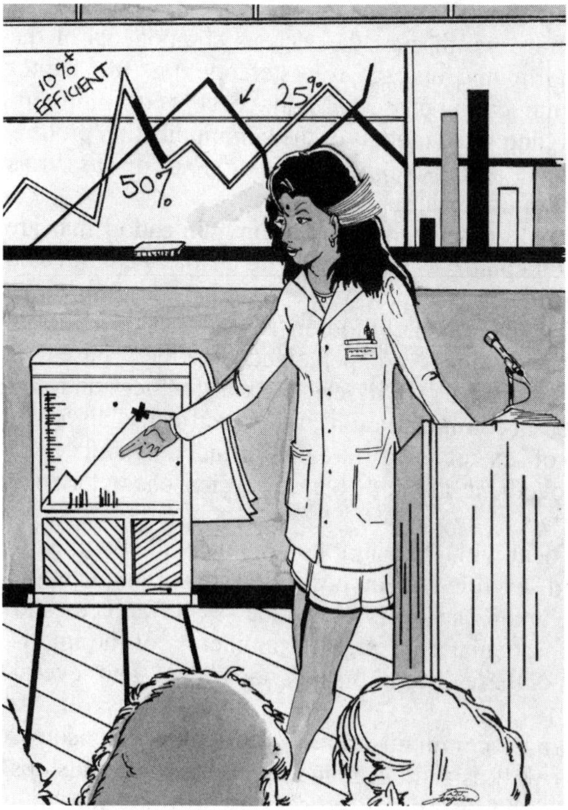

Some women are assuming traditional men's roles.

Finally, sex differences and sex-role stereotypes may affect our communication today in particular ways, but communication behaviors can be changed. We need to explore *strategies* that can be used to improve our communication environment. For example, language that perpetuates sex-role stereotypes can be eliminated from our writing. Teachers can encourage participation from all students in their classes. Men and women can learn to communicate more equally in intimate relationships.

Overview

In this book, we examine the role of sex differences and sex-role stereotypes in the communication process in various contexts. Before we can meaningfully discuss communication in specific contexts, however, you need to understand some basic concepts in the development of sex differences and sex-role stereotyping. To accomplish this, in Chapter 2 we present an overview of the factors that influence the development of sex differences. In addition, we discuss the various components of the concepts of sex role, androgyny, and sex-role stereotyping. In Chapter 3, we introduce the communication process. Major concepts in communication theory are defined, and three models of the communication process are presented. Several basic axioms of communication are discussed as well as the functions of communication.

Language and nonverbal cues are modes of communication that are used in all communication contexts. Thus, separate chapters are devoted to each of these phenomena. In Chapter 4, we examine the differences in language used by male and female children and adults. In addition, we describe how these differences are perceived by others based on sex-role stereotypes. In Chapter 5, we describe sex differences and sex-role stereotypes in nonverbal communication cues. Specifically, this chapter includes a discussion of sex-related differences in encoding and decoding, proxemics, body movement, affect displays, physical characteristics, vocal qualities, and artifacts.

The last five chapters deal with the major communication contexts in which sex differences and sex-role stereotypes influence communication behavior. Each chapter contains an overview of the sex differences and sex-role stereotypes in a particular context, an examination of the implications and consequences of these differences and stereotypes, and several strategies for change.

In Chapter 6, we examine communication in intimate relationships. We focus on marriage as well as same-sex and opposite-sex friendships because communication is the underlying process used to develop both types of relationships.

In Chapter 7, we deal with how the educational context fosters sex-role stereotyping. We discuss sex-role stereotyping in curriculum materials and sex differences in communication patterns.

In Chapter 8, we explore the images of men and women in various media, including films, television, popular music, children's literature, adult literature, cartoons and comic strips, and advertising.

In Chapter 9, we discuss the occupational context for communication and how sex-role stereotypes influence participation in this context.

After reading this book, we hope you will have a clearer understanding of the nature of the issues involved in sex differences and sex-role stereotypes in communication contexts. We hope you will be able to use some of the strategies we suggest to become aware of your own communication behavior and how it affects others.

Suggested Activities

1. In a group of four to five people, list as many differences between men and women and between boys and girls as you can in 30 minutes. List any differences you can think of; do not try to exclusively list differences in communication. For example, males talk louder than females; women earn less money than men; boys are more aggressive than girls. After 30 minutes, each group should write their list on the chalkboard under the headings "Males" and "Females." After these lists are compiled, discuss each item individually. Decide whether the item is a true sex difference between males and females (e.g., on average, males are taller than females) or based on sex-role stereotypes (e.g., women talk more than men do). What are the implications of each of the items on your list for communication between the sexes?

2. Take the list you compiled in Activity 1 and categorize each item in terms of communication context (e.g., does the difference occur in intimate relationships, the educational environment, the media, or the workplace)? Does sex-role stereotyping occur in a particular context or across all contexts? What type of sex-role stereotyping occurs more frequently in each context? What are the implications of your observations for communication between the sexes in each communication context?

3. Have a male and a female in your class role play that they are married and are buying a used car. Observe their behavior and list which of their behaviors are sex differences and which are based on sex-role stereotypes. Have the "couple" re-enact the situation with the male playing the "wife's" role and the female playing the "husband's" role. Which behaviors do you feel are based on sex differences and which are based on sex-role stereotypes? How did the "used car salesperson" react to the couple in

each situation? How do sex differences and sex-role stereotypes affect our communication behavior in this type of situation?

4. The examples of uncomfortable situations discussed at the beginning of this chapter are more likely to happen to women than to men. What types of situations are likely to make men uncomfortable? If you are a male student, describe a situation in which you felt uncomfortable because you were a man. If you are a female student, describe a situation you think would make you uncomfortable if you were a man. Do men students feel uncomfortable in the same types of situations that make women students uncomfortable? In what communication contexts are men more likely than women to feel uncomfortable? Why?

For Further Reading

Chafetz, J. S. (1974). *Masculine/feminine or human? An overview of the sociology of sex roles*. Itasca, IL: Peacock Publishers.

Eakins, B. W., and Eakins, R. G. (1978). *Sex differences in human communication*. Boston: Houghton Mifflin.

Frieze, I. H., Parsons, J. E., Johnson, P. B., Ruble, D. N., and Zellman, G. L. (1978). *Women and sex roles*. New York: W. W. Norton.

Gilligan, C. (1982). *In a different voice*. Cambridge, MA: Harvard University Press.

Kopp, C. (Ed.). (1979). *Becoming female*. New York: Plenum.

Schaef, A. W. (1981). *Women's reality*. Minneapolis: Winston Press.

The Development of Sex Differences and Sex Roles

2

In a scene from the Rodgers and Hammerstein musical *Carousel,* a young man discovers he is about to become a father for the first time. In song, this father-to-be fantasizes about the son he hopes for. His son will be tall and tough—no one will boss him around. His mother may teach him manners, but she will not be allowed to make a sissy of him. He will be good at wrestling, herding cattle, driving spikes, and piloting a riverboat. Suddenly, this expectant father realizes his child *may* be a girl. As the music changes to a gentle theme, so, too, do his fantasies. His daughter will be sweet and petite; she will wear ribbons in her hair and have many suitors. Above all, she must be protected and raised in an environment where she can find the "right" kind of man to marry. Finally, this expectant father brags that his daughter will be half again as bright as girls are supposed to be. Although this is an imaginary scene from the Broadway stage, the sentiments are ones expressed by expectant parents everywhere—my child will embody all that the ideal girl or boy should be.

When a couple learns that they are parents-to-be, they begin to impart an identity to their unborn child. The importance of that identity may differ from one couple to another, or even from one parent to another, but that identity most likely will include male or female characteristics. Throughout history, as couples began to speculate on the sex of their unborn infant, they turned to superstition and folklore for predictions of sex—boys are carried high during pregnancy, and girls are carried low; an active fetus that kicks a great deal in the womb is likely to be a boy. With the development of medical technology, however, parents-to-be may know the sex of their infant several months prior to its birth; as a result, they may impart a sexual identity to their infant long before she or he is born (Lewis, 1972). Thus, the assignment of sex roles begins long before a child is even born.

In this chapter, we examine various theoretical explanations of the development of sex differences and sex-role stereotypes. We then discuss

Boys and girls may be treated differently by their parents.

what we know about actual sex differences, the influence of these sex and sex-role differences, and strategies for changing some of the traditional stereotypes of sex roles.

Theoretical Explanations of Sex Differences and Sex-Role Development

Scholars in many academic fields have explored the nature of sex and sex-role differences and how they develop. Generally, three major theoretical explanations have been posited: biological, psychological, and social. After we discuss the historical background on how sex differences and sex-role development have been viewed, we will describe the three theoretical explanations of sex differences and sex-role development.

Historical Background

As discussed in Chapter 1, sex roles are "the psychological traits and the social responsibilities that individuals have and feel are appropriate for them because they are male or female" (Pleck, 1977, p. 182). Traditionally, sex roles in our society have been viewed as a biological dichotomy—male or female. In recent years, however, there has been a shift from a traditional perspective on sex differences and sex roles to a new perspective.

The *traditional perspective* on sex differences and sex roles is rooted in five key propositions:

1. Women and men differ substantially on a wide variety of personality traits, attitudes, and interests.
2. These differences, to a large degree, are biologically based.
3. A major part of these psychological differences between the sexes results from a psychological process called "sex identity development." In this hypothetical process, males and females psychologically *need* to develop the constellation of "masculine" or "feminine" traits that society defines as appropriate for their sex, in order to have a "secure" sex identity. This process is consistent with, but goes beyond, the psychological sex differences which are directly biologically based.
4. Developing sex identity is a risky affair. Many individuals, particularly males, fail to develop the psychological traits traditionally appropriate for their sex, or develop traits thought appropriate to the other sex. These individuals have profound difficulties in their personality and life adjustment, including homosexuality.
5. Psychological differences between the sexes, as well as individuals' psychological need to develop and maintain a normal sex identity, simultaneously account for and justify the traditional division by sex of work and family responsibilities. (Pleck, 1977, pp. 183–184)

The traditional perspective, then, emphasizes biologically-based sex differences, notes social differences that are learned, and suggests that men and women *need* to be different. Sex-role stereotyping results from this either/or dichotomy of sex roles. Sex roles are placed into rigid categories of appropriate "male" and "female" behavior.

As with any stereotyping, this sex-based stereotyping tends to encourage people to view others as objects rather than as individuals with unique human qualities. Such sex-role stereotyping can place both females and males into inflexible role prescriptions that dictate communication behavior. For example, a recent "TV Week" in the *Chicago Tribune* (Douglass, 1984) illustrates that sex-role stereotyping is alive and well in the 1980s. Robyn Douglass describes what it was like to play both the male

(Carl Perkins) and the female (Carly Perkins) roles in a TV movie, "Her Life as a Man." She recounts that when she was Robyn-as-Carl on the set, her suggestions were taken more seriously; when she was Robyn-as-Carly, her suggestions were perceived as more demanding and difficult. When such sex-role stereotyping leads to sexism—discrimination by members of one sex against the other—the problem becomes a double-edged sword and is detrimental to both sexes.

A *new perspective* on the development of sex differences and sex roles has evolved from studies that focus on male/female similarities and differences, the development of sex-role identity ("masculine" and "feminine" rather than "male" and "female"), and the emergence of psychological androgyny (a blend of masculine and feminine identities, which will be discussed in more detail later in this chapter.) This perspective recognizes biologically-based sex differences, but also *emphasizes* the importance of the social environment on shaping behavior and *de-emphasizes* the idea that people have an inherent need to have sex-appropriate masculine or feminine traits. The following chart compares the traditional and new perspectives on the development of sex differences and sex roles (Pleck, 1977, p. 195):

Comparison of Traditional and New Perspectives on the Psychology of Sex Roles

	Traditional Perspective	New Perspective
1. Extent of psychological sex differences.	Large differences between men and women on most traits.	Some sex differences on some traits (certain intellectual skills and aggression), but considerable overlap between the sexes.
2. Biological basis for psychological sex differences.	Psychological sex differences rooted in biological differences.	Psychological sex differences are biologically based in part, but are nonetheless highly trainable and influenced by environment.

3. Psychological needs in personality development.	Innate psychological need to learn sex-appropriate personality traits and interests, thus establishing secure "sex identity."	Psychological need to have accurate self-classification of one's gender (i.e, male or female), but no psychological need to have sex-appropriate masculine or feminine traits; such traits are learned because of societal pressure, not innate psychological need.
4. Potential problem in personality development.	Failure to develop sex-appropriate masculine or feminine traits, resulting in psychological maladjustment relatively frequent.	(1) Failure to develop accurate self-classification of one's gender, occurring only in a small minority (1 percent to 2 percent). (2) Developing *only* sex-appropriate masculine or feminine traits, leading to psychological handicaps.
5. Implications of psychology for women's and men's social roles.	Psychological sex differences and needs for sex identity account for and justify women's and men's social roles.	Psychological sex differences and presumed need for sex identity do not account for women's and men's different social roles; sources of these differences in social roles lie elsewhere.

Most of the psychological and behavioral differences between men and women conform to culturally-defined appropriate sex roles. For example, every culture has a sexual division of labor (Kon, 1975). Although some of the divisions can be explained by physical differences (men do tasks that demand greater physical strength), other divisions are not so easily explained. In some societies, men are the wood carvers while women are the grain millers. Although jobs are clearly divided by sex within many societies, the variations among societies can be great. Thus, individual societies mold the behavior of the people within that society through the communication process.

June 26

Susan's father arrived today. He will be driving her mother home tomorrow; this is the first he has seen Amanda.

All the thoughts I've been having about the difference between men and women when it comes to babies were reaffirmed with Mr. Koebel. When Susan's mother first arrived here, her natural instinct was to start talking to the baby and to pick her up. With Mr. Koebel, it was more awkward; he looked at Amanda, and he was clearly moved to see her, but he didn't know quite what to do.

When she started crying he looked around for someone else to do something. While Susan and her mother took turns carrying Amanda around the living room, he sat in a chair and watched. I knew exactly how he felt. When Amanda is crying and won't stop, I do what I can to help—but I know, in the end, that it is Susan's responsibility. That may sound like a pretty archaic thing to say, but there's no getting around it.

When Susan or her mother hold Amanda, it seems right; when Mr. Koebel or I hold Amanda, it seems unwieldy. When she cries and Susan or her mother sit for a few minutes without reacting, it seems as if they are neglecting her; when she cries and Mr. Koebel or I just sit there, it seems as if we merely don't know what to do.

I am aware this is contradictory to what we are being told the world is becoming. Women and men, we read, need to take equal roles in the care of a baby. And I'm not saying that the differences are genetic—not exactly. But when the four of us are in the room, and Amanda cries for attention from the nursery, it is clearly Mrs. Koebel and Susan who instinctively know what to do. It is not an inherent lack of capability on the part of the men. Leave me out for a moment; Mr. Koebel landed fighter planes on aircraft carriers during World War II, and he can take care of himself. But when it comes to a two-week-old baby, there's something that has been passed down through the ages, culturally, that makes women think they can handle it, and men doubt that they can. At least this is what I'm coming to believe.

[Bob Greene, letter dated "June 26" from *Good Morning, Merry Sunshine*. Copyright © 1984 John Deadline Enterprises, Inc. Reprinted with permission of Atheneum Publishers, Inc.]

Biological Difference Theories

Scientific research concerning the structure of the brain and its effect on female and male hormonal differences continues to support the claim that males and females *are* genetically different. It is not the intent of this book to dwell extensively on those biological differences scientists have identified; sex differences in physical size, anatomy, and sexual functions are obvious. Beyond these differences, however, scientists believe there are even more fundamental distinctions that separate males and females. According to Gelman and his associates (1981):

> Males and females seem to *experience* the world differently, not merely because of the way they were brought up in it, but because they feel it with a different sensitivity of touch, hear it with different aural responses, puzzle out its problems with different cells in their brains. (p. 72)

Perhaps even more significant than the innate sensory differences experienced by males and females, however, is the variation in maturation rates between males and females. In general, beginning before birth, female physical development advances more quickly than male physical development. As Tibbetts (1976) notes, "this acceleration in the rate of growth is maintained by the female . . . to the age of 17½ years" (p. 31). Although we know the rate of maturation differs between females and males, we may find it difficult to appreciate fully the potential impact of these differing rates. Inevitably tied to maturation rates are skills that may be developed to a greater or lesser degree in males and females. For example, Firester and Firester (1974) describe the impact of maturational differences on the simple, physiological capability of manual dexterity:

> The female superiority in wrist movement, fine finger movement, and manual dexterity continues throughout childhood. At age two the girl is biologically six months older than the boy. This difference continues to increase until by the age of thirteen, the girl is biologically two years older than the boy. (p. 31)

Even with a simple, physiological difference such as manual dexterity—one that occurs primarily because of the maturation process—a variety of social problems may result. For example, girls may be rewarded in school for displaying neatness in such tasks as coloring, drawing, and penmanship. Boys, on the other hand, may be labeled as "messy," "clumsy," or even "inept" simply because they do not possess the physiological maturation necessary to compete with girls on these basic motor skills (Simmons & Whitfield, 1979). Since the potential impact of such labeling by peers and adults can be significant, the development of a child's sexual identity moves from simply being an issue of nature, or biologically-based sex differences, to one of nurture, or socially-based differences. The socialization process that enhances the development of a child's sexual identity is inherently tied to the communication process; communication is the medium through which this socialization occurs. We will examine this concept more fully later in this chapter when we discuss the psychological theoretical approach to sex-role development.

Two other sex differences may be explained biologically: verbal ability and aggression. Some evidence suggests that females' superior verbal ability may be a result of sex differences in the functioning of the brain hemispheres, although much research remains to be done before conclusive evidence is available (Goleman, 1978). That males are more aggressive than females may also be a result of biological differences; prenatal doses of androgen in males influence the development of the males' potential for aggression (Stockard & Johnson, 1980).

Lest we give biological theory more than its due, remember that biology influences the threshold at which given behaviors may appear. These thresholds can be altered by social influences and often are. As a matter of fact, most of the sex differences in a society are learned (Stockard, Schmuck, Kempner, Williams, Edson & Smith, 1980).

Psychological Theories

Systematic attempts to communicate sex-role standards and to shape sex-role behaviors of females and males begin at birth. *Sex-role socialization*—the process by which children acquire the values and behaviors seen as appropriate to their sex—has been examined by many researchers. According to Bandura (1969):

> Sex-role differentiation usually commences immediately after birth, when the baby is named and both the infant and the nursery are given the blue or pink treatment, depending upon the sex of the child. Thereafter, indoctrination into masculinity and femininity is diligently promulgated by adorning children with distinctive clothes and hair styles, selecting sex-appropriate play materials and recreational activities, promotion associations with same-sex playmates, and through non-permissive parental reactions to deviant sex-role behavior. (p. 215)

Scholars interested in the impact of nurturing or sex-role socialization have focused their attention on the acquisition of sex-role information. The two major theories that attempt to explain sex-role development from this perspective are social-learning theory and cognitive-developmental theory. Proponents of both theories posit that same-sex modeling through communication with others is crucial to the process of sex-role development.

Social-Learning Theory

According to *social-learning theory,* information provided by same-sex models both at home and in the media, coupled with reinforcement for sex-appropriate behaviors from significant others, serves as the foundation for acquiring sex-typed behaviors. This theory claims that "boylike" and "girllike" behaviors are shaped by significant others during the preschool years. For example, this theory emphasizes the important modeling a mother provides for her little girl when she buys the groceries, prepares the meals, or works outside the home. The modeling behavior a father provides for his little boy when he repairs the car, leaves for work, or runs the vacuum cleaner leads to the development of sex-appropriate behaviors in his son. Children as young as three can tell you "what boys do" and "what girls do." Social-learning theory claims that this knowledge develops as children model their parents' behavior.

When we assign certain attributes to male or female behaviors, we may be able to observe directly or hypothesize how we will vary our communication behavior based on these assigned male/female attributes. For example, male and female adults were asked to respond to a nine-month-old infant (on videotape) who was reacting to an emotional stimulus. Half the adults were told they were observing a female infant, while half the adults were told they were observing a male infant. Across all situations, the attributed "boy" was perceived as displaying more pleasure and less fear than the attributed "girl." Generally, negative emotions displayed by the infant were more likely to be labeled "anger" when the infant was thought to be a boy, and the same emotions were more likely to be labeled "fear" when the infant was thought to be a girl (Condry & Condry, 1976). Further, the perceived knowledge of an infant's sex makes a difference in the interpretation of nonverbal displays of emotion. Female infants tend to be perceived as more "angry, fearful, or distressed" when adults think they are boys, while male infants tend to be perceived as more "joyful or interested" when adults think they are girls (Haviland, 1977). Thus, in terms of overall dispositional characteristics, infant girls are perceived as more pleasant and passive, while infant boys are perceived as more distressed and aggressive.

The impact of these labels on parental behavior toward the infant, regardless of sex, is apparent. An infant perceived as "angry" is usually treated differently than an infant perceived to be "afraid." A "frightened" infant is usually held and cuddled by parents; an "angry" infant might be reprimanded or completely ignored. The characteristic of fear, which is more often attributed to girls, may explain why infant girls tend to be held and cuddled more than infant boys (Condry & Condry, 1976).

Perhaps as a result of this differential treatment, female infants tend to be more socially oriented during infancy than males (Beckwith, 1972). Observations of infants at six, nine, and twelve months of age indicate that girls tend to be more responsive than boys when mothers speak to them and that girls initiate more interaction with their mothers than boys do (Gunnar & Donahue, 1980). By twelve months of age, girls also demonstrate a greater social competence. As such, girls direct more positive communication behaviors and more proximity-seeking responses to their mothers than do boys (Klein & Durfee, 1978). Finally, tests designed to measure levels of positive involvement during interactions between seventeen-month-old infants and their mothers indicate that girls demonstrate a higher level of positive involvement (Clarke-Stewart, 1973). At various stages throughout infancy, then, girls are perceived to be more socially oriented than boys. This characteristic is attributed to girls during infancy because of their perceived ability to initiate more interaction, to demonstrate more positive involvement behaviors, and to direct more proximity-seeking responses toward mothers than do boys.

As infants begin to develop the turn-taking skills of conversation, parents again relate differently to boys than they do to girls. In a study of parents interacting with their nineteen-month-old infants, fathers spoke less and took fewer conversational turns with both boys and girls than did mothers. While speech patterns, such as average length of response or use of directives, questions, and repetitions, do not differ between mothers and fathers in these interactions, parents, in general, take more conversational turns with boys than they do with girls (Golinkoff & Ames, 1979). These turn-taking patterns in infant/parent conversation reinforce two important sex-role expectations: (1) fathers, as male role models, do not engage in as much verbal interplay with infants of either sex as do mothers as female role models; and (2) girls are more verbal and in less need of parental intervention.

As children grow, these differences continue. Conversational interaction observed between two-year-olds and their mothers indicates that compared to mothers of boys, mothers of girls talk more, ask more questions, repeat their daughters' utterances more often, and use longer utterances. As a result, mothers are more actively engaged in verbal interaction with their daughters than they are with their sons. This differential treatment of boys and girls may be attributed to two basic sex-role expectations: (1) a general sex-role expectation that girls should be more verbal than boys; and (2) a general sex-role expectation that boys should be encouraged to move away from their mothers. By encouraging such physical independence, verbal interaction becomes difficult (Cherry & Lewis, 1976, 1978).

Although parents are the primary communicators of appropriate sex-role behaviors to their children, once these roles are learned, they are reinforced by other children. Preschoolers take advantage of opportunities to shape each other's behavior. From about three years of age, children both reinforce their peers for sex-appropriate behaviors and punish their peers for sex-inappropriate behaviors (Lamb & Roopnarine, 1979). Boys are more likely than girls to administer both positive and negative reinforcements for sex-related behaviors. Positive reinforcements for sex-appropriate behavior are more common than punishment; further, boys are more likely to be positively reinforced by peers for male-typed behaviors than girls, while girls are more likely to be positively reinforced by peers for female-typed behaviors than boys (Fagot, 1978). Because a clear sense of sex-role identity is established by three years of age, positive reinforcement for male-typed activities is more effective for boys, while positive reinforcement for female-typed activities is more effective for girls.

Cognitive-Developmental Theory

From a slightly different perspective, *cognitive-developmental theory* claims that a child's concept of sex role—what is "masculine" and "feminine"—develops in stages until five or six years of age. At that time, proponents of this theory suggest, the child recognizes sex roles as stable variables that remain constant regardless of changes in external characteristics such as clothing or hairstyle. Ruble, Balaban, and Cooper (1981) explain the importance of this sex-role constancy when they write that "this stage of gender [sex-role] constancy is thought to be critical; specifically, it is assumed that children become interested in same-sex models and perceive sex-appropriate behaviors as reinforcing because of the newly acquired sense of inevitability of their gender [sex-role], rather than the reverse" (pp. 667–668). Unlike social-learning theory, cognitive-developmental theory posits that constancy is attained at a specific point in time during sex-role development; when this occurs, the child's role shifts from one of passive receiver of sex-role reinforcement to one of active seeker of sex-role reinforcement. This theory reinforces Maccoby and Jacklin's (1974) observation that the process of imitation is crucial to the child who actively seeks sex-role information. Once a child has established a sense of sex-role constancy, she or he begins to seek out same-sex behavior to imitate.

Regardless of the timing of this developmental process and regardless of whether it is viewed as primarily passive or active, the acquisition of sex roles has much of its basis in the communication process. Significant others who provide appropriate sex-role modeling or who are actively sought as role models do so through the process of communication.

Thompson (1975) observed toddlers at twenty-four, thirty, and thirty-six months of age to assess the extent to which sex-identified labels and sex-role development occur at each age. Children as young as two years old possess the ability to identify sex differences; two-year-olds are capable of discriminating between the sexes even when they see pictures of females with "masculine" characteristics such as short hair or pants. At thirty months of age, toddlers are able to identify the two sexes and to use the pronouns "he" and "she" correctly when identifying a specific sex. In addition, toddlers are able to sort their own picture into the correct sex-based classification and, while they do not express a preference for same-sex or opposite-sex labels, toddlers identify such objects as household articles and clothing using sex-typed labels. For example, the broom belongs to the woman and the hammer belongs to the man.

Three-year-olds are quite confident of another person's sex, are clearly able to identify their own sex, and are certain of some cultural sex-role stereotyping. Unlike their younger counterparts, however, three-year-olds consistently express a preference for same-sex rather than opposite-sex labels as well as objects associated with those labels. For example, toddlers consistently select the adjective "good" as an appropriate label to be attached to same-sex labels and objects. By three years of age, toddlers both accept and prefer their sex label ("he" or "she").

Social Roles Theories

Some scholars have examined sex-role development in terms of the learning of roles and role-behavior rather than the learning of individual or discrete behaviors, such as aggression or verbal ability. *Roles* are a set of behavior patterns that define the expected behavior for individuals in a given position or status. All roles have a complementary role associated with them. For example, one must have a wife to be a husband, a teacher to be a student, an employer to be an employee.

Two strands of thought are distinguishable in the social roles perspective of sex-role development. One is derived from Talcott Parsons (Parsons & Bales, 1955; Parsons, 1964) and deals with the learning of sex roles in early life. The other, symbolic interaction, is derived from the work of George Herbert Mead and analyzes the learning of sex roles throughout the life cycle.

Parsons (1964), a more traditional theorist, suggests that males and females first develop their social roles through interaction in the family. Parsons explains the development of sex roles in early childhood as an identification with or rejection of the mother. For girls, the process of sex-role development is a process of identifying with the mother. For boys, it is one of rejection of the mother's female role. As a male child grows older, he realizes that he cannot be like his mother because he is male, not female. He must deny his early identification with his mother in order to develop his male identity. This theory was developed at a time when mothers were assumed to be the primary socializing force for their children. More recent theories include the role of the father in developing sex roles in children.

Symbolic interaction suggests that individuals develop their view of self from their perceptions of the expectations of significant others (Mead, 1934; Blumer, 1969). In terms of sex-role development, expectations of appropriate behavior for males and females are communicated from other people. Boys may be told, "Don't run like a girl," "Big boys don't cry," and "Don't act like a sissy." Girls may be told, "Act like a lady," "Don't be so bossy," and "Good girls don't hit people." As children perceive the expectations of others, they interpret and evaluate these expectations and act in accordance with them.

In sum, cognitive-developmental theory suggests that children decide which behaviors are appropriate for their sex role and adopt those behaviors. Social-learning theory suggests that sex-role development is the result of reinforcement or encouragement of appropriate behaviors. Social role theory focuses on social roles and social institutions as determinants of sex-role development.

Sex Differences

How accurately do some of the sex-role stereotypes discussed previously reflect differences in the actual behavior of males and females? Maccoby and Jacklin (1974) reviewed over fourteen hundred studies that focused on sex differences. From their extensive review of literature, they concluded that only *four* primary differences have been well-established:

1. Girls have greater verbal ability than boys.
2. Boys excel in visual-spatial ability.
3. Boys excel in mathematical ability.
4. Males are more aggressive. (pp. 351-352)

Table 2.1 summarizes the findings of Maccoby and Jacklin and others.

These researchers suggest that there are other assumptions made concerning sex differences that are open for interpretation; in these instances, the research findings simply have not been consistent in one direction or another. For example, some of the literature suggests that fear, timidity, and anxiety are generally perceived to be greater in girls than boys, but these characteristics may be more closely tied to the specific situation than to sex differences. Further, some research clearly suggests that boys

Sex roles among children are changing.

Table 2.1 Actual, mythical, and equivocal sex differences.

Actual Sex Differences

Physical, motor, and sensory	Girls are physically and neurologically more advanced at birth and earlier in walking and attaining puberty. Boys have more mature muscular development, larger lungs and heart, and lower sensitivity to pain at birth. With increasing age boys become superior at activities involving strength and gross motor skills. Boys are miscarried more, have a higher rate of infant mortality, and are more vulnerable to disease, malnutrition, and many hereditary anomalies. Females are definitely not the weaker sex in terms of physical vulnerability.

Cognitive

Even in infancy girls are superior in verbal abilities and this superiority increases markedly in the high school years. This includes vocabulary, reading comprehension, and verbal creativity. From about age 10 boys excel in visual-spatial ability, which is involved in such tasks as manipulating objects in two- or three-dimensional space, reading maps, or aiming at a target. Boys excel in mathematics beginning at about age 12. Almost all children labeled as exceptionally talented in mathematics by the junior high school level are male.

Social and emotional development

Boys are more often the aggressors and the victims of aggression, particularly of physical aggression, even in early social play. Girls are more compliant to the demands of parents and other adults as early as 2 years of age. Boys are more variable in their responses to adult directions. Sex differences in compliance are not consistently found in peer relations, although preschool boys are less compliant to the demands of girls than they are to boys, or than girls are with partners of either sex.

Sex differences in atypical development

Boys are more likely to have school problems, reading disabilities, speech defects, and emotional problems.

Equivocal Sex Differences

Activity level

When differences in activity level are found, it is usually boys who are more active than girls. Many studies find no differences in activity level.

Dependency

There is no difference in dependency in younger children. However, older children and adult females tend to rate themselves as more dependent.

Fear, timidity, and anxiety

In young children consistent differences in timidity between boys and girls are not found. However, older girls and women report themselves as being more fearful, and males are more likely to involve themselves in physically risky recreations and occupations.

Exploratory activity

A number of studies of early exploratory activity have found boys to be more venturesome and curious and likely to attack barriers intervening between themselves and a desirable object. However, differences on these behaviors are not consistently found.

Table 2.1 *continued*

Vulnerability to to stress	Recent findings suggest that males are more vulnerable to family disharmony and interpersonal stress. This is supported by the overrepresentation of boys in child guidance clinics. However, further research needs to be done before conclusions can be firmly drawn.
Orientation to social stimuli	There is some evidence that infant girls may orient to faces more than boys, and may recognize their mother's face at an earlier age.
Mythical Sex Differences	Boys are not less social than girls. Boys and girls spend as much time with others and are equally responsive to others. Girls are not more suggestible. Girls are not more likely to conform to standards of a peer group or to imitate the responses of others. Girls are not better at rote learning and simple repetitive tasks. Boys are not better at tasks involving the inhibition of previously learned responses or complex cognitive task. Boys are not more responsive to visual stimuli and girls to auditory stimuli. Boys do not have more achievement motivation than do girls. Differences in achievement motivation and behavior vary with the type of task and conditions involved. Under neutral conditions girls are often more achievement-oriented than boys. However, competition is more likely to increase the achievement motivation of boys than girls. Girls do not have lower self-esteem than boys. There are few sex differences in self-satisfaction. However, girls rate themselves as more competent in social skills, and boys view themselves as strong and powerful.

From Hetherington, E.M., and Parke, R.D. (1979). *Child psychology: A contemporary viewpoint,* 2nd ed. (pp. 569-570). New York: McGraw-Hill. Some of this material is also adapted from Maccoby and Jacklin (1974). Reprinted with permission.

are more active and competitive; however, other studies indicate that adults relating to children encourage and reward physical activity and competition in boys while discouraging the same characteristics in girls. As a result, these characteristics may be more closely tied to the socialization process than to innate sex differences. There is evidence to suggest that even the four differences noted by Maccoby and Jacklin are not as prevalent today as they were in 1974.

Finally, Maccoby and Jacklin note that there are several perceptions of male/female differences that simply are unfounded. First, while girls are often perceived as more social than boys, both boys and girls engage in active, social relationships; there is no significant difference between the levels of male and female socialization. Play styles may differ for boys and girls (girls are more passive and boys are more active in their play), and girls may stay closer to their mothers than boys during play, but these behaviors should not necessarily be linked directly to the socialization process. Second, girls are not more suggestible than boys. Although girls are usually more compliant to maternal commands during their infancy, research that examines compliance during the toddler and preschool years of development suggests boys are considerably more susceptible to influence than are girls. Compliance-gaining behaviors typically associated with suggestibility, then, may be more closely related to the issue or topic than to sex. Third, the literature does not support the assumption that girls lack achievement motivation. Boys traditionally have been labeled as more competitive than girls; competition, however, should not be equated with achievement motivation. Girls are highly motivated and use the appropriate strategies necessary for success in cooperative settings. Also, research that explores the broadening perceptions of girls concerning career options and aspirations clearly suggests that girls exhibit achievement motivation in areas such as science and mechanics.

Strategies for Change

An alternative to the rigid sex-role division prevalent in our society is the concept we discussed earlier in this chapter—androgyny. Morse and Eman (1980) argue that the dichotomous biological classification of male and female offers little explanation about why people think and behave the way they do. As we discussed earlier, traditional sex roles have labeled males as aggressive, assertive, active, and independent and have labeled females as passive, subjective, noncompetitive, and dependent.

In 1974, Sandra Bem popularized the concept of androgyny, which maintains that individuals can blend both masculine and feminine identities. In general, Bem identifies four gender orientations: androgynous (high association with both masculine and feminine characteristics); masculine (high association with masculine and low association with feminine characteristics); feminine (high association with feminine and low association with masculine characteristics); and undifferentiated (low association with both characteristics). A variety of studies have used Bem's measure of psychological orientation and found it to be more appropriate than sex when measuring communication similarities and differences.

Most notably, much research has focused on the relationships among sex, sex role, and social influence. Findings have indicated that "feminine" people, regardless of biological sex, are more likely to use tears, emotional alteration, and subtlety to influence others. "Feminine" females, "masculine" males, and androgynous people tend to have a higher need for approval than cross-sex-typed persons; in addition, androgynous and masculine people receive more positive peer evaluations than feminine people (Falbo, 1977). Androgyny and masculinity are more closely associated with self-esteem, body satisfaction, and sexual satisfaction than femininity (Kimlicka, Cross & Tarnai, 1983).

In evaluating individuals' performances in interpersonal situations, the use of sex-role orientations has provided more insight than merely knowing the biological sex of the participants. Since complex interpersonal situations apparently require the use of well-integrated masculine and feminine social skills, androgynous individuals are highly effective in interpersonal situations, and undifferentiated individuals are highly ineffective. For example, androgynous males are able to use warm, complementary social behaviors when these affective responses are necessary; androgynous females are able to use effective refusal social skills when faced with unreasonable requests from others (Kelly, O'Brien & Hosford, 1981). The ability to blend both "masculine" and "feminine" qualities when necessary in interpersonal situations maximizes interpersonal effectiveness.

Several communication variables have been studied in relationship to androgyny. For example, females and androgynous males tend to disclose more information about themselves than "masculine" males (Greenblatt, Hasenauer & Freimuth, 1980). In addition, androgynous females and males report less communication apprehension than "feminine" females (Greenblatt et al., 1980).

Some research focuses on the impact of sex-role-appropriate communication behaviors as opposed to sex-role-inappropriate communication behaviors, regardless of biological sex. In general, individuals exhibiting sex-role-appropriate traits ("feminine" females and "masculine" males) compared to people with sex-role-inappropriate traits ("masculine" females and "feminine" males) are evaluated more favorably by others. Specifically, "masculine" males and "feminine" females are viewed as better adjusted, more likeable, and more competent communicators than "feminine" males or "masculine" females (Harris, 1977; Stoppard & Kalin, 1983). Studies comparing males and females who use sex-role-appropriate language (verbal and nonverbal) with males and females who use sex-role-inappropriate language also have produced some interesting findings. People who use "female" language features are seen as more credible; people who use "male" language features are consistently perceived as more extroverted. Thus, perceptions of a communicator are not based on biological sex but on the use of "male" and "female" language (Berryman-Fink & Wilcox, 1983). (This topic will be discussed further in Chapter 4.)

Much of the research in communication has shifted away from distinguishing male/female differences based on biological sex and instead has shifted toward sex-role differences based on the psychological orientations

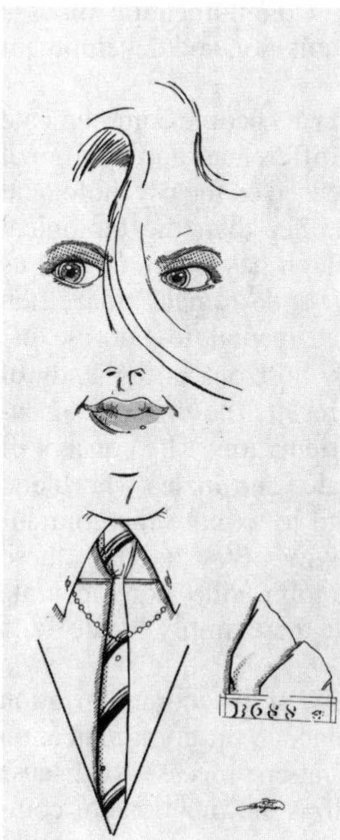

Androgyny is a popular concept.

of masculine and feminine. From such a perspective, the concept of androgyny allows us to consider individuals who are able to blend masculine and feminine qualities rather than rely solely on biological distinctions. This sex-role orientation often provides more accurate descriptions and a broader base of interpretations when explaining *why* people communicate and behave the way they do.

Conclusion

An integral part of every individual's identity is a sexual identity. Although this sexual identity has its roots in biological differences, which account for distinctions in sensory processing, physical capabilities, and maturation rates, the differences between males and females extend far beyond biological sex. A vital part of the socialization process includes the development of sex roles; these sex roles reflect the psychological traits and social responsibilities traditionally labeled "male" and "female." Biological, psychological, and social role theorists have attempted to explain the process of acquiring sex roles, yet no one can doubt the importance of communication in this process. Communication plays a vital role in shaping and reinforcing both the acquisition and development of appropriate sex roles.

In recent years, research has sought to explain why people communicate the way they do by searching beyond basic sex differences and traditional male/female sex roles. To do so, research has focused on the psychological orientations of "masculine" and "feminine" rather than the biological distinctions of "male" and "female." This research has begun to lead us away from rigid sex-role definitions of "male" and "female" that often result in sex-role stereotyping and sexism detrimental to both sexes. Instead, this research has begun to explore new horizons in the study of male/female similarites and differences; as a result, the concept of androgyny has emerged as a potential sex-role orientation. The concept of androgyny allows us to better understand females and males who blend both masculine and feminine characteristics and to explore the communication behaviors that can enhance androgyny. By studying these similarities and differences, we have been able to provide more accurate descriptions and explanations of human, rather than simply "male" and "female," behavior.

The following chapter presents an overview of the communication process in general terms. We define major concepts in communication theory and present three models of the communication process. We discuss several basic axioms of communication as well as the functions of communication. This material will be used in later chapters as we discuss sex differences and sex-role stereotypes in various communication contexts.

Suggested Activities

1. Place the headings "masculine behavior" and "feminine behavior" on top of two sheets of paper. List as many adjectives as you can under each heading that describe a person exhibiting each type of behavior. Were the lists difficult to generate? Do any words appear on both lists? What types of words appear exclusively on either list? In general, how is masculine behavior described? How is feminine behavior described? Which of these descriptions is based on sex-role stereotyping? How are these stereotypes developed?

2. Find examples of three magazines sold to parents-to-be or to parents of young children. What types of sex-role stereotyping occur in these magazines (e.g., ads for trucks picturing only boys, articles on how to dress your little girl in pretty clothes, advice on what type of behavior parents can expect from boys and girls)? In general, what types of messages about sex-role stereotyping are being communicated to parents?

Using the same magazines, look for examples of more equal sex-role portrayals (e.g., ads for computers picturing both boys and girls, pictures of fathers feeding their infants, articles on non-sexist childrearing). Overall, are there more ads and articles portraying sex-role stereotyping or portraying a more equal role for boys and girls?

3. Visit a daycare center or elementary school. Keep a journal and record activities that young children engage in. Code your observations in terms of the sex of the child you are observing. List as many activities as you can. For example, what types of toys do the children play with? How much time does each child spend interacting with others? How much time does each child spend in solitary play? What types of activities are conducted? How much running takes place? After you have completed your observations, summarize your findings and draw some conclusions about sex differences in play and interaction behavior in young children. Do your findings agree with the research described in this chapter?

4. Sex-role socialization practices have changed over the years. To determine some of these changes, interview your oldest relative (e.g., a grandparent or someone the same age) and a parent (or someone the same age). Try to get a picture of what it was like for each of these people when they were growing up. Ask questions such as:

> What was your family like when you were growing up? How many brothers and sisters did you have? Were your parents strict? What types of things were you allowed to do, and what types of things were you forbidden to do? Why? What did your parents want you to grow up to be? How do you know this?

Where did you go to school—elementary school, junior high, high school, college? Were the schools large or small? What was it like to be a student in school at the time? What sorts of things concerned students? Did you enjoy school? Why or why not?

When you were growing up, who were your friends? Who was your best friend? Describe him or her. What kinds of things did you do with your best friend (e.g., go to the movies, attend dances, play sports)?

When you were in school, what did you want to become when you graduated? Did you realize this ambition? Why or why not?

From the information you have gathered, draw a picture of what it was like growing up in your parents' and grandparents' generations. How were sex-role expectations communicated to them? For example, were they told what career to pursue or discouraged from pursuing a particular career? Were they encouraged to excel in school or sports? Were they expected to marry and raise a family? In general, how has the sex-role socialization process changed over the years? How are the sex-role messages you received different from the messages your grandparents and parents received?

For Further Reading

Evans, R.G. (1984). Hostility and sex guilty: Perception of self and others as a function of gender and sex-role orientation. *Sex Roles, 10,* 207–215.

Isaacs, M.B. (1981). Sex role stereotyping and the evaluation of the performance of women: Changing trends. *Psychology of Women Quarterly, 6,* 187–195.

Kutner, N.G., and Levinson, R.M. (1978). The toy salesperson: A voice for change in sex-role stereotypes? *Sex Roles, 4,* 1–7.

Malone, M.J., and Guy, R.F. (1982). A comparison of mothers' and fathers' speech to their 3-year-old sons. *Journal of Psycholinguistic Research, 11,* 599–608.

McCroskey, J.C., Simpson, T.J., and Richmond, V.P. (1982). Biological sex and communication apprehension. *Communication Quarterly, 30,* 129–133.

Montgomery, C.L., and Burgoon, M. (1980). The effects of androgyny and message expectations on resistance to persuasive communication. *Communication Monographs, 47,* 56–67.

Pitcher, E.G., and Schultz, L.H. (1983). *Boys and girls at play: The development of sex roles.* New York: Praeger.

Sherman, M.A., and Haas, A. (1984, June). Man to man, woman to woman. *Psychology Today,* pp. 72–73.

Simmons, B., & Whitfield, E. (1979). Are boys victims of sex-role stereotyping? *Childhood Education, 56(2),* 75–79.

The Nature of Communication

3

The word "communication" is abstract and, like all words, has several meanings. For example, one textbook includes 126 definitions of communication (Dance & Larson, 1976). Some definitions are simple; some are complex. Some define communication from the perspective of the receiver, others from the perspective of the source, and others from the perspective of both. It is not our purpose to argue the pros and cons of various definitions, but merely to note their complexity. In this book, we will use the word "communication" to mean the process of transmitting and receiving symbolic cues—both verbal and nonverbal. Verbal communication is the spoken word. Nonverbal communication consists of cues that are not words. These nonverbal symbolic cues include proxemics (the use of space), physical characteristics (such as height, weight, facial features), artifacts (such as jewelry, make-up, clothing), body movement, touching behavior, and paralanguage (such as voice qualities and characterizers). (We will discuss nonverbal communication cues and their relationship to sex differences and sex-role stereotypes in Chapter 5.)

Shared meaning, created through communication, allows us to convey our own identity and to convey our expectations for others' identities. Since all identities are based, in part, on how people communicate with us, and, as noted in Chapter 1, people communicate differently to males and females, communication plays a key role in the development of sex roles. To explore sex differences and sex-role stereotypes from a communication perspective, we need to begin with a basic understanding of the communication process itself.

The Communication Process

One of the most effective ways to illustrate the process of communication, as well as the components of communication, is through a model, or visual representation. The use of models is not new. In fact, people use models every day. A map is a visual representation of a territory; a pattern is a visual representation of a finished article of clothing; a blue print is a visual representation of an architectural structure. A model, because it is visual, helps us to organize and analyze communication. However, models provide only partial views. A map provides us with only a partial view of the territory: it does not show us all the trees, flowers, roads, or houses that are actually in the territory. Because a model gives an incomplete view, it may make the communication process appear simpler than it actually is. As you examine the models we present, be sure to keep their limitations in mind.

There are numerous models of communication, and each depicts its author's view of communication as linear, interactional, or transactional. These three views of communication are distinguishable in terms of the relationship between sending a message and receiving a message. The linear view depicts communication as one-way—one person sends a message; the other receives it. The interactional perspective views communication as a turn-taking, two-way process—one person sends a message; the other person receives it and, in turn, responds. Finally, in the transactional view of communication, participants are simultaneously sending and receiving messages. As we briefly examine each of these three views, keep in mind that for our discussion of communication, sex differences, and sex-role stereotypes, we will focus on the transactional perspective because we believe it to be the most accurate model for our purpose.

The *linear model* views communication as a one-way phenomenon: I send a message to you. Figure 3.1 depicts this view. The emphasis of the linear model of communication is on the performance skill of the message sender. Suppose you are telling a friend where and at what time

Figure 3.1 Linear Model

the two of you should meet to study. You arrive at the appointed time and place, but your friend never arrives. You learn later that your friend thought you were to meet an hour earlier and left after waiting for you for half an hour. According to the linear view, you (the message sender) did not communicate accurately. Perhaps you spoke too fast or your message was disorganized. Whatever the reason, you failed to get your message across.

The *interactional model* of communication examines the relationship between the person talking and the person listening, and the way this relationship affects communication (Berlo, 1960). Figure 3.2 presents a model of the interactional view. When two people interact, they put themselves into each other's shoes, try to perceive the world as the other perceives it, and try to predict how the other will respond. Interaction involves reciprocal role-taking, the mutual employment of empathic skills. In other words, communication is circular and two-way, an interaction in which the participants take turns being the source and the receiver, or a process of reciprocal influence: you (source) talk to me (receiver) and I (source) answer you (receiver). *Feedback*—signals that allow communication participants to monitor and evaluate the success of their communication—is important to the interactional view.

To some theorists, the interactional perspective falls short of describing what actually occurs in communication. Barnlund (1970), for example, suggests that communication is *transactional* rather than interactional in nature. In a transaction, communication participants do not take turns being the source and the receiver. Instead, each is both source and receiver simultaneously. In other words, a transaction is a process of simultaneous

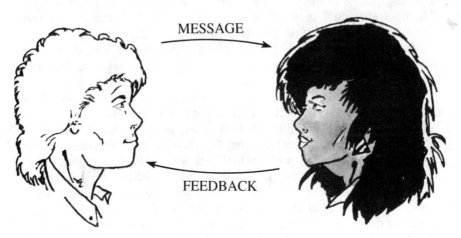

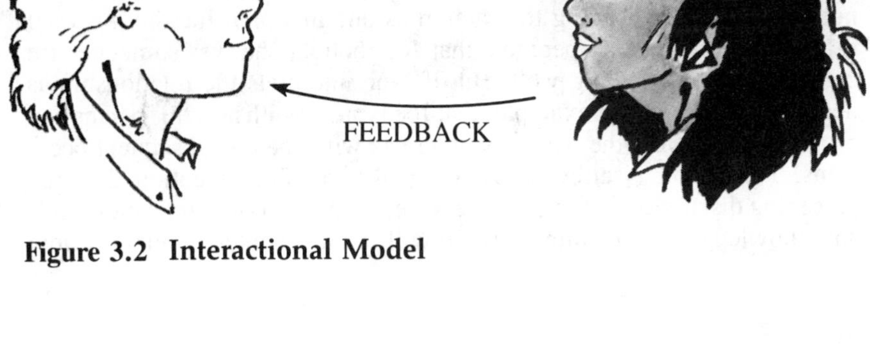

Figure 3.2 Interactional Model

influence. A simple communication event can serve as an example. Jane meets Joe on the street and says, "Hi, how are you?" Joe answers, "Fine, thanks." This exchange sounds simple enough, yet as Jane greets Joe, Joe also receives Jane's look of recognition, maybe even a smile. Both are sending and receiving messages at the same time. As Joe answers Jane's greeting, Jane receives an image of Joe. Thus, Joe is both sending and receiving messages. In other words, designating who is the source and who is the receiver is quite difficult. Like the old chicken-and-egg problem, as one person acts as a source ("Hi, how are you?"), he or she also acts as a receiver of the other person's visual cues (nonverbal communication). Thus, the transactional view of communication presents the communication process as dynamic, complex, and continuous.

Figure 3.3 depicts a transactional model of the communication process. Each person perceives and interprets verbal and nonverbal messages sent and received through various channels (any of the senses). In other words, each person is sending *or* receiving verbal messages, as well as sending *and* receiving nonverbal messages. In order to demonstrate the simultaneous nature of the transactional view, participants are labeled A and B rather than sender and receiver. The arrows also suggest this transactional perspective. In addition, the model depicts other important variables in the communication process, such as beliefs, attitudes, values, and experiences. These variables help to determine what messages are sent and how they are received and, thus, affect the relationship between the participants.

Each person in the communication event defines the other person and the relationship between them. They don't just send and receive the words in the message; they communicate how they view one another and the relationship. For example, if Jane smiles when she meets Joe and says, "Hi, how are you?" and Joe answers, "Fine, thanks," but frowns and moves hurriedly on, Joe defines the relationship at that point in time. His words imply a greeting, yet his expression and his actions define the relationship, at least for the moment, in a negative way—he does not want to talk to Jane.

Our perceptions of the relationship message and the communication event as a whole will affect our subsequent communication. Jane may not perceive the preceding transaction as one in which Joe did not want to talk to her. She may perceive that Joe thought she was someone else or that he wasn't feeling well. But if Jane interprets the relationship as negative and thinks, for example, that Joe is angry with her, this perception probably will affect the way Jane interacts with Joe on subsequent occasions. Perception is affected by all of the variables mentioned in the preceding discussion—values, beliefs, self-concept, communication skill, and knowledge. For example, as we will see in Chapter 7, females' low

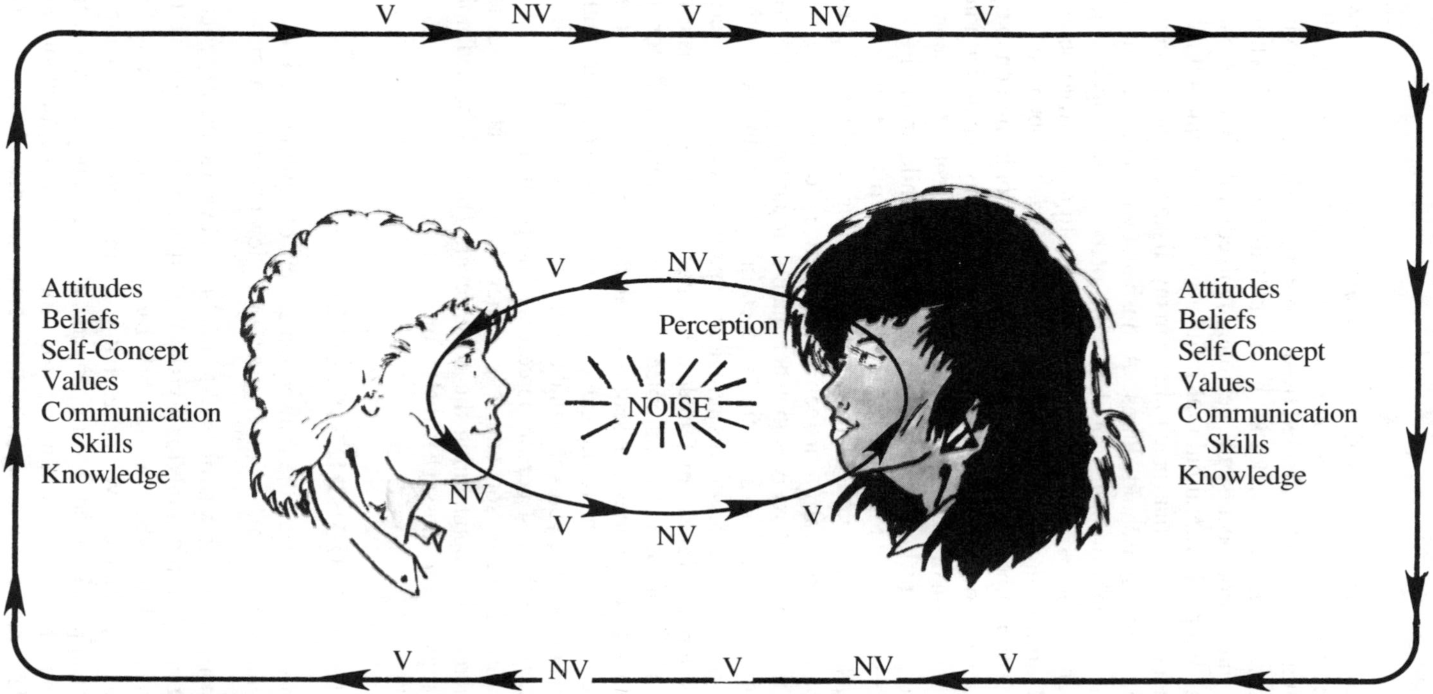

V - Verbal messages
NV - Nonverbal messages

Figure 3.3 Transactional Model

self-concept of their mathematical ability affects how they perceive a teacher's communication with them as well as their achievement in math.

Perceptions also can be affected by the context in which the communication occurs. Context includes such variables as the physical setting in which the interaction occurs, the persons involved in the interaction, the time of the interaction, and cultural influences. It is not uncommon for couples in a two-career marriage to have many disagreements concerning responsibility for household duties. A husband who believes that the home is a woman's domain probably will not be overly eager to help with household chores, and will be in conflict with a wife who believes household duties should be shared because she has a job outside the home. The couple does not agree on appropriate behavior in this context.

Finally, perceptions can be affected by noise, or any signal that interferes with reception of a message. Noise is always present in the channels, and can be physical (horns honking, dogs barking, children crying), but is not necessarily auditory. For example, a piece of dust under your contact lens during a lecture can be quite distracting, or "noisy." Noise can also be psychological (your feelings, prejudices, daydreaming). For example, if a woman perceives that her male companion is insensitive, she will interpret what he says and/or does in light of this perception. Likewise, if a man perceives his female companion as too domineering and values submissiveness in females, he may decide to terminate the relationship. All of these are examples of distraction that can distort the message; therefore, the message sent is not always the message received. If you have ever played the rumor game, in which a message is transmitted through several people, you know that the original message is far different from the message the last person perceives. The problem here is one of additive noise. Each person adds his or her noise to that of the next person, increasingly heightening the noise level. This heightened noise level accounts for the message's distortion.

Axioms of Communication

To help you understand the transactional view of communication, this section includes five axioms of the transactional view of communication.

1. Communication is a process. Many of us have had the experience of moving and then returning for a visit. We expect everything to be the same, to just pick up where we left off. But we are disappointed to find that things have changed. We have changed; our friends have changed; our relationships with them have changed. We may enjoy the visit, but it is just not the same. Communication, like life, is unrepeatable and irreversible. Our communication is different; time has passed and our relationship with the other person has changed. Thus, communication is a process; it is dynamic and ever-changing. Communication does not take place in a vacuum; each person is influenced by time, place, circumstances, and the other person or persons in the communication event.

2. Communication is complex. Whenever two people communicate there are actually six people present: who you think you are, who your partner thinks you are, who you think your partner thinks you are, and the three equivalent "persons" of your partner.

All of these perceptions enter into the messages you send and the messages you receive. If Sam perceives that Jill can influence his chances for promotion, he will communicate with her differently than if he perceives she has no power over his career. Sam's communication also is affected by his perception of himself and how he perceives Jill. A similar situation exists for Jill. Remember that in addition to these six "persons," the variables of time, place, and circumstances also affect Sam and Jill's communcation (see figure 3.4).

3. Messages, not meanings, are communicated. In David Berlo's words, "Communication does not consist of the transmission of meanings. Meanings are not transmitted, not transferable, and meanings are not the message; they are the message-user" (1960, p. 175). Meanings are in people, not in words. When someone says, "What a pig," a message has been transmitted, but not a meaning. Perhaps you visualize a four-legged animal. Someone else receiving the same message might visualize a police officer; another might visualize a sloppy eater. Thus, the meaning wasn't transmitted, only the message. Each person receiving the message puts a meaning to the message—perhaps the same meaning the source intended, perhaps not.

4. You cannot not communicate. Whenever you are perceived by another person, you communicate. This tenet suggests the importance of nonverbal communication. For example, when several people in an elevator together do not speak to each other and avoid each other's glance, they very clearly communicate their desire not to have any contact with the others in the elevator.

5. All communication has two messages—a content message (a linguistic message) and a relational message (a message that tells how you view the relationship). Often the content is communicated primarily through the verbal channel, the relational message through the nonverbal channel. For example, if you are conversing with a close friend (content message), your relaxed posture, close seating arrangement, and frequent eye contact (relational message) communicate that you feel comfortable with the relationship.

Figure 3.4 Perceptions in the communication process.

Communication Functions and Contexts

In additional to the three views of communication, understanding the communication process requires a knowledge of two additional concepts—communication functions and communication contexts.

Communication Functions

Functions (Allen & Brown, 1976) refer to our reasons, or purposes, for communicating. These purposes include:

Informing: The major purpose of informing is to secure or share information. Informing activities include receiving information, questioning, naming, acknowledging, and comprehending. When you listen to a lecture or tell someone about an incident that happened to you, you are using the informing function.

Controlling: This function involves persuasion, both trying to persuade and being persuaded. Often this function is associated closely with message senders. Listeners, however, also must be active participants in the process of controlling behavior through such acts as responding to commands, accepting ideas, responding appropriately to threats and warnings, bargaining, rejecting, arguing, and acknowledging. For example, the controlling function occurs when you try to persuade a professor to give you a higher grade.

Imagining: Imagining forms of communication include those activities involving communicators in such imaginary situations as fantasizing, storytelling, or role-playing. If you rehearse in your mind what you will say to your parents to explain the dent in the car, you are involved in the imagining function.

Feeling: The major purpose of feeling forms of communication is to express or respond to feelings. Such activities as responding to emotional states, commiserating, blaming, and showing emotional responses are forms of the feeling function.

Ritualizing: Ritualizing forms of communication are the primary means of facilitating interactions socially and of maintaining relationships. These acts include greeting, taking turns in conversations, and participating in social amenities.

Communication Contexts

As we noted in Chapter 1, to fully understand the communication process, we need to consider not only the functions of communication, but also the varying situations in which communication occurs. These communication contexts include:

Intrapersonal: This context involves "talking" to oneself, including self-analysis, setting goals, rationalizing, praising, blaming, and creating self-concepts.

Interpersonal: This context is communication between two people or in small, informal gatherings. Activities include interacting with friends or parents, and formal and informal interviewing situations.

Small Groups: This context involves small groups of people (from five to ten), interacting in a face-to-face situation, who have an awareness of a group identity. These groups include families, peer groupings, athletic groups, and committees.

Public: Public communication involves presentations delivered before larger groups of people, including public speeches, lectures, court deliberations, and legislative deliberations.

Media: This is communication from one person transmitted to another through some intervening technology, such as radio, television, or film.

Organizations: This context involves communication within complex organizations that are structured to complete some task or provide some type of service.

In the remaining chapters of this book, we will discuss these contexts of communication and how they relate to sex differences and sex roles.

Conclusion

This book focuses on the function of sex differences and sex roles in the process of communication in various contexts. This chapter has focused on the communication process. Three views of communication—linear, interactional, and transactional—were presented. In addition, five axioms of communication were discussed. Finally, the concepts of communication functions and communication competence were introduced. In subsequent chapters we will use the concepts in this basic introduction to communication to explain how the process of communication is influenced by sex differences and sex-role stereotyping.

Suggested Activities

1. As discussed in this chapter, there are five communication functions (informing, controlling, imagining, feeling, and ritualizing) and six communication contexts (intrapersonal, interpersonal, small groups, public,

media, and organizations). List the five communication functions across a sheet of paper and the six communication contexts down the side. Draw a grid of 30 squares. In each square, describe a communication situation you observed or participated in that occurred in the appropriate communication context and fulfilled the appropriate communication function. For example, you were talking to a group of four people at a party (small group context) and one of the people told you that the midterm in one of your classes was postponed (informing function). Or—you saw an ad on television (media context) for perfume (controlling function).

Examine your completed grid and note which of the situations you described reflect sex differences and sex-role stereotypes in communication behavior. Which communication functions and communication contexts are more likely to either create or maintain sex differences and sex-role stereotypes? Why?

2. Bring a picture of the door to your dorm room to class. If you do not live in a dorm, bring a picture of your refrigerator door or someplace that you display things. If you cannot bring a photo, draw a picture of the door or bring in some of the objects on it. Describe your door to the class. What kinds of items do people display on their doors? What communication functions do these items serve? Are there differences in the items displayed by men and women? What types of sex-role stereotypes are contained in these messages?

3. List the various communication contexts you encounter each day (e.g., at work, in school, with your family). How do sex-role stereotypes influence your communication in each of these contexts both in terms of how you communicate with others and how others communicate with you? Do others communicate with you differently in particular contexts based on sex-role stereotypes (e.g., customers' reactions to male and female servers)? In which contexts do sex-role stereotypes seem to have the greatest effect on communication? Why?

For Further Reading

Dance, F.E.X. (Ed.). (1982). *Human communication theory: Comparative essays*. New York: Harper & Row.

Galvin, K., and Book, C. (1984). *Person to person: An introduction to speech communication*. Skokie, IL: National Textbook Co.

Littlejohn, S.W. (1983). *Theories of human communication*, 2nd ed. Belmont, CA: Wadsworth.

Miller, G.R. (Ed.). (1976). *Explorations in interpersonal communication*. Beverly Hills, CA: Sage.

Patton, B.R., and Griffin, K. (1981). *Interpersonal communication in action: Basic text and readings,* 3rd ed. New York: Harper & Row.

Roloff, M. (1981). *Interpersonal communication: The social exchange approach*. Beverly Hills, CA: Sage.

Ruben, B.D. (1984). *Communication and human behavior*. New York: Macmillan.

Stewart, J. (Ed.). (1977). *Bridges not walls,* 2nd ed. Reading, MA: Addison-Wesley.

Watzlawick, P., Beavin, J.H., and Jackson, D.D. (1967). *Pragmatics of human communication: A study of interactional patterns, pathologies, and paradoxes*. New York: W.W. Norton.

Wilmot, W.W. (1980). *Dyadic communication,* 2nd ed. New York: Random House.

4

Sex Differences and Sex-Role Stereotypes in Language Usage

Imagine that you have overheard the following conversation:

Person A: I've had a really rough day. My head is killing me.
Person B: I'm so sorry. Let me get you an aspirin.
A: Thanks. I think I flunked the chemistry exam. I hate that guy. He keeps giving us formulas we've never seen before. I'd like to meet him in a dark alley some night. I'd show him.
B: What do you think . . .
A: Yah, get even pretty good.
B: Let's go to a movie tonight.
A: I told you—I'm tired! I'm going to crash for a while and then maybe get a pizza.
B: That's okay with me.

What do you know about the people in this conversation? Describe them. You know Person A is probably a college student because he just took a chemistry exam. He might be a high-school student, but he is definitely some type of student. *He*? Of course. But how did you conclude that? What evidence did you use to make your conclusion? He just sounded like a man, right?

And what about Person B? Is B a male or female? How did you reach this conclusion? Are men usually interrupted? Do they calmly reply to a verbal assault? Of course they do sometimes, but, according to sex-role stereotypes and research evidence, women are more likely to take a conciliatory position in a conversation.

This example demonstrates some of the sex differences and sex-role stereotyping associated with our language behavior. In Chapter 2, we examined parents' use of sex-role stereotyping when communicating with their children. In this chapter, we will discuss the differences in language used by male and female children and by women and men, how these differences are perceived by others, and how language is used to describe men and women. We will also suggest some strategies for change.

Sex Differences in Language Usage

Language Differences in Children and Adolescents

One common sex-role stereotype—that girls talk before they walk, and boys walk before they talk—has evolved into the belief that girls demonstrate language competence at an earlier age than boys. This stereotype may not be true, however, depending on the language function observed. To explore the emergence of specific language functions, uses, and strategies, Haslett (1983) observed preschoolers engaging in conversations. Her research emphasizes some interesting distinctions between boys' and girls' linguistic skills.

According to Haslett (1983), language serves four functions for children that are similar to the functions of communication we discussed in Chapter 3: a directive function (directing actions and operations), an interpretive function (communicating the meaning of events and situations the child witnesses), a projective function (projecting and exploring situations, which the child is not actually experiencing, through imagination and past experiences), and a relational function (establishing and maintaining relationships with people).

Three-year-olds primarily use language to fulfill the interpretive function. Through language, they master information about their environment. In addition, three-year-olds use language to serve the relational function of expressing their own ideas and needs. As three-year-olds use them, both of these functions tend to reflect an egocentric or self-centered view of the world. As children grow to four years of age, however, a developmental shift that emphasizes the projective function of language begins to emerge. Children start to use imagining strategies to create new roles and play contexts. In addition, they begin to use relational functions directed more toward others.

Girls develop these strategies at an earlier age than boys. As a result, girls develop greater cognitive complexity and communicative adaptability in using these strategies during the toddler and preschool years. For example, at three years of age, boys only comment on imagined contexts in play, but girls are able to hold up an object like a wooden block and imagine it is something else, and they can imagine that they are a character from a story and speak appropriately for that character. According to Haslett (1983), boys alter the context, but girls alter "their identity through enacting different roles in their play" (p. 125). When boys comment on the imagined contexts of play, inevitably this commentary is in the form of sounds (for example, growls associated with animals or crash noises associated with cars) that accompany the play activity. Girls, in contrast, use commentary concerning imagined contexts with much greater complexity: they usually elaborate in great detail on the imagined play context and its imaginary actions or problems. Overall, girls are able to rename or reidentify people and objects in the play context, to use language associated with specific roles in play, and to comment extensively on the imagined context. This sequence of imagining strategies appears later in boys.

In addition to using imagining strategies, three-year-old boys and girls use self-maintaining strategies—language used to identify their own needs and protect their own self-interests, such as "I'm hungry" or "Leave my doll alone." As we might expect from traditional sex-role stereotypes, almost half of the self-maintaining strategies used by three-year-old girls emphasize "other" rather than "self." At approximately four years of age, there is a significant drop in the frequency of self-maintaining strategies. This reduction in self-maintenance strategies reflects children's decreasing egocentricity and growing social and communicative knowledge. By age four, children begin to realize the necessity of acknowledging the feelings of others and the rights of others to achieve desired goals. Girls, by using other-emphasizing strategies more than self-emphasizing strategies, develop these linguistic strategies earlier than boys do. According to Haslett, these strategies reflect sex-role socialization patterns that reinforce females for being nurturing and other-directed and reinforce males for being aggressive and self-assertive.

This difference in aggression and self-assertiveness is seen in mixed-sex play groups (Esposito, 1979). Three- and four-year-old boys in mixed-sex groups interrupt conversations more often than girls do. In general, boys interrupt twice as often as girls. There is no difference between boys and girls in verbal behaviors such as overlaps in conversation, lapses in conversation, and conversational initiation. Boys, however, do talk more in same-age dyads than in mixed-age dyads; girls talk the same amount regardless of the play partner's age (Langlois, Gottfried, Barnes & Hendricks, 1978). This difference may be accounted for by the nature of the dyadic interaction. Older boys often use verbal instructions to direct younger boys, who obey and rarely respond verbally in the dyad. Girls are more likely to try to establish a reciprocal relationship, which encourages more verbal interaction regardless of the play partner's age. Again, this differential behavior may be tied to sex-role socialization that reinforces cooperative behaviors for girls and reinforces competitive behaviors for boys.

Children and adolescents, ranging in age from five to fifteen years, learn the rules that are appropriate for friendly conversation primarily in same-sex peer groups (Maltz & Borker, 1982). Since boys' groups tend to be more hierarchical, with language used primarily to assert dominance and to attract and maintain an audience, boys assume different rules for friendly conversations. Boys view friendly conversation among members of their peer group as training for verbal aggression. Girls interact in same-sex groups that are more egalitarian. As a result, girls use friendly conversations as a training ground for cooperation. Their speech patterns tend to reflect a desire for cooperation and a desire to negotiate shifting alliances in the group. These patterns may be related to a supportive goal of cooperation and signaling attention found later in adult women's speech (Sgan & Pickert, 1980). If different purposes for conversation exist between boys and girls, then these purposes, reinforced by peer groups during childhood and adolescence, may help to account for the differences in adult male/female communication discussed later in this chapter.

Although the research discussed above suggests that boys develop communication patterns more conducive to competition and girls develop communication patterns more conducive to cooperation, Sgan and Pickert (1980) note that girls use assertive behaviors just as often as boys do. They analyzed children's verbal indicators of assertiveness (for example, use of commands, instructions, and suggestions) in working together to complete a task. Kindergarten and first-grade boys use assertive verbal indicators more often than girls do, and they direct those verbal indicators toward boys more often than toward girls. However, this behavioral trend is equalized by the time children reach the third grade. By this age, girls use just as many assertive verbal indicators as boys do and they direct those verbal indicators toward both boys and girls. Assertive behaviors are not necessarily the same as the aggressive behaviors often identified with competition, but neither are they the same as the passive behaviors often identified with cooperation and compliance. This discrepancy in findings may be explained by examining the definition of the task the children were asked to complete. Perhaps girls used as many assertive verbal indicators as boys did because boys reacted to the nature of the task. In a task that is defined for them as cooperative, boys may use fewer assertive verbal indicators than when they are interacting in all-male peer groups. Girls, on the other hand, may be reacting to the presence of boys in the task group. Although girls tend to be more egalitarian in all-female play groups, they may use more assertive verbal indicators in mixed-sex play groups.

In addition to demonstrating sex differences in language usage, children are aware of sex-role stereotypes concerning male and female speech. Language characterized as "male" or "female" by adults is consistently identified and labeled "male" or "female" by children (Fillmer & Haswell, 1977). First-grade through fifth-grade children can identify statements that reflect sex-role stereotyped language. For example, according to sex-role stereotypes, a man is more likely to say "It's a nice day," and a woman is more likely to add an intensifier—"It's such a nice day." Children's ability to identify stereotyped language differences demonstrates their awareness of different attributes given to male and female language usage.

Language Differences in Adults

Studies of the language differences between men and women have focused on areas ranging from differences in rate of speech to type of graffiti (see "Women's Wallflowerings" for an example of this material). In this section, we will discuss the research in three of these areas—verbosity (amount of speech), interruptions, and conversational initiation. We will also summarize the research on an area of speech behavior that has been called "women's language."

Women's Wallflowerings

"I Regina love Allan so damn much. If I can't have him I shall die. This is no joke. I must divorce my husband and make Allan mine or I do not want to continue on."

"Dear Regina, Just have an affair with Mike—Edith."

"Regina, run away with Allan. Be happy."

Women's graffiti often respond to one another in this way. In a recent inquiry, Laura Tahir, a doctoral candidate in social psychology at New York City's New School for Social Research, gleaned 517 markings from 54 different women's toilet stalls in New York City libraries, restaurants, and bowling alleys. Almost a third of the entries explicitly replied to other graffiti. For those women, graffiti-making appears to be a kind of collective conversation in a common space.

Until the 1970's, Tahir notes, graffiti collectors reported a scarcity of wallscratching by women, sometimes attributing the lack to traditional female scruples against public display and the defacement of property. Though Tahir has no direct evidence of an increase, she thinks her own abundant harvest in 1978 may reflect women's liberation into more assertive—even aggressive—behavior.

Overtly political messages were scarce, however. In classifying her "latrinalia" into 20 categories, Tahir found that only 2.4 percent of the graffiti talked about politics, although gay rights commandeered another 8 percent. The hottest topic—with 16.6 percent of the entries—was romance. "Abraham thinks of me," ran one; "I think of Abraham."

Many responses were advisory: "Should I love one man just to keep from being lonely when there are so many good men around?" "No." Or,

"Ladies, what should I do? I fell in love with this terrible guy. He's a bum, a hustler, SCUM. Intellectually he's wrong, but I love him. Do I just have to get over him?" "Yes," said one reply. A second suggested, "Love yourself first."

Other remarks frequently ranged into realms of high feeling, such as:

The chauvinistic: "New York is the world's largest mental ward: Commit yourself today!" In response: "New York . . . has the most cultural diversity, the most open-minded liberal people." "What's so great about liberals? They mess a lot of things up—especially government."

The aesthetic: "Dew evaporates and all our world is dew . . . so dear, so fresh, so fleeting."

The flip: "If Batman was so smart, why did he wear his underpants outside his pants?"

The scientifically arch: "Quarks have charm." "If you take them out to dinner."

The admonitory: "Obey God, Read the Bible, Go to church." "And only have sex in the mercenary [sic] way."

The triumphal: "I love you and I'm sober."

The hortatory: "Wages for housework from all governments for all women!"

And the champion response-getter:

The mournful: "1977 losses—Maria Callas, Ethel Waters, Leopold Stokowski, Groucho Marx, Alfred Lunt, Sebastian Cabot, Joan Crawford, Freddy Prinze." Responses were added, one by one: "Stupid Elvis Presley," "Anais Nin," "Thomas Schippers," "Rosalind Russell," "Howard Hawks," "Me, almost." To which: "Welcome back."

Some locations had a tone peculiar to their clientele: sentiments expressed in the toilet of a lesbian bar tended to concentrate on romance and gay rhetoric: "You don't have to have a lover to be a lesbian; a woman without a man is like a fish without a bicycle." Writers in a bowling alley inscribed no more than "Elvin and Violet," or "Lisa and Mingo, '71." Little can be guessed, however, about the class or proclivities of the writers in one New York Public Library exchange:

"Love is the answer!"
"No, Christ is the Answer!"
"But Christ is God and God is Love!"
"Well I'm from England and I don't recall having these types of problems."

—*Linda Asher*

Tahir is at the Department of Psychology, New School for Social Research, 66 West 12 St., New York, N.Y. 10011.

Verbosity

The typical sex-role stereotype holds that women talk more than men. However, research evidence shows that men talk more than women. For example, when men and women are given as much time as they desire to describe a picture, on the average, men talk over four times as long as women (Swacker, 1975). Men use more words per utterance than women do, especially if they are given negative feedback about their performance (Wood, 1966). An extensive review of research found that in mixed-sex dyads or small groups, men tend to speak more often and at greater length than women (Eakins & Eakins, 1976).

These observations hold up in writing as well as in speaking. When people are asked to write a transcript of a conflict between a man and a woman, both men and women give more dialogue to the man than to the woman (Konsky, 1978). Look back at the dialogue at the beginning of this chapter and you will see that Person A has considerably more words to say than Person B. This difference in number of words probably contributed toward your reaching the conclusion that Person A was a man.

Perhaps the stereotype of the talkative woman arises because women spend more time initiating and maintaining conversations than men do. In a study of marital interaction, to maintain a conversation, wives asked five times as many questions as their husbands did (Fishman, 1978). The questions were used to engage their husbands in dialogue. Only 36 percent of the topics introduced by the wives succeeded, but almost all of the topics (96 percent) introduced by the husbands were discussed. Both partners seemed to take for granted that any topic introduced by the husband was worth discussing (Metts, 1984). (We will discuss this topic in more detail later in this chapter.)

Interruptions

Look back at the conversation at the beginning of this chapter. One of the clues that may have led you to conclude that Person A was a male was that Person A interrupted Person B. In mixed-sex conversations, men tend to talk longer and interrupt women more often than vice versa (West & Zimmerman, 1983). This conversational pattern occurs as early as three years of age (Eakins & Eakins, 1976). Boys interrupt girls twice as often as girls interrupt boys (Esposito, 1979). In one study of adults' conversations, 96 percent of all interruptions occured when men interrupted women (Zimmerman & West, 1975). In contrast, interruptions are fairly equally distributed when the conversational partners are either both males or both females.

When talking to women, men initiate more interruptions primarily to control the conversation. Women do not invite interruption by seeming to tolerate it, and men do not interrupt simply to get a word in edgewise; if anything, the reverse is true. After observing adult use of interruptions with children, West and Zimmerman (1977) likened this pattern to adult mixed-sex interruption patterns; both women and children have restricted rights to speak, and both men and adults use interruptions to display dominance.

Conversational Initiation

As discussed previously in this chapter, topics introduced by men are noticed and carried on by other conversationalists, but topics introduced by women typically die a sudden death even though women tend to initiate more topics than men. The following example may sound familiar to you.

Imagine that you are at a restaurant observing a couple having dinner together. For a while they read their menus, then she asks him, "What are you going to order?" He says, "I'm going to have the prime rib." She says, "That sounds good. I think I'll have the broiled sole." After the server takes their order, there is a moment of silence. Then she says, "I went to the mall today to look for a dress for my sister's wedding." He replies, "Um." She continues, "but I couldn't find anything I liked. I guess I'll have to keep looking." He remains silent. She tries again by asking "Did you get the new tires for your car?" He says, "No, they didn't have time to balance them today so I have to go back tomorrow." Then she says, "Are they a good deal? Should I get some for my car?" He replies, "You don't really need new tires. Wait awhile until they wear more." She says, "Okay. I talked to your mother today. She wants us over for dinner on Tuesday." He looks over her shoulder and says, "Oh."

This example illustrates one way in which men speaking with women inhibit conversations. Giving minimal responses, such as "um," to topics introduced by women violates the turn-taking rules for conversation. Since topics initiated by women receive only minimal responses, the conversation breaks down (Parlee, 1979b). Thus, men can control a conversation with little effort by failing to respond to topics initiated by women, while having the topics they bring up accepted (Fishman, 1978). Women work harder in conversations because they initiate more topics and also respond to topics initiated by men (Parlee, 1979b). The impact of male interruptions and ability to "kill a topic" is most likely a reflection of power. As Key (1972) notes, women with money or power are not interrupted. Since, for the most part, men are the ones with power, they are the ones who are not interrupted.

Women's Language

In a widely-read and controversial book, Robin Lakoff (1975) proposes that, in general, women speak differently than men. Lakoff has been criticized for comparing the language used by women to a male standard (Spender, 1985). Her critics argue that she implies that any deviation from the male standard is a deficiency on the part of women and should be changed. From our perspective, if women and men use language differently, that usage is a reflection of the reality they perceive and not a deficiency on the part of either men or women. With this perspective in mind, we will examine Lakoff's ideas, which have generated a great deal of research as well as controversy. Women's language, according to Lakoff, has eight primary features.

Large vocabulary. Women have a large number of words to describe things that interest them or that are generally delegated to them as women's work. For example, according to Lakoff, women use more words to describe colors than men do. A woman might ask for a mauve dress or a beige scarf. If a man uses words like mauve or lavender, he may be considered sarcastic or perhaps effeminate. Although Lakoff contends that women develop these vocabularies because they are relegated to unimportant areas that do not concern men, such as color discrimination, a larger vocabulary can be an advantage in certain situations. For example, people with larger vocabularies are able to more accurately describe their surroundings.

Empty adjectives. According to Lakoff, both men and women use neutral adjectives such as "great" and "terrific." Women alone use adjectives such as "adorable," "charming," "sweet," and "lovely." Although women may freely use the neutral words, men are ostracized for using the women-only words. A woman is in danger, however, if she chooses from the women-only list in an inappropriate situation. For example, a female business executive might be ostracized by her male colleagues if she said, "That's a divine idea!" From our perspective, men are also limited because they are not allowed to use "women-only" words in some circumstances.

Question intonation, tag questions, and hedges. In perhaps the most controversial part of her book, Lakoff contends that women often end a statement with a rising intonation. For example, in response to a question such as "What's your name?", a woman might say, "Mary Smith?" In particular, Lakoff believes that women end sentences with inappropriate tag questions such as "It's really hot, isn't it?"

Lakoff maintains that women's speech contains more hedges, such as "well," "you know," and "kinda," than men's speech. These words convey the impression that the speaker is unsure of herself or of the accuracy of her statements. Of course, the use of hedges may be appropriate when there really is doubt, but even when they are stating facts, women tend to start sentences with "I think," "I guess," or "I wonder." Lakoff argues that women use these linguistic devices more than men do because women have been socialized to believe that asserting themselves is not ladylike or feminine.

Research evidence does not totally support Lakoff's observations about hedges and tag questions. Men do use tag questions and hedges. An analysis of taped conversations from a university workshop showed that males used thirty-three tag questions while females used none (DuBois & Crouch, 1975). In addition, the sex of the listener may influence the use of hedges in a conversation. Martin and Craig (1983) observed that males and females use about the same number of qualifying words, such as "maybe" and "sort of," when talking to males, but males use fewer and females use more qualifying words when talking to females. Both males and females use more false-start nonfluencies when speaking to someone of their own sex than when speaking to someone of the opposite sex.

In a small group situation, when women *do* use tag questions and disclaimers (that is, "introductory expressions that excuse, explain, or request understanding or forbearance"), they are perceived less positively and are less influential than women who state their views more directly (Bradley, 1981). Males in small group situations are viewed as intelligent and well-informed even if they fail to support their arguments or if they use verbal qualifiers (statements such as "Well, I'm no expert, but . . ."). In contrast, women who fail to support their arguments and who use verbal qualifiers are perceived as less intelligent and less knowledgeable. Thus, the way in which linguistic devices are perceived depends on whether they are used by men or women. Bradley (1981) concludes that qualifying phrases may be seen as indicators of uncertainty and nonassertiveness when used by women but as "tools of politeness and other-directedness" when used by men (p. 90).

Men may sound more precise than women when, in fact, they are not. Swacker (1975) asked males and females to describe a picture. In discussing a bookshelf in the picture, the women made statements such as "about six books," "six or seven books," or "around five or six books." The men consistently responded with "five books," "six books," "seven books." Even when the men were clearly guessing and not giving an exact count, they did not use a qualifier, whereas half of the time females used qualifiers.

Language differences sometimes conform to sex-role stereotypes.

Intensive "so." According to Lakoff's observations, a woman is more likely than a man to hedge on strong feelings by using the word "so." For example, instead of saying "I'm very unhappy," a woman might say "I'm so unhappy." The use of "so" decreases the intensity of the emotion and hides the strength of the woman's feelings.

Hypercorrect grammar. As Lakoff (1975) says, "Women are not supposed to talk rough" (p. 55). Little boys often drop the *g* in words like "running" and "going," whereas little girls are less apt to omit the final consonants in words.

Superpolite forms. Related to their use of hypercorrect grammar, women are expected to speak more politely than men. As Lakoff notes, women are experts at euphemism. In terms of sex-role stereotypes, a man may be excused from the social amenities, but a woman rarely is.

Lack of jokes. Lakoff contends that women do not tell jokes. She notes the sex-role stereotype that women are incapable of telling jokes because they ruin the punch line or mix up the sequence. You may or may not have noticed this difference. According to the sex-role stereotype, women are humorless, yet many women are adept at joke telling. Some women today earn their livings as comedians. One study has even found that college students tell more jokes that discriminate against men than discriminate against women (Pearson, Miller & Senter, 1983).

Italics. According to Lakoff, the more feminine you are, the more you speak in italics. For example, a woman might say, "I really *think* you *should* consider staying in *school*." Although at first glance it might appear that italics strengthen an utterance, in actuality, they diminish its strength by giving the listener directions on how to act. The speaker is not sure that she can convince the listener to do something, so she uses double force to make sure her meaning is clear.

Examine your own experience with the language usage of males and females. Do you observe women using Lakoff's categories of women's language? In what kinds of situations does this usage occur? What effect does it have on the communicators?

Implications and Consequences of Language Differences

We think that the language features discussed above can be better described as powerless language rather than as women's language. The linguistic devices used by women are devalued *not* because the devices are inherently weak, but because women often have less status in society than men do, and the language women use is, therefore, devalued (Bradley, 1981).

The style of interaction in mixed-sex communication reflects male control and dominance. The greater number of interruptions by males in mixed-sex communication, the discovery that men talk more than women, more positive evaluations of male performance, and greater male influence all suggest that sex differences in communication are a function of status characteristics (Berger, Rosenholtz & Zelditch, 1980). Women's use of language that suggests uncertainty, their increased use of such language with men, and men's propensity to interrupt women suggest continued male dominance in mixed-sex interactions (McMillan, Clifton, McGrath & Gale, 1977).

In general, people with power, regardless of their sex, do not speak as politely as less powerful people (Baxter, 1984; Kramarae, 1981). Females use more polite communication tactics than males do. For example, females use fewer face-threathening actions and more negative and positive face-redress tactics than males do. Face-saving behavior is consistent with the polite style of communication typically associated with females (Baxter, 1984). Women are expected to speak more politely than men, regardless of the sex of the addressee or the nature of the requested action (Kemper, 1984). Men, on the other hand, are expected to use different forms of requests for men and women addressees. A man is expected by his listeners to adopt a "ladylike" form of speech if he requests a woman to do something, but a woman is not expected to use powerful language, regardless of the sex of the person she is talking to. For example, a man is expected to say, "Would you please make some tea?" because making tea is a sex-role stereotyped feminine act. It is acceptable for a man to say "Rake the leaves" without the "please" if he is addressing another man. Women are expected to use polite forms (such as "please" and "Can you?") regardless of the sex of the listener or the topic of the conversation (Kemper, 1984).

Other communication behaviors that reflect deference versus power and control are closely tied to the polite communication style. The qualities of language described by Lakoff (1975) and others have been termed "deferential language" to show how they function in interaction. To determine whether these characteristics affect the perceptions of speakers, Liska, Mechling, and Stathas (1981) asked students to evaluate a transcript of a group discussion involving speakers who used deferential language and speakers who used nondeferential language. The students evaluated the speakers who used deferential language as more submissive, less assertive, and less willing to take a stand than the speakers who used nondeferential language. In addition, the speakers who used deferential language were more likely to be perceived as feminine. In general, the students perceived the speakers who used deferential language as having less power and more personal warmth. The authors conclude that "masculinity is a characteristic attributed to those who have been judged as dominant rather than dominance being the characteristic attributed to those who have already been judged as masculine" (pp. 44–45).

The deferential style of communication is closely associated with femininity. For the most part, men use a variety of communication behaviors to develop control in their relationships with others. Because controlling communications is important to males, males are expected to use more verbally–aggressive persuasive message strategies than females do; to use fewer of these messages would violate sex-role expectations and would weaken male persuasive impact. Females are expected to be less verbally aggressive and to use more prosocial message strategies; females are often penalized for deviating from this expected strategy.

Berryman and Wilcox (1980) examined perceptions of male and female sex-role stereotyped language. They note that male speakers are perceived as significantly less accommodating and, as a result, more in control. Berryman and Wilcox suggest that the use of questions and incomplete sentences by females contributes to the perception that females are flexible, and that the use of obscenities, slang, and nonstandard grammar by males contributes to the perception that males are inflexible.

Wheeless (1984) tested the theory of speech accommodation, which holds that because of their lower status women are especially aware of and adapt to the communication behavior of others. For example, as we will discuss in Chapter 5, women are better encoders of nonverbal cues than men are. Because of this heightened awareness, women tend to accommodate their speech to others, especially men. Wheeless asked men and women to respond to several conversational situations. She found that all people use both feminine and masculine language forms, yet, respondents who identify themselves in terms of the traditionally masculine or feminine sex roles that we discussed in Chapter 2 differ in the amount of conversational accommodation they use. Feminine individuals are more accommodating than masculine individuals. In other words, people who conform to a feminine sex role use speech that is more considerate, cooperative, helpful, sensitive, sincere, submissive, and sympathetic.

How Language Describes Women

The language used to describe women is different from the language used to describe men. According to Spender (1985), men have controlled the development of language, provided themselves with more positive words to describe themselves, and given themselves more opportunities to use those words. Simply stated, as the English language developed, the people in charge of the changes were men. For example, the seventeenth- and eighteenth-century prescriptive grammarians who tried to dictate standard language usage were men. Throughout history, the predominant holders of power were men (leaders, fighters, scholars, clerics), and powerful people set the standards for language. Of course, women had some influence and will presumably have more as they assume positions of power in society, but, overall, men have set the standards of language usage outside the home.

How does this "man made language," as Spender (1985) terms it, treat women? To begin with, the masculine form of a word is often taken as the standard, and the feminine form is derived from it. For example, men are authors, poets, princes, actors, and governors. Women are "-esses." "Authoress" and "poetess" are passing from usage as more and more women are successful in these professions, but we still use "princess," "actress," and "governess." Notice how the word "governess" is not the female equivalent of governor. A governor governs a country or state. What does a governess govern?

Words used to describe women often have sexual connotations. For example, men are described with animal names like pig, rat, ape, or snake, but even though these words are used in a negative sense, they generally do not have sexual connotations. Animal names used to describe women (for example, cow, fox, chick, and mother hen) involve strong sexual connotations (Strauss-Noll, 1984). Think of the sentence "_____ is a pro." This sentence has somewhat different connotations if you begin it with "She is" or with "He is."

Words used to describe women often take on a negative connotation that the male equivalent does not have (Spender, 1985). For example, both "spinster" and "bachelor" refer to unmarried adults, but "old spinster" has negative connotations that "old bachelor" does not.

The current debate over the term "Ms." is a good example of differential treatment of women. The popular form of address for a man is "Mr.," which gives no indication of marital status. Up until a few years ago, a woman was always identified as "Miss" or "Mrs.," clearly identifying her as unmarried or married (or at least formerly married). Even today the term "Ms." is not in total usage. Some people argue that "Ms." is difficult to pronounce or that it really means "manuscript." Widely read newspapers such as the *New York Times* continue to identify females by their marital status.

Thus, language is used to treat men and women differently. Language usage is a reflection of the society in which we live. As long as society defines men and women in terms of sex-role stereotypes, differences in language usage will persist.

Strategies for Change

Although language will not totally cease to be sexist until society ceases to be sexist, some people have urged that language change be used as a means to change society. The following sections describe some of the ways that have been suggested to change language to reflect less sex-role stereotyping.

Generic Pronouns

Complete the following sentences:

As the construction worker surveyed the building site, . . .

The nurse who works on the fifth floor is very helpful. In fact, yesterday . . .

When a person wins the lottery, . . .
After a judge instructs the jury, . . .

Did you have any difficulty adding the appropriate pronouns to each of these sentences? Was your choice of pronouns determined by traditional sex-role stereotypes? People are more likely to use "he" when considering traditional male roles such as judge and construction worker and "she" when considering traditional female roles such as nurse and secretary (Wheeless, Berryman-Fink & Sarafini, 1982). Neutral roles (such as winning the lottery) are identified as either "he" or "they" even though "they" may be grammatically incorrect in a particular context. Thus, traditional sex-role stereotypes affect our language choice.

Language also affects our perceptions of the world. When people read or hear sentences containing generic pronouns such as "he" (for example, Everyone deserves his right to a fair trial), they are more likely to believe that the sentences refer to men than to women. People perceive words, that end in "man" (such as "chairman" or "spokesman") as more likely to refer to men than to women, but perceive words that end in "person" (such as "chairperson" or "spokesperson") as equally likely to refer to men or women (Todd-Mancillas, 1981).

To overcome the tendency to exclude women from sentences using generic pronouns, writers have suggested a number of alternative approaches. The noncontrived approach advocates using "him or her," "he/she," or "s/he" instead of generic pronouns (Todd-Mancillas, 1981). As you have probably noticed, we use "he or she" throughout this book. A more contrived alternative is to coin new words to refer specifically to men and women. Densmore (1970) advocates "herm" to mean "her or him" and "heris" to replace "her or his." Millett and Swift (1972) suggest "tey" for "he or she," "ter" for "his or her," and "tem" for "him or her."

As you probably are aware, these alternatives to generic pronouns are not in common usage. Language habits are slow to change. We are likely to pick up new language forms if influential people use them or if we hear or read them in the media. For example, until the 1970s, Watergate was an apartment complex, not a term referring to a national scandal. Since the media or other influential sources are not using pronouns like "ter" or "heris," the general public is unlikely to pick up this usage. In addition, we may not be using words like "ter" because contrived pronouns may be more difficult to understand (Todd-Mancillas, 1984).

Todd-Mancillas (1981), and others, have suggested less-contrived alternatives. First, existing language options can be used instead of "man"-linked words and masculine pronouns. For example, sentences can be pluralized ("Students are expected to type their papers" instead of "A student is expected to type his paper"), and "people" or "human beings" can be substituted for "man" or "mankind." Second, we can use constructions that call specific attention to both males and females; i.e., "he or she," "women and men," or "her or his." In addition, neutral words such as "salesperson" or "worker" (instead of "workman") should be used.

Guidelines for Nonsexist Language Usage

Sorrels (1983) lists eight guidelines for nonsexist communication:

1. Commit yourself to remove sexism from all your communication.
2. Practice and reinforce nonsexist communication patterns until they become habitual. The ultimate test is your ability to carry on a nonsexist private conversation and to think in nonsexist terms.
3. Set a nonsexist communication example and direct or persuade others to adopt your example.
4. Use familiar idiom whenever possible, but if you must choose between sexism and the unfamiliar, use the unfamiliar until it becomes familiar.
5. Take care not to arouse negativism in the receiver by using awkward, cumbersome, highly repetitious, or glaring revisions. A sufficient variety of graceful, controlled, sex-positive, dynamic revisions exist so that you can avoid entirely bland or offensive constructions.
6. Use the full range of techniques for correction of sexist communication, including reconstructions, substitution, and omission.
7. Check roots and meanings of words to be sure that the words need to be changed before changing them.
8. Check every outgoing message—whether written, oral, or nonverbal—for sexism before sending it. (p.17)

Following these guidelines, the nonsexist communicator should use every available means to avoid sex-role stereotyping in language and language that excludes women. For example, using "workers" instead of "workmen," "police officer" instead of "policeman," and "flight attendant" instead of "stewardess" includes all people in these job categories. Avoid labels like "woman superstar," "boy genius," "lady lawyer," or "male hairdresser." Table 4.1 provides further examples of alternatives to sexist language which were suggested by Scott, Foresman and Company, a publisher of textbooks.

Conclusion

In this chapter, we have discussed sex differences in language usage and how those differences are perceived by others. Language differences appear in young children. As preschoolers, girls comment on the imagined

Table 4.1 Alternatives to sexist language usage.

Examples of Sexist Language	**Possible Alternatives**
Early Man	Early humans, early men and women
Mailman	Letter Carrier
Girlfriend/Boyfriend	Friend
In New England, the typical farm was so small that the owner and his sons could take care of it by themselves.	In New England, the typical farm was so small that the family members could take care of it by themselves.
Andrew Wyeth is a fine painter, and Georgia O'Keefe is an exceptional woman painter.	Andrew Wyeth and Georgia O'Keefe are fine painters.
Marie Curie did what few people — men or women — could do.	Marie Curie did what few people could do.
Mary Wells Lawrence is a highly successful woman advertising executive.	Mary Wells Lawrence is a highly successful advertising executive.
The normal dog likes his food moist and meaty.	The normal dog likes its food moist and meaty.
Mother Nature, she. . .	Nature, it. . .
A homeowner and his family. . .	Homeowners and their children . . .
Men are male chauvinist pigs.	Some men consider males superior to females.
Mom, give your child his favorite breakfast—Crunchie Budgies.	Parents, give your children their favorite breakfast—Crunchie Budgies.
The best man for the job . . .	The best person for the job . . .

These examples are adapted from Scott, Foresman and Company (1974) and Sorrels (1983).

contexts in play with greater complexity than boys do. As we might expect from traditional sex-role stereotypes, girls use more other-emphasizing strategies than boys do. As children and as adolescents, boys view friendly conversation among their peers as training for verbal aggression. Girls establish more egalitarian same-sex groups. Girls use friendly groups as a training ground for cooperation.

Although the typical sex-role stereotype holds that women talk more than men, in fact, men talk more than women. In addition, men are more likely to interrupt women than vice versa. In general, males demonstrate more power in interactions. They control conversations, in part, by failing to respond to topics initiated by women.

According to Lakoff (1975), women speak a different language than men. "Women's language" is characterized by a large vocabulary, empty adjectives, question intonation, tag questions, hedges, the intensive "so," hypercorrect grammar, superpolite forms, lack of jokes, and italics. Although there is disagreement over some aspects of women's language (for example, the use of tag questions), speakers who use deferential language are evaluated as more submissive, less assertive, and less willing to take a stand, than speakers who do not use deferential language.

In addition to these sex differences and sex-role stereotypes in language usage, women are excluded from full participation in society through the use of generic pronouns like "he." Generic pronouns and "man"-linked words (such as "chairman") are usually perceived as indicating men rather than women. To correct this omission, writers and speakers should use inclusive forms, such as "worker" or "chairperson," should cast sentences in the plural to avoid using "he," and should avoid all forms of sexist communication whenever possible.

Suggested Activities

1. Role play a situation in which a student is asking a teacher for an extension on a paper. Repeat the role play four times so that you observe a male student/female teacher, male student/male teacher, female student/female teacher, and female student/female teacher. Analyze the language behavior used by the participants in these interactions. Who talked more? When did interruptions occur? What effect did power have on these interactions? In general, how does the language behavior of males and females differ in dyadic interactions?

2. Review the characteristics of deferential language discussed in this chapter. If you are a man, choose a situation in which you normally talk a great deal (e.g., a discussion group, at dinner, or with your family) and try to use deferential language. For example, use hedges, tag questions, and more polite language than usual. How did people react to you? Did you feel comfortable in the situation? Why or why not? If you are a woman, identify a situation in which you tend to use deferential language (e.g., a classroom, on a date, or with a professor) and try to use nondeferential language (e.g., avoid tag questions and hesitations, directly state your opinions and support them). How do people react to you? Were you comfortable in the situation? Why or why not?

3. Ask ten males and ten females to complete the following sentences adapted from Wheeless, Berryman-Fink, and Serafini (1982):

When artists become famous, . . .
Before a judge can give a final ruling, . . .

After a nurse has completed training, . . .
After a college athlete graduates, . . .
When a person loses money, . . .
When an elementary school teacher has a problem child in class, . . .
When the weather is rainy, . . .
When a construction worker completes a job, . . .
After a secretary has taken dictation, . . .
When a person wins a prize, . . .

Count the number and types of pronouns your respondents used to start the second part of these sentences. Were your respondents more likely to use masculine pronouns with occupations that are traditionally masculine (e.g., construction worker, judge)? Were your respondents more likely to use feminine pronouns with occupations that are traditionally feminine (e.g., nurse, secretary)? What alternatives, if any, did they use? What are the implications of your results for sex-role stereotyping in language usage?

For Further Reading

Berryman, C. L., and Eman, V. A. (Eds.). (1980). *Communication, language and sex*. Rowley, MA: Newbury House.

Bradley, P. H. (1981). The folk-linguistics of women's speech: An empirical examination. *Communication Monographs, 48,* 73–90.

Haslett, B. J. (1983). Communicative functions and strategies in children's conversations. *Human Communication Research, 9,* 114–119.

Kramarae, C., Schulz, M., and O'Barr, W. M. (1984). *Language and power*. Beverly Hills, CA: Sage.

Liska, J., Mechling, E. W., and Stathas, S. (1981). Differences in subjects' perceptions of gender and believability between users of deferential and nondeferential language. *Communication Quarterly, 29,* 40–48.

Miller, C., and Swift, K. (1977). *Words and women*. Garden City, NY: Anchor Books.

Sorrels, B. D. (1983). *The nonsexist communicator*. Englewood Cliffs, NJ: Prentice-Hall.

Spender, D. (1985). *Man made language,* 2nd ed. London: Routledge and Kegan Paul.

Todd-Mancillas, W. R. (1981). Masculine generics = sexist language: A review of literature and implications for speech communication professionals. *Communication Quarterly, 29,* 107–115.

5 Sex Differences and Sex-Role Stereotypes in Nonverbal Communication

Visualize this scenario. The department head enters the room where the weekly staff meeting is about to begin. Pat is a middle-aged manager with short, silver-grey hair and penetrating blue eyes. Walking briskly, the department head enters the room and slams the door. Pat approaches the large rectangular table where six staff members are seated, stands erect at the head of the table, places a brown leather briefcase on the table, slowly opens the briefcase, removes several folders, slowly closes the briefcase, and places it on the floor. Laying the folders in several carefully arranged stacks, Pat pauses and looks intently at the staff members seated around the table. Frowning, Pat nervously taps fingers on the tabletop and slowly sits down in the large chair at the head of the table. With a quick glance at the clock on the wall, Pat coughs once and begins to speak.

This scene was described through the use of words, but the department head *has not* yet uttered a single word—there was no dialogue. Although the department head has not yet communicated verbally, there is no doubt that this person *has* communicated to those staff members in the room. Remembering this scene, indicate the judgments you were able to make about the department head on the scales below:

happy :___:___:___:___:___:___:___:unhappy

stimulated :___:___:___:___:___:___:___:relaxed

dominant :___:___:___:___:___:___:___:submissive

satisfied :___:___:___:___:___:___:___:unsatisfied

excited :___:___:___:___:___:___:___:calm

influential :___:___:___:___:___:___:___:influenced

hopeful :___:___:___:___:___:___:___:despairing

frenzied :___:___:___:___:___:___:___:sluggish

controlling :____:____:____:____:____:____:____:controlled

masculine :____:____:____:____:____:____:____:feminine

Social psychologist Albert Mehrabian (1981) has estimated that no more than 7 percent of the social meaning in face-to-face communication is carried through the verbal message; the remaining 93 percent of the social meaning is carried through nonverbal communication channels. Nonverbal communication most often reveals our emotions, our attitudes, and the nature of our relationships with others. At the core of these messages, however, nonverbal communication reflects our sex and sex-role stereotypes. By understanding nonverbal communication differences between men and women, we can become more sensitive and responsive in our communication with others.

There are many frameworks used to examine nonverbal communication. Perhaps the simplest definition is that *nonverbal communication* includes *all* communication except that which is coded through words. With the introduction of such popularized books as Julius Fast's *Body Language* in the 1970s, the general population has come to define nonverbal communication as those behavioral cues transmitted exclusively by visual sensations. Such a definition typically includes facial expression, eye contact, gestures, posture, physical appearance, and clothing. However, this limited definition excludes the vocal characteristics that surround the verbal message—such characteristics as vocal range, pitch, inflection, vocal quality, rate of speaking, and the use of pauses. Nonverbal communication, then, includes *both* the visual cues that communicate and the vocal characteristics that surround the verbal message. Together, these sets of cues comprise all communication except that which is coded through words.

As we noted in Chapter 3, communication is the process by which we transmit and receive symbolic cues—both verbal and nonverbal. Chapter 4 focused on sex differences and sex-role stereotypes in verbal (or language) cues, the implications and consequences of these differences, and strategies for change. In this chapter, we will explore such differences in nonverbal (or nonlanguage) cues, discuss the implications and consequences of these differences, and suggest strategies for change in nonverbal cues. Specifically, this chapter focuses on differences in the ability to encode and decode nonverbal messages, personal space and touching behavior, body movement and posture, facial expression and eye behavior, physical appearance, vocal characteristics, and the use of physical objects or artifacts.

Sex Differences and Sex-Role Stereotypes

Encoding and Decoding Abilities

In this chapter, *encoding* is the formation of messages that are communicated through nonverbal channels; *decoding* is the translation of nonverbal behaviors into meaningful messages. In general, females are more proficient than males at forming and interpreting nonverbal messages—a difference that emerges in childhood.

Girls, at all stages of development, tend to be better interpreters of emotional expression than boys are (Trotter, 1983). One reason for this superiority may be that mothers are far more restrictive in the range of emotions they display and encourage with boys than with girls. Male infants are not typically exposed to as many emotional displays as are female infants; therefore, girls, who are exposed to these emotions throughout their development, are provided with a broader base for interpreting emotional displays and greater latitude in the emotions they are allowed to display. The most obvious example of this difference is that in our culture it is traditionally considered feminine and acceptable for a female to cry, but it is traditionally considered unmasculine and unacceptable for a male to cry; as a result, women report crying (both privately and publicly) significantly more often than men do (Lombardo, Cretser, Lombardo & Mathis, 1983).

The Profile of Nonverbal Sensitivity (PONS), developed by Robert Rosenthal and colleagues, is a test commonly given to assess nonverbal decoding ability; it provides 220 two-second segments of a woman's face, body, and voice (content free, but retaining vocal tone) in various combinations. From a choice of two, the observer is then asked to select the scenario enacted by the woman. Invariably, research using this test demonstrates that women are better at selecting the correction situation than men are (Rosenthal et al., 1979). Some researchers have criticized the PONS test because the encoder in the scenarios is female and they believe that females may be better decoders of nonverbal messages sent by females. This phenomenon may account for the research findings that favor males. Regardless of this concern, however, the PONS test continues to be a primary measure of nonverbal sensitivity. A review of seventy-five studies on gender differences in the ability to assess another person's feelings using vocal or facial cues indicated that in 84 percent of these studies females were better nonverbal decoders than males (Hall, 1978). While this percentage alone is not conclusive, it strongly suggests that women generally tend to be more proficient than men at nonverbal decoding.

Although we know that women tend to be more proficient at nonverbal encoding/decoding than men, we still have no definitive explanation for this proficiency. Hall (1979) offers a suggestion based on the role of women in society compared to the role of men in society. He argues that greater nonverbal sensitivity is required of those persons who are oppressed in a society—women. To survive, women must be better interpreters of the nonverbal messages around them. This message-interpreting capability provides women with the information necessary to predict the behavior of the more dominant members of society (men) accurately and to adjust accordingly. Men do not have this survival need. Since they are the dominant members of society, they are not as motivated as women to be proficient in nonverbal encoding and decoding.

Further, women maintain this encoding/decoding advantage primarily with obvious, rather than subtle, nonverbal cues (Rosenthal & DePaulo, 1979). Women are especially proficient in decoding nonverbal cues that facilitate relationship maintenance—empathic facial expression, head nods that indicate agreement and support, and touch to seek affiliative responses. Since women are traditionally socialized to maintain smooth relationships, they are more likely to become sensitive to nonverbal cues that facilitate and reinforce a close, supportive relationship.

A second explanation might be that femininity is associated with better nonverbal sensitivity because females are given more of an opportunity to practice nonverbal decoding in traditionally feminine occupations. Buck (1976) found that fine arts majors and business majors were relatively good nonverbal decoders and science majors were relatively poor nonverbal decoders. Women probably major in fine arts and business more often than they major in science. Perhaps women are drawn to college majors that require and encourage greater nonverbal sensitivity; as a result, women pursue occupations that require and encourage greater nonverbal sensitivity. For example, greater nonverbal sensitivity has been linked with those who are in the helping professions. Nursing, teaching, and flight attendanting are professions that permit submissiveness and expressiveness, and professions that are traditionally occupied by women (Isenhart, 1980).

Whether we accept or reject these explanations for sex differences in nonverbal encoding and decoding abilities, they do reflect sex-role stereotyping. Women traditionally have been perceived to hold the submissive role in our culture and to function as facilitators and accommodators in the development of relationships. Women have traditionally sought work in the helping professions and, as a result, women may be *expected* to become more nonverbally sensitive.

Personal Space and Touching Behavior

Sommer (1959) defines *personal space* as an invisible bubble that surrounds us, moves with us, and separates us from others. Each of us has a personal space. Think for a moment about the last time you used an elevator. Imagine the door opening and imagine walking into that empty elevator. Where did you stand? You probably stood at the back of the elevator or near the buttons. What happened when the elevator stopped at a floor and another person stepped in? Did you move or stand firm to defend your territory? The two of you probably moved to opposite corners of the elevator. How would you feel if you were on an elevator with only one other person and that person stood right next to you? Would you feel uncomfortable or crowded? This example illustrates the concept of personal space. In some situations we prefer to maintain our distance from others, but in other situations we prefer closeness and even touch. Male and female differences in the use of personal space begin in infancy and continue into adulthood.

The use of space between parents and infants (as well as touching behavior) indicates basic sex differences. In general, girls seek and receive more touching and less space than boys do. For example, by about six months of age, boys are hustled away from touching contact with their mothers, who believe that boys should be independent and should explore the world around them. As a result of this parental behavior, boys, by as early as thirteen months of age, demonstrate more exploratory and autonomous behavior than do girls. Boys tend to venture farther away from their mothers than girls, remain away from their mothers longer than girls, and look at, as well as talk to, their mothers less than girls. With this newly-discovered independence, boys play more actively with toys and other objects, such as doorknobs and light switches. Boys also respond to frustration with more overt aggression than girls do; girls tend to respond with passive crying. Based on both of these activities, boys may assume that parents are not expected to be in close physical proximity (Lewis, 1972).

In general, infants ranging from ten to sixteen months of age demonstrate strong attachment behaviors to their mothers. However, girls look at, touch, and remain significantly closer to their mothers than do boys at the same age (Brooks & Lewis, 1974; Cohen & Campos, 1974). Two-year-old girls ask to be held by both parents almost three times as often as do boys. As a result, parents are more likely to react positively when girls ask to be held than when boys make the same request. When girls ask to be held, they are perceived to demonstrate dependence, and this characteristic is given positive attributes; when boys are perceived to demonstrate dependency by asking to be held, they are often criticized. Because dependency is thought to be an inappropriate attribute for boys, parents encourage boys to explore their physical world independently, while girls are rewarded for seeking help or trying to help others within their physical world (Fagot, 1978).

Since girls are not encouraged to be assertive, independent, or exploratory, they remain closer to their mothers during play than do boys. When playing with other children, girls paired with boys are more likely to stand watching passively or withdraw toward their mothers than boys paired with other boys or girls paired with other girls (Jacklin & Maccoby, 1978). In addition, toddlers ranging in age from three to five years orient their bodies farther away from opposite-sex peers during interaction than from same-sex peers. This body-orientation preference occurs regardless of age (within three to five years), status, or even familiarity with the play partner (Wasserman & Stern, 1978). Passive behavior demonstrated by girls paired with boys, as well as the tendency for girls to orient their bodies away from boys and to move toward their mothers, is consistent with socialization practices encouraged by parents during infancy.

When interacting with adults, both male and female toddlers appear to be more comfortable approaching females. Toddlers and preschool childern move closer to adult females than to adult males, though the distance for both sexes decreases with increased social interaction (Eberts & Lepper, 1975). Toddlers and preschoool children interacting with adults during free play are more likely to approach female adults than to approach male adults. In general, girls maintain greater distances with adults of either sex than do boys (Beach & Sokoloff, 1974). One explanation for the ease with which children of both sexes approach female adults may be that children typically spend more time with female adults—traditionally with mothers, day-care workers, and babysitters. The reluctance of girls to approach adults of either sex appears to be an extension of sex-role stereotyping, which encourages boys to explore their physical environment (including people) and discourages girls from the same activity.

In addition to sex differences in their own behavior, children maintain traditional sex-role stereotypes in assigning personal space to others. Boys differ from girls when asked to position cutout characters engaged in interactions with differing emotional contexts. Girls place significantly greater distances between cutouts of two "angry" men or cutouts of an "angry" man and an "angry" woman than between cutouts of two "angry" women (Melson, 1976). This difference suggests that both toddler and preschool girls perceive male anger as an emotion that commands more space than female anger, regardless of the other person's sex. More significantly, however, this difference suggests that toddler and preschool girls perceive males as higher in status; therefore, males are able to command more space regardless of the emotional context.

Sex differences in the use and perception of personal space continue as children grow. Boys command more space than girls during childhood and adolescence. Boys learn to need and use more territory at earlier ages than girls do (Harper & Sanders, 1975). For example, boys tend to spend more time outdoors, cover more geographical areas, and use between 1.2 and 1.6 times the amount of space as girls. When confronted with situations involving crowding (a psychological perception of closeness that may or may not be related to physical proximity), fourth-grade to eleventh-grade boys report feeling considerably more uncomfortable, tense, and annoyed than girls do.

To gain a better understanding of the socialization process during childhood and adolescence, we will examine the use of personal space among peers. Specifically, boys and girls position themselves closer together when using space in same-sex dyads than when they are in opposite-sex dyads. This preference shifts during adolescence, however, when attraction to the opposite sex becomes an important consideration and attraction to the same sex is viewed as inappropriate. Mixed-sex dyads require more space than same-sex dyads (Severy, Forsyth & Wagner, 1980). In general, however, sixth-, seventh-, and eighth-graders move closer to opposite-sex peers (Meisels & Guardo, 1969; Whalen, Flowers, Fuller & Jernigan, 1975). The proxemic preference for opposite-sex peers comes earlier for girls, but the preference is clearly established for most boys by the time they reach the ninth grade. When children and adolescents do interact with same-sex peers, both boys and girls use less perceived distance with same-sex peers they describe as interpersonally attractive (Guardo, 1975).

Touch is also more desirable with same-sex peers during childhood. In children who are in kindergarten through the sixth grade, touch is more frequent and includes a greater variety of body areas when touching occurs between same-sex peers rather than between opposite-sex peers (Whalen et al., 1975; Willis & Hofmann, 1975). Sex differences in touching behavior may reflect the differences in the ways parents touch their children. Parents limit their touch of children primarily to the head and arm regions. Fathers touch their daughters more frequently than their sons, but they touch both sons and daughters in the same general regions. In contrast, mothers touch both sons and daughters the same amount and in the same general regions (Rosenfeld, Kartus & Ray, 1976). Research on proxemics continues to confirm the existence of cultural sex-role stereotyping that suggests male–female touch and female–female touch are more appropriate than male–male touch.

In adulthood, the personal space bubbles that surround women are generally smaller than those that surround men (Evans & Howard, 1973); women command less space than men. Women react more negatively to an indirect, side-by-side invasion of their space; men react more negatively to a direct, face-to-face invasion of their space (Fisher & Byrne, 1975). These sex differences, as well as the observation that women tend to be more cooperative and less aggressive than men in high-density situations (Freedman, O'Hanlon, Oltman & Witkin, 1972), reflect sex-role stereotyping. Women are perceived to be more social, more affiliative, and of lower status; as a result, space surrounding women is considered more public and accessible than space surrounding men.

Also, women are touched more than men; in fact, men touch women about twice as much as women touch men (Henley, 1977). This distinction becomes even greater when such status cues as age and socio-economic level are removed. Women receive considerably more touch than men, and women make more specific distinctions concerning the meaning of that touch. For example, both the type of touch (patting, stroking, squeezing) and the place of touch (hands, face, arms, genitals) are essential for women to distinguish between love/friendliness and sexual desire. For men, type of touch is a distinguishing factor in meaning, but place of touch is not (Nguyen, Heslin & Nguyen, 1975). Sex-role stereotyping associated with status and dominance in men may explain why men initiate more touch and women receive more touch; and sex-role stereotyping associated with affiliative behavior in women may account for the greater levels of distinction women make in attaching meaning to touch.

Body Movement and Posture

Think for a moment of the woman in the Impulse perfume commercial. As she walks down the street, her strides are long, her head is held high, and she moves at a brisk pace with her arms swinging freely. She communicates self-confidence and control as well as sex appeal. Obviously, the producers of this commercial and the makers of this perfume hope to appeal to the independent, self-confident woman of the 1980s who is comfortable with her own sexuality. Even the name of the product conveys that certain strength and independence of a changing female image. The manner in which men or women carry themselves and move communicates a great deal about how they perceive themselves and others. These nonverbal aspects of individual behavior reflect not only personality traits and attitudes, but also sex differences and sex roles in our society.

Sex differences in body movement and posture begin to emerge in toddler and preschool children. For example, by three and four years of age, girls use three specific gestures significantly more often than do boys: (1) the limp wrist gesture; (2) arm flutters; and (3) flexed elbows (Rekers, Amoro-Plotkin & Low, 1977). By four and five years of age, girls use these same gestures, as well as hand claps and palming gestures (indicating questioning), significantly more often than boys do (Rekers

& Rudy, 1978). Gestural differences remain consistent throughout early adolescence, but some of these gestures (limp wrists and arm flutters) are stereotypically associated with a feminine sex role in adulthood. In fact, males who exhibit these behaviors as adolescents and adults are often perceived as unmasculine and may be perceived as homosexual.

Other gestural behaviors that reflect male/female differences in toddlers and preschool children include the use of *emblems*—gestures that represent direct verbal equivalents. Such common emblems as gestures that communicate "I don't know," "yes," "no," "I'm tired," and "come here" are frequently used by children as early as three years of age (Kumin & Lazar, 1974). As a child's repertoire of emblems increases, such common emblems as "I won't listen," "blowing a kiss," and "I won't do it" are added by four years of age. In general, girls use more emblems than boys do at both three and four years of age—a phenomenon consistent with the development of early language competency in girls. Although boys generally are better at decoding the meaning of such emblems at age three, girls surpass boys in decoding capability by age four and, as we noted earlier, maintain this superiority into adolescence.

The development of sex-role stereotyping in body movement for children often occurs during free play. After observing videotapes of children (whose average age was eight and one-half years) in free play sessions with parents, Tauber (1979) noted that parents of girls are more likely to engage them in social play that focuses on the development of interpersonal relationships and enhancement of the socialization process. Parents of boys are more likely to engage in physical play that focuses on the development of physical activity. In addition, daughters of supportive mothers are more likely to engage in physical contact-seeking behavior than are daughters of supportive fathers. In general, the relationship between mother and daughter during play is similar to the relationship between mother and son during play; fathers, however, do not relate to daughters in the same way they relate to sons. Fathers tend to be very supportive of boys who engage in active play, but they tend to withhold support from girls who engage in active play. Thus, fathers' behavior toward children during free play again reinforces male independence and activity and female affiliation and passivity.

Adult men and women also differ in their body movement and posture. Women tend to present their bodies as a moving entity; they walk with their legs close together (small steps) and their arms close to their sides, presenting the image of a moving whole. Men tend to be more independent in their movement from the trunk up; their legs are spread at a ten to fifteen degree angle while their arms are angled five to ten degrees away from the trunk of their bodies (Eakins & Eakins, 1978).

In comparing gestures used by males and females, Peterson (1976) noted several differences. While gestures are used by both men and women to illustrate and supplement the verbal message, men generally use more gestures than women. Women tend to use more gestures when communicating with men than when communicating with other women. Further, men use or display more dominant gestures, such as the closed fist, pointing, and sweeping gestures. Women are more likely to engage in submissive gestures, such as holding their hands in their laps or playing with their hair and dress ornamentation. In posturing, men usually stretch their legs out and cross them at the ankles while sitting, but women usually tuck in their legs and cross them at the knees. This posture difference is another indication that men command more space than women.

Men and women exhibit stereotyped nonverbal cues.

Posture differences in males and females may reflect a perceived status difference. Women sit with their arms closer to their sides and their legs crossed at small angles. Men sprawl out more—stretching their arms and legs out in front of them and crossing their arms and legs at larger angles. Despite women's superior anatomical flexibility, they are generally less relaxed in their posture than men. Relaxed posture is most likely a reflection of a perceived higher status among men because high-ranking men are comparatively more relaxed than low-ranking men when communicating (Mehrabian, 1972).

After observing the carrying behavior of college men and women, Jenni and Jenni (1976) noted some of the same postural differences. Female college students tend to wrap their arms around their books and balance them in front of their bodies—a more compact carrying position. Male college students tend to support their books with their arms at the side of the body—a more expansive carrying position.

It appears, then, that both movement and posture reflect male/female differences. Males use body movements and postures that command more space; females are more compact in both their body movement and posture. These sex differences, begun in childhood and maintained throughout adulthood, tend to reinforce male independence and activity and female dependence and passivity.

Facial Expression and Eye Behavior

Recall that scenario of the department head described at the beginning of this chapter. Pat never spoke, yet we made judgments about Pat based on nonverbal cues, including facial expressions and eye behavior. Remember, Pat looked intently at the staff members, frowned, and glanced quickly at the clock before beginning to speak. Facial expression and eye behavior are typically thought to be the keys to an individual's personality and emotional state. When we try to determine if someone is happy, sad, frustrated, lying, or being honest, we most often focus our attention on the person's facial expression and eye behavior. It seems quite appropriate, then, to explore male/female differences in this key set of nonverbal cues used to communicate vital aspects of our personality, attitudes, and relationships with others.

Affect displays are facial expressions that convey our emotions. There are few sex differences in affect displays portrayed during infancy; however, affect display differences between boys and girls do begin to appear in children. Buck (1976) discovered that mothers who view televised images of children watching emotionally-arousing slides report that six-year-old boys use fewer facial expressions in general than do four-year-old boys. It appears that boys inhibit and even mask their overt responses to emotion as they get older, while girls continue to respond openly and freely.

According to researchers who studied the eye-gaze behavior (length and direction of eye contact) of toddlers and preschool children ranging from three to five years of age, sex differences are readily apparent (Kleinke, Desautels & Knapp, 1977). Girls in this age range use eye gaze directed toward others longer and more often than do boys. In addition, boys tend to react more negatively than girls to others (both males and females) who gaze at them for longer periods. Girls, on the other hand, tend to like and respond more positively to others who gaze at them for longer periods of time.

Finally, toddlers and preschool children continue to demonstrate a marked preference for same-sex peers, rather than for opposite-sex peers, through facial expression. Preschool children smile more often when they are interacting with their peers than they do at other times (Cheyne, 1976). However, both boys and girls smile considerably more with same-sex peers than they do with opposite-sex peers. Consistent with child development literature, children at this stage of development are most comfortable with and even prefer same-sex peers.

As children continue to develop, girls both receive and use more affect displays than boys. Feldman and White (1980) made an interesting discovery concerning children's use of facial expression to deceive others. According to their research findings, the degree to which deception is revealed through facial expression decreases for girls as they get older; however, the degree to which deception is revealed through facial expression increases for boys as they get older. It appears, then, that as they get older, boys are less able to control "leakage" of deception cues.

Most of the research that compares facial expressions of adult males and females focuses on smiling and eye contact. The results of these studies tend to reinforce the previously reported research findings on children. In general, women use more facial expression than men (Mehrabian, 1972). More specifically, women smile more often than men (Parlee, 1979a), women are more likely to return smiles from others (Henley, 1977), and women tend to be attracted to people who smile (Lau, 1982).

In addition, women engage in more overall eye contact than men. This finding has led many researchers to conclude that visual information plays a far more significant role in the social field of women than in the social field of men, and that the visual activity of women is more sensitive to social field conditions than that of men. Eye contact is often associated with people of lower status who are seeking approval; therefore, frequent use of eye contact by women may relate to a sex-role stereotype associated with lower status for women. Women's greater sensitivity to the visual field may also be related to sex-role status. Some researchers speculate that women are more sensitive to facial expressions and eye contact because women are the submissive sex in society; to survive, women *must* be more sensitive to the dominant sex in society—males. Sex-role stereotyping rather than biological differences, may account for male/female differences in facial expressions and eye behavior.

Physical Appearance

The old adage, beauty is in the eye of the beholder, may lead us to believe that the physical characteristics we label beautiful are based on unique and individual standards; however, in our culture there is a relatively high level of agreement concerning what *is* and what *is not* attractive. The specific physical characteristics that constitute beauty may differ from person to person, but the total look that is created from these individual physical characteristics is labeled attractive or unattractive with relative consistency. The physical characteristics of models like Brooke Shields and Cheryl Tiegs differ considerably, the physical characteristics of actors such as Tom Selleck, Ben Vereen, and Richard Gere vary greatly, and the physical characteristics of recording artists like Michael Jackson, Bruce Springsteen, and Mick Jagger span a wide range; yet millions of people around the world find these individuals physically attractive.

The physical differences between males and females are numerous and obvious. Perhaps more important than the physical differences themselves, however, is how males and females perceive these physical characteristics in themselves and others. After all, for both males and females, physical appearance is an important determiner of how we feel about ourselves and about those around us.

Boys and girls who are considered attractive also are thought to be more independent in their behavior—they are not nearly as afraid of others and usually require less assistance with tasks they attempt (Bennetts, 1979). In conjunction with this positive attribution of independence, attractive children of both sexes also are perceived to be more socialized; that is, attractive children are more likely to relate well to others. As a result of this socialized label, attractive children are characterized as playing in feminine ways that use more socialization. Unattractive children of both sexes are characterized as playing in masculine ways (often alone) with masculine toys that stress independent activity rather than sharing and human interaction (Langlois & Downs, 1979).

Physical characteristics can include hair color and length, facial and body hair, skin color and complexion tones, and physical handicaps. We will focus primarily on the perception of body size; specifically, we will examine body shape, height, and weight. For boys, sex-role stereotypes concerning body build and social acceptance are clearly established by six years of age. For example, males six to ten years of age view mesomorphs (muscular body types) as more socially acceptable than ectomorphs (thin, weak, tall, and underdeveloped body types) (Staffieri, 1967; 1972). Males between the ages of nine and twenty believe that physical attractiveness leads to social acceptance, and they assign more positive behavioral descriptors to the mesomorph body type and more socially negative behavioral descriptors to the endomorph and ectomorph body types (Kelck, Richardson & Ronald, 1974; Lerner, 1969).

In general, males are more satisfied with somewhat larger body size than females are (Jourard & Secord, 1955). Women tend to feel most attractive when they are considered small and slim—characteristics they typically associate with being pretty (Berscheid, Walster & Bohrnstedt, 1973). The desire to be small and slim accounts, in part, for the rise during the past decade in such eating disorders as anorexia nervosa and bulimia, particularly in adolescent women who are high achievers. Eating disorders have led many adolescent females to poor health and even death in striving for social acceptance through beauty.

Female preferences for the male physique also reinforce male perceptions. For example, women prefer men with V-shaped physiques—medium-wide trunks or medium-thin lower trunks and thin legs; women least prefer men with pear-shaped physiques—wide lower trunks. Traditionally, women who perceive themselves as "feminine" prefer muscular men, and women who perceive themselves as "liberated" prefer thinner, more linear men. Large women are typically attracted to large men, but research indicates that probably the best determiner of female preference is the physique of the man with whom she is involved at the time (Lavrakas, 1975).

Women also prefer men of average height; however, if given a choice, women prefer tall men to short men. According to survey research, tall men are considered more attractive, datable, and likeable than are short men (Graziano, Brothen & Berscheid, 1978).

In general, being perceived as attractive is important to both males and females, but can one ever be *too* attractive? Research suggests that attractive males and females are more effective than unattractive males and females in influencing others, but that males are allowed to be more attractive than females and still retain credibility. Beyond a certain level of attractiveness, very attractive women are perceived as less effective persuaders than unattractive women (Hoffman, 1977). If a woman is perceived as too attractive, she loses credibility in presenting her ideas to others. In fields such as sales or broadcast journalism, moderately

Chart 5.1

"When you first meet someone, which one or two things about physical appearance do you tend to notice first?"

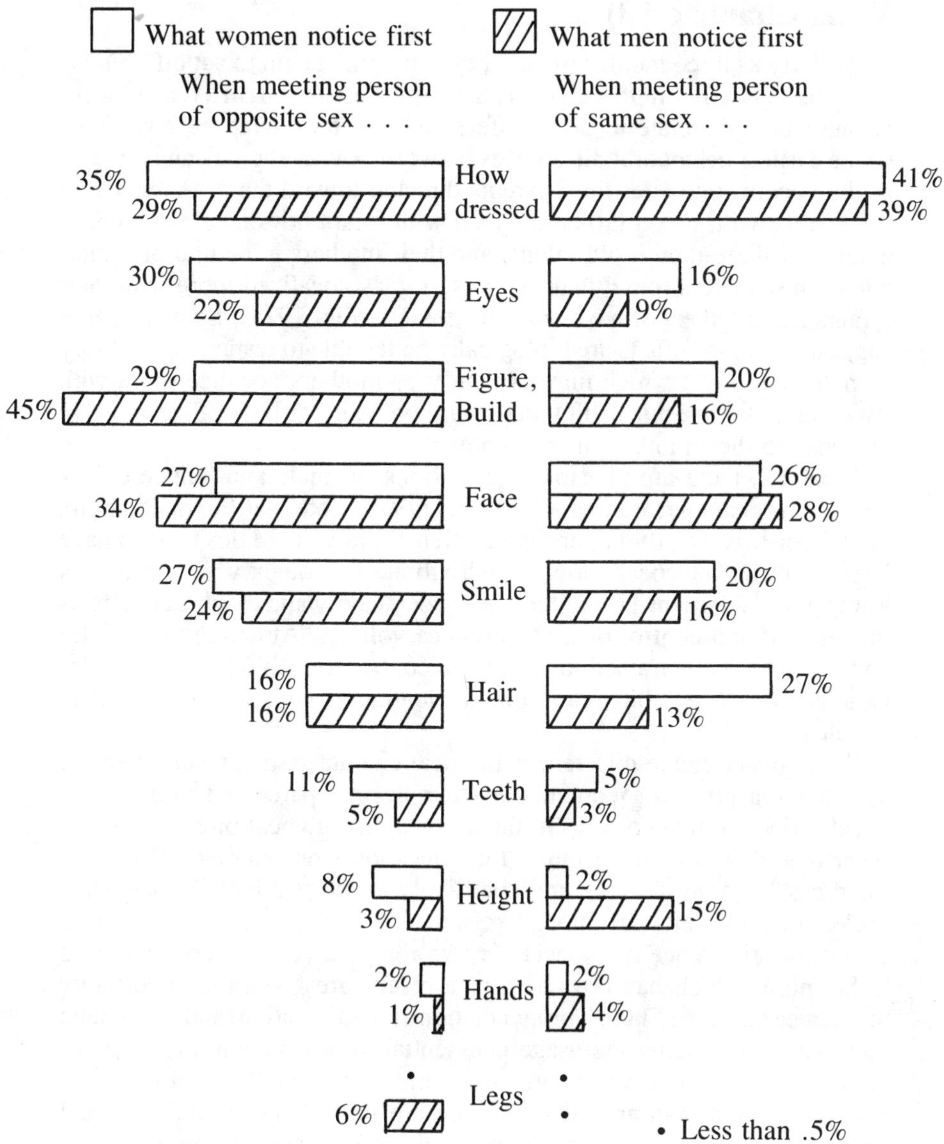

[*Source:* Data from a survey by the Roper Organization reported in *Public Opinion* (Volume 6, No. 4). Adapted from *Psychology Today*.]

attractive women may be more successful than extremely attractive women; for men, however, extreme attractiveness does not appear to be as closely tied with credibility.

Vocal Characteristics

As early as three months of age, boys and girls begin to act differently. As we noted earlier in this chapter, many of these initial differences occur because parents relate to boys differently than they relate to girls. One of the earliest behavioral differences between boys and girls can be traced to the vocalization cues their parents directed toward them. Parents tend to vocalize with infant girls more than with infant boys. For example, in a study of three-month-old infants and their mothers in natural play situations, researchers found that mothers of girls vocalized more with their infants than mothers of boys did (Lewis & Freedle, 1973). Some research suggests that girl infants are biologically better able to respond to auditory stimuli than boys, which may explain why mothers vocalize more with daughters. As a result of this maternal behavior, girls vocalize more in response to their mothers than do boys.

In adults, there are physiological reasons for male and female differences. For example, Eakins and Eakins (1978) note that the male larynx (vocal cord) is usually larger than the female larynx. Males tend to have larger and thicker vocal cords, which vibrate less quickly and produce a lower pitch. Also, the size of the upper body cavity and diaphragm affects the amount and control of air to produce volume. Although both males and females can be trained to use breath control to their advantage, males naturally produce a bit more volume (loudness) with their voices than females.

Some male/female differences in vocal characteristics result from the socialization process. Women, for example, are perceived to use more vocal inflection that conveys hesitancy — a rising vocal pitch on a statement that should confirm rather than question (for example, "You like my dress?"). Also, females are more likely to use standard English when speaking, and males are more likely to use nonstandard dialects. This dialectical difference may occur for two reasons: (1) girls are socialized to be more verbal than boys and, as a result, are given the opportunity to practice standard English pronunciation and articulation; and (2) women may realize that language usage is essential to *any* recognition of status in society and, as a result, are much more attuned to developing the necessary skills than are men. Women are more likely to be evaluated on *who* they are; and men are more likely to be evaluated on *what* they do. Language skill may be more important in developing a female's identity, and job and task accomplishment may be more closely identified with a male's identity.

A study conducted by Addington (1968) is a particularly thorough exploration of the personality perceptions typically associated with nine vocal qualities. Results of the study indicate that finer personality distinctions are made concerning the vocal qualities of women; i.e., we are more likely to judge women by vocal qualities than we are to judge men by vocal qualities. Some of the most significant male/female differences discovered in the study indicate that more negative judgments are made about women than about men.

For example, breathiness in the voice suggests to listeners that a female is feminine and pretty, but it also suggests that she is shallow. For a male, however, breathiness in the voice suggests that he is young and perhaps artistic; there is no judgment made about the quality of his personal credibility. Vocal tenseness in a female voice suggests youth, emotion, and lack of intelligence; however, vocal tenseness in a male voice suggests maturity and steadfastness. A throaty quality in the female voice suggests laziness, masculinity, and lack of intelligence; this same quality in the male voice suggests age, a realistic attitude, maturity, and sophistication, and also suggests to listeners that he is well-adjusted. It appears, then, that a women whose vocal qualities are typically considered feminine is accepted as consistent with her sex role, but this feminine sex role often implies immaturity, shallowness, and lack of intelligence. A male whose voice is consistent with his masculine sex role is considered intelligent, mature, sophisticated, and well-adjusted. Again, the sex-role stereotype is that males are active, independent, and dominant, and that women are passive, dependent, and submissive.

Vocal qualities in males and females also reflect and reinforce many of the same power and status issues raised by other nonverbal cues. Men tend to use nonverbal cues that reflect power and status; women tend to use nonverbal cues that reflect subordination. For example, women often add a questioning tone to their voices by using rising vocal inflections that seem to seek approval; men tend to use downward vocal inflections that convey certainty. Vocal patterns appear to remain constant in both same-sex and mixed-sex interactions, and they tend to reinforce a perception of male power and dominance and female uncertainty and submission.

Artifacts

When one of the authors' baby niece was brought home from the hospital, she was cuddled in a soft, pink blanket. Her new room had been painted pink; it was filled with pink toys and pink stuffed animals. Her new first gift from her aunt was a pink, frilly dress designed to make her look as feminine as any female infant only one week of age can look.

The *artifacts* or objects with which we surround an infant are often reflections of the attributes we believe the infant possesses. This important link between objects and the attributes we believe a baby possesses is underscored when we note that both toy and activity preferences during play conform to sex-role stereotypes for infants by about three years of age (Bell, Weller & Waldrop, 1971). For example, observations of infants ranging in age from twelve to twenty-four months indicate that boys engage in active play with transportation toys and generally forbidden objects, such as light switches, more often than girls do. Girls more often play with soft toys and dolls (Smith & Daglish, 1977). Further, boys are given more play objects that encourage activities directed away from the home, and girls are given play objects that encourage activities directed toward the home (Rheingold & Cook, 1975). Such parental toy selection clearly indicates that boys are expected to identify with activities outside the home environment, but girls are expected to identify primarily with objects within the home environment.

Barbie: In Shape and Dressed for Success

With her business suit and attaché case, she looks like many young working women in the '80s. She can sit for hours in front of her computer terminal or charge hundreds of dollars worth of clothes on her new credit cards—without a single change in expression. Barbie, the doll, follows all the trends, so it's hardly surprising that lately she's adopted the Yuppie life-style.

The person who understands Barbie best is Tom Wszalek, marketing director for Mattel toys, her manufacturer. This year's avatar is called Day to Night Barbie, says Wszalek, because the skirt of her suit reverses for evening wear and because she comes not only with a bedroom, "with a vanity and all those things you associate with Barbie's world, but also with a complete modern office environment." Tiny magazines, a tiny calculator and extremely tiny credit and business cards are also part of the package intended to make Barbie "a woman of substance, a woman of the '80s." Ogilvy & Mather has even come up with a Virginia Slims-ish slogan for Barbies: "We girls can do anything—right, Barbie?"

In part, Day to Night Barbie may be an attempt to improve Barbie's image. She isn't exactly a favorite with feminists, but her new professionalism might enhance her status. And the enterprising Mattel company, which last year marketed Great Shape Barbie dressed in Jane Fonda-like leotard and leg warmers (this year there's a workout center complete with exercise bike, weights and pulleys), is hoping that the latest modifications will keep her on the marketing fast track. Wszalek, however, takes a less cynical view toward Barbie's changes. "She," he argues, "has always had the potential to be multidimensional."

In general, parents select toys to initiate play with three-month and six-month-old infants based on perceived sex differences (Severy et al., 1980; Will, Self & Datan, 1976). When infants are actually girls or are labeled girls, both male and female parents are more likely to seek feminine toys, such as dolls, to initiate play. When an infant is actually a boy or is labeled a boy, fathers are more likely to use a neutral toy, such as a teething ring, to initiate play than to use a male-typed toy. The choice of a neutral toy may signal a trend away from sex-role stereotyping with infant toys and, though limited to toys for boys, may signal changes in sex-role stereotyping during infancy. These changes are especially significant considering that male sex-role stereotyping is usually stronger and more predominant than female sex-role steretoyping at this age (Severy et al., 1980).

There is additional evidence of a shift in sex-role stereotyping regarding toy preferences. Zucker and Corter (1980) observed the interaction of adults with four-month-old infants during play, and noted that both male and female adults spend considerably more time using neutral toys than they spend using toys traditionally identified as male or female. Since these findings include male and female adults as well as male and female infants, the implications are broader in scope than previous research. Parents who use neutral toys may encourage a more androgynous orientation toward play—one that becomes acceptable and even preferred by both male and female infants. Once toys become more neutral, or androgynous, in nature, the attributes that accompany them when given to infants of both sexes will become more androgynous. As a result, infants may be better able to explore and develop both feminine and masculine attributes at an early stage of development.

As we noted earlier, male sex-role stereotyping is considerably stronger than female sex-role stereotyping for toddler and preschool children. Thus, boys probably will identify and prefer male-typed toys, and girls possibly will identify and prefer female-typed toys (Eisenberg-Berg, Boothby & Matson, 1979). Boys clearly prefer male-typed toys by two years of age, but their ability to conceptualize the sex-role dimension of the toy is not apparent in their responses (Blakesmore, LaRue & Okejnik, 1979). Girls, however, do not demonstrate a stong preference for girl-typed toys by age two, nor do they possess the ability to conceptualize the sex-role dimension of the toy independently. If the sex-role dimension of the toy is brought to girls' attentions, they are aware of it, but they apparently do not use this information consciously to determine a toy preference.

Parents of preschool children indicate that they fully expect their children to play with the appropriate, culturally defined, sex-typed toy; however, only boys fulfill this general expectation (Schau, Kahn, Diepold &

Cherry, 1980). Specifically, boys play with masculine-typed toys more than they play with either feminine-typed or neutral toys. Girls, however, play most often with neutral toys and equally with feminine-typed and masculine-typed toys. When boys do play with feminine-typed toys, such as a dollhouse or child's kitchen mixer, they invariably play with the toys in a masculine rather than feminine manner. For example, boys are likely to use a child's mixer as a drill or a machine gun rather than for its culturally-defined purpose in the home.

Finally, when preschool children are asked to select toys that would be appropriate for a specific sex and then to justify their choices, boys are more likely than girls to choose sex-inappropriate toys as the most disliked and sex-appropriate toys as the most liked by other boys (Eisenberg, Murray & Hite, 1982). This finding further substantiates the considerable pressure for boys to behave in ways conforming to sex-role

Children play with sex-role stereotyped toys.

stereotypes. As a result, girls do not appear to exhibit as many sex-role stereotypes at this age as do boys.

Our discussion of artifacts has focused primarily on children and their toys, but these artifacts often serve as the foundation for reinforcing sex-roles and sex-role stereotyping in our culture. The powerful images of masculine and feminine created by the media and discussed in Chapter 8 carry tremendous impact in reinforcing artifacts associated with masculine and feminine sex roles for adults. The use of dress, make-up, jewelry, and hairstyle often becomes an extension of sex-role expectations in social settings. Further, the toys we give children are often associated with jobs and occupations traditionally considered masculine and feminine — a nurse's kit versus a doctor's bag, G.I. Joe versus a Barbie doll, or a sewing kit versus a chemistry set.

Giving mom an electric mixer for her birthday and dad a power drill for his birthday may reflect an extension of sex-role expectations for mothers and fathers. Even a man's choice to purchase a particular model of car may differ from a woman's choice for the same purchase because very different images may be associated with different models, and a portion of that image may be sex-role related. It appears, then, that from the toys of childhood to the toys of adulthood, the objects with which we surround ourselves communicate, in part, an extension of our sex-role identity.

Implications and Consequences of Nonverbal Differences

Albert Mehrabian, in his 1981 book, *Silent Messages,* examines the impact of nonverbal communication by asking one simple question: How is it possible to have agreement in using and understanding nonverbal cues when, unlike language, definitions for nonverbal cues are rarely, if ever, explicitly discussed or taught? His answer to this question is based on the premise that only *three* basic dimensions of human feelings and attitudes are conveyed nonverbally: immediacy (liking-disliking), status and power (degree of influence), and responsiveness (activity-passivity). In the next section, we will explore how nonverbal cues influence and reflect these three dimensions in male and female communication.

Nonverbal Cues of Immediacy

Nonverbal cues of *immediacy* indicate the degree of liking or disliking felt in the communication. In general, we are drawn toward people or objects we like, evaluate positively, and prefer. At the same time, we tend to avoid people or objects we dislike, evaluate negatively, or do not prefer. Regardless of the verbal message a communicator may be sending, the degree of liking or disliking that a communicator is feeling may readily be detected through nonverbal cues.

Mehrabian indicates that nonverbal cues usually considered to indicate a high degree of immediacy, or liking, include the following: standing close to rather than far from an individual, leaning forward rather than leaning backward in a chair while listening, facing another individual directly rather than turning to one side, touching, establishing direct eye contact, and using gestures that indicate a desire to reach out to the other person. In addition to these visual nonverbal cues, vocal characteristics may indicate the degree of liking we have for another person. A rich, resonant voice may indicate warmth and friendliness, and such vocal reinforcers as "ah," "uhm," and "uh-huh" may be used by an attentive listener as encouragement in conversation.

Although use of these nonverbal cues probably varies more from situation to situation than from males to females, females traditionally are more likely to demonstrate immediacy cues of liking than are males. Because of the affiliative and nurturing behavior parents more often direct to girls than to boys as they are growing up, girls are more likely to move close to other people, to touch other people, and to make eye contact with other people than boys are. As a result of this socialization, females are more comfortable demonstrating nonverbal cues typically associated with liking, and males are more comfortable with the nonverbal cues of independence and distance often associated with disliking. Unfortunately, men in general may be perceived as being cold and unfeeling because they are not socialized to feel comfortable demonstrating the immediacy cues of liking; and women may be perceived as passive or as seeking approval because they are socialized to demonstrate the immediacy cues of liking. Perhaps most important to realize is that these sex differences are not biologically based; instead, they stem from socializing experiences with parents, peers, and others. Socialization reinforces and enhances traditional masculine and feminine sex roles.

Nonverbal Cues of Status and Power

Nonverbal cues of *status and power* indicate a degree of influence or control rather than a submissive and dependent attitude. The person who is perceived to have a high degree of status and power is able to regulate the degree of immediacy that will be demonstrated in interactions with others; this person becomes the controlling superior in the interaction.

At the same time, the individual who is perceived to be of lower status and power may be viewed as weak or subordinate; this person does not have the right to increase immediacy cues with someone of higher status and power.

Mehrabian discusses several nonverbal privileges that are afforded the individual perceived to be of higher status and power. For example, the high-status individual is provided with a greater expanse of space in which to move and use gestures. As a result, high-status individuals usually feel comfortable assuming a confident, relaxed posture and using expansive gestures that encroach on the space of lower-status individuals. Further, the high-status person is often allowed to refuse eye contact or to initiate touching behavior with a lower-status person. The high-status individual usually projects vocal confidence by speaking with greater volume, at a faster rate, and with fewer pauses. In general, the nonverbal behavioral cues of high-status individuals indicate power through control—the ability to control the amount of approach afforded a lower-status individual.

The literature discussed in this chapter suggests that men traditionally demonstrate the nonverbal cues associated with power and control. As we noted earlier, from infancy, boys command more space in play than girls do and are encouraged to explore away from their parents. As adults, men continue to command more space because they spread their arms and legs out, and use broader body movements and a greater number of large gestures. Women use more eye contact than men; and men are better able to refuse eye contact from both men and women—a sign of power and control. Vocally, men hold the biological advantage of having deeper, more resonant voices, which can often project more volume. These characteristics, too, are often perceived as reflecting high status.

The implications and consequences of men being perceived as having higher status than women are fairly obvious. Perhaps the most significant consequences can be found in the work force, where higher status usually translates into higher salaries. As long as women are perceived as subordinates in the work force, as well as in other communication contexts, their ability to demonstrate power and control will be limited. Women, however, may not be the only losers in this status disparity. As long as men are perceived as having high status, the burdens often associated with decision making will have to be carried by men—burdens of power and control that can create tremendous stress for men in our society. Although some sex differences are biologically based (larger body size and deeper voices), the socialization process, beginning with parents, reinforces traditional sex-role expectations. Boys are encouraged to be independent, exploratory, and task-oriented; these behaviors clearly are linked to power and control. Girls, on the other hand, are encouraged to be dependent passive, and facilitative; these behaviors clearly are linked to submissiveness. Again, socialization tends to reinforce and even encourage traditional masculine and feminine sex-roles associated with status and power cues.

Nonverbal Cues of Responsiveness

Nonverbal cues of *responsiveness* indicate the extent of awareness and reaction to people—the sheer intensity of our communication with others. According to Mehrabian, the highly responsive individual is able to communicate a wide range of emotional responses easily—anger, frustration, happiness, and hurt. The less responsive individual, however, appears withdrawn and oblivious to those around him or her.

Several nonverbal cues are associated with responsiveness. The highly responsive individual typically uses body movements and gestures that are lively and larger than life, commands and uses more space, and initiates more touching behavior. In addition, the highly responsive person demonstrates vocal variety with the fullest use of pitch range and verbal pacing. Adjectives commonly used to describe the highly responsive person include active, dynamic, vital, and involved; the less responsive individual, however, is often described as passive, dull, disinterested, and uninvolved.

As with responsiveness, this communication attribute is probably more directly related to individual personality and situations than it is to being male or female. Men are more responsive on some cues, and women are more responsive on others. For example, men command more space—more broad gestures, greater body expanse, and more initiation of touch. Women, on the other hand, demonstrate a broader range of facial expressions, more direct eye contact, and a greater range of vocal variety. Men tend to demonstrate more responsive cues indicating status and power, and women tend to demonstrate more responsive cues indicating emotional affiliation. Responsiveness may be found in both men and women, but the nature of that responsiveness and the attributes associated with it may differ between men and women. Sex-role stereotyping males as having higher status and women as having lower status and sex-role stereotyping women as affiliative and men as nonaffiliative may constrict the opportunities for both sexes to explore these attributes in their personalities.

Strategies for Change

Just as verbal communication cannot be interpreted out of context, nonverbal communication cannot be interpreted independent from the verbal message; further, one set of nonverbal cues cannot be viewed separately from other nonverbal cues. Both verbal and nonverbal messages come together to complete the communication process. Using Albert Mehrabian's framework of dimensions that may be communicated nonverbally, we can identify nonverbal cues both sexes should strive to adopt.

Immediacy Cues

Traditionally, females more easily display the immediacy cues of liking than do males. This male/female difference has no biological basis; instead, it appears to develop as a result of the socialization process. Almost from birth, girls are socialized to be affiliative and dependent; they are encouraged to express their feelings and emotions, including the immediacy cues of liking. Boys are socialized to be task-oriented and independent; they are encouraged to mask their true feelings, especially the immediacy cues of liking. Since these behaviors are learned through the socialization process, they can be adapted for more effective communication. Consider the following suggestions to encourage more effective communication of immediacy cues.

Both males and females should be encouraged to use nonverbal cues that accurately reflect feelings and emotions, including the immediacy cues of liking. Although females appear to be more comfortable in doing this, both sexes should be taught that masking true feelings (liking *or* disliking) is unproductive in the communication process. For communication to be effective, we must use both verbal and nonverbal cues that are consistent and accurately reflect the message being sent. Masking one set of cues (usually nonverbal cues) will only confuse our intended message.

Because the immediacy cues of liking are learned, parents can play a vital role in encouraging the development of those cues, especially in boys. For example, boys can be socialized from an early age by parents to feel comfortable seeking affiliation with people they like. Parents can encourage boys to engage in social play rather than independent play. They can be taught and encouraged to move closer to people around them (both male and female), to use a wider range of facial expressions and vocal characteristics to express feelings of liking, to use more eye contact directed toward both males and females to draw people into relationships, and to touch both males and females as an indication of liking rather than as an indication of power and control. If parents are willing to encourage and reinforce these behaviors for boys in childhood, they can lay the groundwork for modifying sex-role expectations that often lead to sex-role stereotyping.

Women, too, can play a significant role in assisting men in adapting nonverbal immediacy skills. Women can encourage and positively reinforce men's use of nonverbal immediacy cues to indicate liking. Whether in the interpersonal relationships of friend, spouse, parent, or co-worker, men need to be encouraged to open up and express their true feelings. If men are able to do so, however, women may face a challenge they have never encountered before: women will have to acknowledge and cope with the newly-expressed feelings. While men have become adept at masking their true feelings, women have become adept at ignoring men's true feelings. Although neither of these behaviors leads to productive communication between the sexes, masking and ignoring feelings is considerably easier for both sexes. The real challenge for both men and women comes with expressing feelings and seeking to understand feelings as part of the total communication process; only then will the parameters of sex-role expectations be broadened and the likelihood of sex-role stereotyping be reduced.

Status and Power Cues

Status and power cues are the nonverbal cues most often associated with men rather than with women. Men may possess some physical attributes in adulthood that enhance the perception of power and control (larger body physique and deeper, louder voices), but research suggests that power and status cues are more closely tied to the socialization process than to biological differences. Because these status and power cues also are learned in the socialization process, they too can be adapted for more effective communication. Consider the following suggestions to encourage more effective communication of status and power cues.

Both males and females should be encouraged to use nonverbal cues that reflect status and power when such cues are appropriate to the communication situation. Instead of using these cues as a reflection of sex-role stereotyping (men are always dominant and women are always submissive), both sexes should use these cues when the situation calls for them. For example, it may be appropriate for a woman to use status and power cues as the manager of her office just as it may be inappropriate for her male secretary to demonstrate such cues in the office. We should remember that the nature of the situation, not biological sex or sex-role stereotyping, dictates the use of status and power cues in interpersonal communication.

Because status and power cues are learned, parents can play a vital role in encouraging the development of those cues, especially in girls. Accompanied by the verbal strategies discussed in Chapter 4, girls should be encouraged to use voice and body cues that convey competence and self-confidence in a variety of communication situations. For example, girls should be encouraged to command more space, use more expansive gestures, and use more volume in projecting their voices when assuming leadership roles. These nonverbal cues, coupled with verbal assertiveness, can enhance a female's ability to command the authority and respect often necessary to influence others.

Men, too, can play a significant role in assisting women with learning to use status and power cues. Often when a woman uses assertive nonverbal cues to communicate status and power, she is labeled as aggressive and abrasive. For example, if a woman raises her voice or pounds her fist on the desk to emphasize a point, she may be criticized for behaving aggressively and inappropriately for her sex role. If a man demonstrates these same behaviors, he is considered assertive and authoritarian. Both men and women are guilty of negative sex-role labeling, but men can play a particularly vital role in modifying these stereotypes. Men can prepare women to feel comfortable using status and power cues when they are appropriate. When women do demonstrate these cues, men can label them as assertive and appropriate rather than as aggressive and inappropriate. In addition, men can work to become more comfortable when they relate to women using these nonverbal behaviors. Assertive communication behaviors should be an option afforded to both sexes and should be viewed positively when used by either sex. (See Chapter 9 for a more extensive discussion of assertive behavior.) After all, an equal distribution of power and control between the sexes provides the foundation for a truly democratic society—one that grants members of both sexes the opportunity to rise to the top of the political and economic structure.

Responsiveness Cues

Finally, we have noted that both men and women have the capability to be responsive; unfortunately, men may be limited to responsive cues that reflect status and power, and women may be limited to responsive cues that reflect immediacy and affiliation. Responsiveness on both sets of cues is important, and both men and women need to expand the range of responsiveness in their repertoire of nonverbal cues. From an early age, boys need to be encouraged to use more affiliative behaviors (moving closer to others, using more touch to demonstrate caring, using more facial expression and vocal range to reflect emotions). Learning to use nonverbal responsive cues is crucial if men are to become more expressive in the communication process. Women need to explore and develop responsiveness that reflects power and control in their communication

Fashion affects our projection of self.

rather than subordination (commanding more space, using more expansive gestures to create an image of confidence, using stronger volume to portray competence and command). A willingness to explore the range of responsiveness available in the use of nonverbal cues and the willingness to encourage and reinforce new behaviors in both men and women will provide the foundation for change in sex-role expectations. These behavioral adaptations should reduce sex-role stereotyping for both sexes and enhance the quality of communication between the sexes.

Conclusion

Sex differences and sex-role stereotyping occur in nonverbal cues. In general, women are more adept at encoding (forming) and decoding (translating) nonverbal cues than men—a difference that emerges in childhood and continues into adulthood. In general, men are given and use more personal space than do women. Boys tend to venture farther away from their mothers than do girls, stay away from their mothers longer than girls, and look at as well as talk to their mothers less than girls do. Sex differences in the use and perception of personal space continue as children grow; boys command more space than girls during childhood, adolescence, and into adulthood. In addition, men and women attach different meanings to both place of touch and type of touch in the communication process. Men also initiate more touch than women—usually for the purpose of power and control rather than nurturance and affiliation.

In body movement and posture, toddlers and preschool children tend to use different gestures depending on their sex. Girls tend to use more emblems (nonverbal gestures with verbal equivalents) than boys use. Throughout childhood development and into adulthood, men continue to command more space in both posture and general body movements than women command. Although there are few sex differences in affect display (facial expressions) and eye behavior during infancy, boys tend to inhibit and mask their overt responses to emotion as they grow older, and girls continue to respond freely. As children develop, girls both receive and use more affect displays than boys. As a result, females tend to be better than males at encoding and decoding affect displays throughout their lives.

Although the common sex-role stereotype holds that women are more concerned than men with personal appearance, the majority of what we know from research about perceptions of physical appearance is about men. For men, stereotypes about body build and its link to social acceptance are clearly established by six years of age. Mesomorphs (people with athletic bodies) are perceived as more socially acceptable than are ectomorphs (people with very thin bodies) or endomorphs (people with short, chubby bodies). Women believe that small and slim are important determinants of their physical attractiveness. Unfortunately, diseases such as anorexia nervosa and bulimia have increased as a result of young women striving to meet this sex-role expectation.

Vocal qualities reflect the same sex-role stereotypes as verbal cues. Mothers vocalize more to female infants than to male infants; as they grow older, boys express less emotion in their voices than girls do. As adults, women add questioning tone to their voices by using rising inflections that seem to seek approval; men use downward vocal inflections that convey certainty.

Sex-role stereotypes are also reflected in artifacts, such as toys. As infants, boys play with transportation toys and forbidden objects, such as light switches, more than girls do; girls more often play with soft toys and dolls. Boys are given play objects that encourage activities directed away from the home; girls are given play objects that encourage activities directed toward the home. Recent research, however, suggests that parents are beginning to offer neutral toys to their children. This finding indicates a shift away from some traditional sex-role stereotypes.

Overall, nonverbal behaviors reflect the same sex-role stereotypes we observed in verbal behavior in Chapter 4. Boys and men demonstrate nonverbal cues that conform to sex-role expectations of independence and dominance. Girls and women demonstrate nonverbal cues that conform to sex-role expectations of dependence and submission. Unfortunately, conforming to these sex-role expectations leads to sex-role stereotyping, which can have negative repercussions for both sexes. Because these nonverbal behaviors are taught in the socialization process, males and females can be taught to expand their repertoire of nonverbal cues and break away from rigid sex-role stereotypes. We hope that exploring new behaviors will broaden both male and female communication options and will enhance their communicative capabilitities.

Suggested Activities

1. Spend an hour in a location where people gather, such as a shopping mall, a fast food restaurant, or an outdoor park. Observe the proxemic behavior (use of space) of as many people as you can. Be sure to note their sex and approximate age. What can you conclude about how people use space? How much touching behavior did you observe? When did it occur? Were there any differences in touching behavior between men and women and people of different ages? What did the touching behavior you observed indicate to you about the relationships between the people you were observing? What are the implications of the nonverbal behavior you observed for communication between the sexes?

2. Look through magazines and newspapers and find pictures of male and female mesomorphs, male and female ectomorphs, and male and female endomorphs. Try to find people who are approximately the same age and who are approximately equal in attractiveness except for their body type. Ask ten males and ten females to rate each of the pictures on the following scales:

I think this person is attractive.	Yes	No	Maybe
I would like to be friends with this person.	Yes	No	Maybe
This person is intelligent.	Yes	No	Maybe
I would like to date this person.	Yes	No	Maybe
This person must be lonely.	Yes	No	Maybe
This person is happy.	Yes	No	Maybe

Tabulate the results you obtained for male and female respondents and for males and females of different body types. How are people with each body type perceived? Are males and females perceived differently? Do males and females perceive people with the same body type differently? How do sex-role stereotypes affect our perception of body type?

3. Wear (or bring) your favorite t-shirt to class. Does your t-shirt directly convey a message about sex-role stereotypes (e.g., "A woman's place is in the house--and the Senate," "Men control the world--but women control men")? Could your t-shirt be interpreted differently when worn by a man or a woman (e.g., "It's not easy to be a sex symbol," "Born to be hugged")? Is your t-shirt more likely to be worn by a woman than a man (e.g., "I like the simple things in life--men") or vice versa (e.g., "I used to be disgusted, now I'm just amused")? In general, what does the choice of t-shirts say about the role of sex differences and sex-role stereotypes in the communication process?

For Further Reading

Buck, R. (1976). A test of nonverbal receiving ability: Preliminary studies. *Human Communication Research, 2,* 162–171.

Eisenberg, N., Murray, E., and Hite, T. (1982). Children's reasoning regarding sex-typed toy choices. *Child Development, 53,* 81–86.

Gottman, J. M., and Porterfield, A. L. (1981). Communicative acceptance in the nonverbal behavior of married couples. *Journal of Marriage and the Family, 43,* 817–824.

Henley, N. M. (1977). *Body politics: Power, sex, and nonverbal communication.* Englewood Cliffs, NJ: Prentice-Hall.

Hickson, M. L., and Stacks, D. W. (1985). *Nonverbal communication: Studies and applications.* Dubuque, IA: William C. Brown.

Isenhart, M. W. (1980). An investigation of the relationship of sex and sex role to the ability to decode nonverbal cues. *Human Communication Research, 6,* 309–318.

La France, M., and Mayo, C. (1979). A review of nonverbal behaviors of women and men. *Western Journal of Speech Communication, 43,* 96–107.

Malandro, L. A., and Barker, L. L. (1983). *Nonverbal communication.* Reading, MA: Addison-Wesley.

Mehrabian, A. (1981). *Silent messages: Implicit communication of emotion and attitudes,* 2nd ed. Belmont CA: Wadsworth.

Nguyen, T., Heslin, R., and Nguyen, M. L. (1975). The meanings of touch: Sex differences. *Journal of Communication, 25(3),* 92–103.

Rekers, G. A., and Rudy, J. P. (1978). Differentiation of childhood body gestures. *Perceptual and Motor Skills, 46,* 839–845.

Weitz, S. (1976). Sex differences in nonverbal communication. *Sex Roles, 2,* 175–184.

Communication and Sex Roles in Friendship and Marriage

6

As discussed in Chapter 3, shared meaning created through communication allows us to convey our own identity to others as well as to convey our expectations for others' identities to them. The primary context in which we communicate and develop our identities is in interpersonal relationships involving direct, face-to-face encounters between two people. In particular, these relationships typically are found in friendships, marriage, and the family. Since we discussed the interpersonal dyad of parent and child in Chapter 2 and again in Chapter 5, in this chapter we will focus exclusively on the interpersonal dyads of friendship and marriage.

Friendships, and often marriage, are central relationships in our lives. There are many similarities between these two types of dyadic relationships. First, although marriage is a more institutionalized relationship, both friendship and marriage are uniquely defined and privately negotiated between two people. As a result of this negotiation, both friendship and marriage have the potential to be the deepest, most intimate of all interpersonal relationships. We strive to create relationships that meet our needs. Friendships and marriage give us the opportunity to fulfill such basic relationship (and communication) functions as expressing our feelings, confirming another's identity, serving as a catalyst for change in another, and accomplishing goals outside the relationship. Participating in both friendships and marriage can lead to a fuller, more complete life.

Second, both friendship and marriage require a considerable investment of emotional energy; both demand a commitment between the two people developing the relationship. Friendships range in level of intimacy from acquaintances to casual friends to intimate friends. The amount and depth of the information we disclose to another person increases as we develop a more intimate relationship. An intimate friendship (as well as an intimate marriage) requires continual sharing of yourself, your ideas and feelings, as well as a respect for the other person. Disclosing intimate information makes us vulnerable; thus, *trust* is an essential ingredient for intimacy in both friendship and marriage.

Finally, both friendship and marriage are highly "rhetorical" in nature; that is, they involve people who are self-conscious, intentional, and purposeful in their communication with one another (Rawlins, 1982). Since communication is the underlying process used to define, negotiate, and develop both types of relationships, in this chapter we will explore sex differences and sex-role stereotypes in friendship and marriage, the implications and consequences of these differences, and strategies for change to enhance the quality of these relationships. We will discuss communication in friendships involving only males, friendships involving only females, and friendships between males and females as well as communication in marriage.

Communication in Same-Sex Friendships

Think about the friendships you've experienced over the years. When you first began elementary school, your friends were probably both boys and girls. You walked to school together, you ate lunch together, and you played games at recess together. As you grew from childhood to early adolescence, your circle of friends probably became limited to people of your own sex. Again, you probably walked to school together, ate lunch with these friends and attended after-school activities with them. Although a sexual interest in the opposite sex often emerges with the onset of middle adolescence (as "The Lizzie Pitofsky Poem" shows), our early experiences with same-sex friends and our continued development of these friendships play important roles in our lives.

The Lizzie Pitofsky Poem

I can't get enoughsky
Of Lizzie Pitofsky.
I love her so much that it hurts.
I want her so terrible
I'd give her my gerbil
Plus twenty-two weeks of desserts.

I know that it's lovesky
'Cause Lizzie Pitofsky
Is turning me into a saint.
I smell like a rose,
I've stopped picking my nose,
And I practically never say ain't.

I don't push and shovesky
'Cause Lizzie Pitofsky
Likes boys who are gentle and kind.
I'm not throwing rocks
And I'm changing my socks
(And to tell you the truth I don't mind).

Put tacks in my shoes,
Feed me vinegar juice,
And do other mean bad awful stuffsky.
But promise me this:
I won't die without kiss-
Ing my glorious Lizzie Pitofsky.

[Judith Viorst, "The Lizzie Pitofsky Poem" from *If I Were In Charge of the World and Other Worries*. Copyright © 1981 Judith Viorst. Reprinted with permission of Atheneum Publishers, Inc.]

Men and women exhibit different patterns of same-sex friendships. In characterizing the nature of same-sex friendships, men report many more same-sex friendships than women report; however, women describe their same-sex friendships as intimate more often than men do. According to Lewis (1978), men are probably not as likely to form intimate, same-sex friendships for several reasons. These reasons, for the most part, are associated with sex-role stereotyping in our culture.

First, in our culture the pressure to compete in the work force encourages men to develop many male friendships primarily for the sake of networking, or "making connections." The competitive nature of these same-sex friendships, however, does not encourage the development of intimacy. Instead, these relationships may be with people we consider casual acquaintances or casual friends rather than close, intimate friends. Intimacy in relationships is based on mutual disclosure, which involves trust, and men may not be willing to open themselves up to the risks associated with revealing their feelings to others. In other words, business relationships may be necessary for men to move up the corporate ladder, but men do not share their inner thoughts and feelings with other men who hold the power to hire, promote, or fire them. The costs associated with such intimacy may far outweigh the benefits for men in same-sex relationships.

Second, homophobia, or fear of the label "homosexual," also discourages some men from developing close, intimate male friendships. Men are taught from childhood to value such social concepts as teamwork, brotherhood, camaraderie, and a sense of fraternity, but their close relationships are not supposed to have a sexual connotation. Because homosexuality is still perceived by some people as inappropriate sex-role behavior, any male friendship that might be suspected of such a label may prove difficult for men to develop. As a result, the threat of the "homosexual" label may discourage some men from seeking and developing intimate, same-sex friendships.

Finally, we cannot discount the lack of sufficient role models for men to develop intimate, same-sex friendships. Without the positive reinforcement from interaction with men in close, intimate, same-sex friendships, men may have little motivation to seek intimacy in same-sex friendships and few role models to show them how to develop such intimacy.

Disclosure in Same-Sex Friendships

Regardless of the reason for the differences in intimacy levels between female friends and male friends, observable differences in the disclosure patterns that lead to intimacy do occur. *Disclosure* refers to the sharing of information with another person through the communication process.

More specifically, *self-disclosure* occurs when one person voluntarily communicates information about himself or herself that the other person is unlikely to know or discover from other sources (Pearce & Sharp, 1973). Disclosure should not be confused with intimacy (we can know a lot about someone and still not feel close to that person), but both disclosure and self-disclosure are essential for the development of any intimate, interpersonal relationship. Among its many dimensions, disclosure can differ in its intent, or purpose; its breadth, or range of topics; and its depth, or level of intimacy. The nature of disclosure may vary with both the type of relationship and the stage of development within that relationship (Wilmot, 1980). For example, two people brought together through a shared crisis or disaster may self-disclose more and experience more intimacy in that short amount of time than two people who have worked side-by-side in an office for years and have never had time for self-disclosure. Regardless of the circumstances, however, there must be a certain level of trust between two people for self-disclosure to occur and intimacy to develop (Wheeless & Grotz, 1976).

In general, disclosure among women friends focuses on topics that involve personal and family matters. Such topics are closely related to "self" and tend to be characterized as more emotional in nature than men's talk (Haas & Sherman, 1982). Women often are more willing to share intimate details of their personal lives with other women than men are willing to share with other men. Communication among men generally focuses on topics such as current events, sports, money, and music—topics that may reflect images of competition, power, and status (Sherman & Haas, 1984). There is an old saying that "women are valued for who they are while men are valued for what they do." If this saying is at all reflective of social values, then these topics of conversation tend to reinforce traditional sex-role stereotypes for males and females. Women traditionally talk to each other about personal and affiliative issues that reflect *who they are;* men traditionally talk about task and power issues that reflect *what they do*.

As we noted in Chapter 4, a common sex-role stereotype is that women talk considerably more than men talk. If this stereotype were true, female friendships would be never-ending marathons of dialogue, while male friendships would consist of nothing more than a few, brief utterances. In fact, some research suggests that men talk longer about each topic of conversation they discuss than women or mixed-sex friends do (Ayres, 1980). Other research, however, reports that sports is the primary topic about which men talk longer and in greater depth than any topic discussed by women (Aries & Johnson, 1983). As a result of these somewhat conflicting studies, it is difficult to generalize about the amount of time men and women typically spend discussing topics during the course of a same-sex friendship. Remember, though, that women have no single topic equivalent to sports that accounts for a significant portion of their conversational time. As you may have noticed from your own conversation, however, same-sex friends of either sex are likely to talk about people of the opposite sex rather than about people of their own sex. Men talk about other men less than women talk about other women (Sherman & Haas, 1984). Regardless of whether this talk is positive or negative toward other women, this example reinforces the personal nature of women's talk—women talk about people in general more than men talk about people in general.

Several communication behaviors used by men and women in same-sex friendships demonstrate that women are facilitators of disclosure and that men are controllers of disclosure. Talk among women friends is generally characterized by noncritical listening and mutual support. Women are more likely to sense when their women friends are in trouble and, as a result, provide a sympathetic listening ear that conveys understanding and concern. If a man senses that a close male friend is depressed, his first impulse may be to ignore that depression and change the subject in their conversation. While this behavior is insensitive by female standards, it is considered appropriate between men. In fact, men tend to comfort each other by diverting their attention to inconsequential matters during the course of conversation as an indication of common courtesy (Howell, 1981).

Friends sometimes avoid self-disclosure in their relationships. Women avoid self-disclosure to reduce the potential for personal hurt and to avoid problems with their interpersonal relationships. Because women often disclose personal topics, the potential for damage to the "self" is great. Men avoid self-disclosure as a means of maintaining control over their relationships (Rosenfeld, 1979). As a result, men are often willing to talk frankly and intimately with each other when they are total strangers, will probably never meet each other again, and have no need to control the relationship. In ongoing friendships, however, men are often unwilling to develop such intimacy with other men.

Thus there are some basic differences between disclosure in female friendships and disclosure in male friendships. Although males tend to report more same-sex friends than females, females describe a deeper level of intimacy with their same-sex friends. The amount of disclosure, the nature of that disclosure, and even the reasons for avoiding disclosure differ between male friends and female friends.

Communication in Mixed-Sex Friendships

Our discussion of communication in same-sex friendships focused primarily on differences in disclosure; so too does our discussion of communication in mixed-sex friendships. In addition, we will discuss how the communicator styles used to disclose to each other create distinct roles for males and females in mixed-sex friendships. For the most part, these roles reflect the male dominance through control typically associated with sex-role stereotypes.

Disclosure in Mixed-Sex Friendships

There are some interesting differences in the nature of disclosure in mixed-sex friendships compared to disclosure in same-sex friendships (Hacker, 1981). Specifically, unlike self-disclosure in same-sex friendships, there is no significant difference in the amount of disclosure between men and women in mixed-sex friendships. Instead, differences emerge in the nature of the self-disclosure between men and women. For example, when talking to women friends, men tend to confide more about their weaknesses while they *enhance* their strengths. In this way, men are likely to present a balanced view of their strengths and weaknesses when they disclose to women. Women tend to confide about their weaknesses and *conceal* their strengths. These two different disclosure patterns used by men and women in conversation with each other reinforce some common sex-role stereotypes. Men are expected to assume a superior or dominant position through disclosure, so they include and even enhance their strengths when they confide to women about their weaknesses. Women are expected to facilitate the disclosure process by playing a subordinate role in which they confide only their weaknesses and discuss none of their strengths.

Following such a disclosure pattern, this dialogue might occur between mixed-sex friends. Don tells Karen he failed his biology exam, but adds that he passed every other biology exam this semester. In reply, Karen admits that she, too, did poorly on the exam (she does not reveal her grade of "C") and fails to mention that she currently holds a B average in the course. Karen's decision to conceal her accomplishments should facilitate further self-disclosure from Don; however, to assume the role of facilitator she must shift from an equal position in the communication to a subordinate position that reinforces sex-role stereotypes. This superior/subordinate role relationship often found in mixed-sex communication may indicate that females are more willing to be dominated in conversation and that males are more willing to dominate conversation to conform to sex-role stereotypes (Markel, Long & Saine, 1976).

In dating couples, both males and females indicate that they disclose fully to their partners in almost all topic areas. Analysis of the actual disclosure in these relationships, however, indicates that women disclose more than men in several areas, including disclosure of their greatest fears. In general, women are more likely to be considered the partner who discloses more in dating relationships (Rubin et al., 1980). Further, couples who describe their relationships as egalitarian (based on equality) in sex-role attitudes, disclose more to each other than couples who describe their relationships as traditional (based on inequality) in sex-role attitudes. Thus, a male role based on equality encourages more self-disclosure and emotional intimacy in a close male/female friendship. As a result, couples who hold more equal sex-role attitudes perceive each other as a source of emotional support and as someone to confide in.

Communicator Style in Mixed-Sex Friendships

Disclosure primarily involves the content of what is being communicated, and communicator style primarily involves how that content is conveyed. *Communicator style* refers to "the way one verbally and paraverbally interacts to signal how literal meaning should be taken, interpreted, filtered, or understood" (Norton, 1978, p. 99). Such characteristics as dominant, animated, relaxed, attentive, open, and friendly are often used to describe a person's communicator style. These characteristics contribute to a person's effectiveness in the communication process.

Women generally use a communicator style that others consider attentive and open, and men tend to use a style perceived by listeners as dominant, relaxed, and dramatic (Montgomery & Norton, 1981). These styles of communication coincide with and reinforce the sex-role stereotypes associated with males and females. For example, as we discussed earlier in this chapter, females are perceived to be facilitators of communication; both attentiveness (letting the other person know she is being heard) and openness (receptivity to communication) facilitate the interpersonal communication process. Men are generally perceived to be controllers of communication. Being dominant (taking charge of the interaction), dramatic (manipulating verbal and nonverbal cues to highlight or understate content), and relaxed (anxiety-free) conveys control in the communication process—a control often associated with status and power.

Although people perceive that men and women use different communicator styles, when men and women are asked to describe their own communicator styles, they indicate minimal differences. For example, of all the variables that constitute communicator style, women perceive themselves only as more animated than men, and men perceive themselves only as more precise than women. Both men and women rate themselves similarly on other aspects of communicator style. Thus, both men and women report more similarities than differences in their communicator style. In addition, both men and women report similar perceptions concerning the stylistic characteristics that are considered to be indicators of effective communication. This research, then, highlights male and female similarities in perceptions of communicator style (Montgomery & Norton, 1981).

Most research that examines communicator styles actually used by men and women in mixed-sex friendships focuses on strategies that reflect dominance as a means of controlling the communication. Specifically, the dominance typically associated with men in communication among mixed-sex friends is reflected by men interrupting more than women, talking more than women, receiving more positive evaluations of their performance in dialogue from both men and women, and by the perception of greater male influence (Berger, Rosenholtz & Zelditch, 1980). For example, women's speech acts tend to be longer than men's speech acts in conversation, but communicators of both sexes talk more when the listener is a woman. When men and women are asked to designate who speaks more often in mixed-sex dyads, women are more accurate in their perceptions than men; when they are incorrect, however, they tend to designate the man as the dominant speaker (Markel, Long & Saine, 1976). As we discussed in Chapter 4, women's use of linguistic uncertainties, their increased use of these uncertainties with men, and men's propensity to interrupt women all suggest that men continue to dominate interactions between mixed-sex friends (McMillan et al., 1977).

Language choice in dialogue between mixed-sex friends also indicates differences in male and female communicator styles. In general, there is a tendency for females to judge verbs used in interpersonal communication with friends as more emotional than males do; in contrast, males tend to judge verbs used in interpersonal communication with friends as more reflective of control than females do. For example, a woman may characterize her own behavior toward a man as protecting him (intending to communicate positive emotions), but she may be surprised when he responds to her actions in terms of the control he perceives her communication conveys. Similarly, a woman may express her admiration for a man without realizing the extent to which this places her in a subordinate position within his conceptualization of the relationship. Even in reacting to the word "trust," men are likely to perceive an emotional dimension that implies subordination as a component of the verb that women do not even consider (Thompson, Hatchett & Phillips, 1981). Again, linguistic choices reflect the sex-role stereotype of a superior role for men and a subordinate role for women.

In conclusion, the amount and type of disclosure is important in creating and maintaining male and female sex roles in mixed-sex friendships. As in same-sex friendships, disclosure (and specifically self-disclosure) is essential to the development of mixed-sex friendships. Although men and women use an equal amount of disclosure in mixed-sex friendships, women's disclosure is more intimate and self-related than men's disclosure. In relationships where men and women are equal to one another, both men and women perceive that more disclosure occurs. Perhaps more important in this discussion, however, is the introduction of differences in the communicator styles used by men and women in mixed-sex friendships. A variety of language strategies, ranging from the use of interruptions and duration of speech to language choice and interpretation, reflect and reinforce sex-role stereotypes in these relationships.

Communication in Marriage

Sex Roles in Marriage

The roles we play in relationships include the rights, responsibilities, obligations, and duties typically associated with occupying these positions. The changing roles of men and women in relation to one another probably reflect one of the greatest social changes we will experience in our lifetimes. How women and men have come to view themselves and each other has changed drastically in the last two decades, and nowhere has that change been felt more and carried with it more social impact than within marriage and the family. "Bertha's Wish" expresses a common desire for another kind of change.

Bertha's Wish

I wish that I didn't have freckles on my face.
I wish that my stomach went in instead of out.
I wish that he would stand on top of the tallest building and shout,
"I love you, Amanda."

One more wish: I wish my name was Amanda.

[Judith Viorst, "Bertha's Wish," from *If I Were in Charge of the World and Other Worries*. Copyright © 1981 Judith Viorst. Reprinted with permission of Atheneum Publishers, Inc.]

Traditionally, the husband has been considered the breadwinner of the family whose primary task is to provide a sufficient income to meet the family's needs. With that role of breadwinner often came the implicit role of decision-maker within the marriage and family structure. This traditional role coincided with and reinforced the traditional male sex-role stereotypes of dominance and control. Wives traditionally worked inside the home, focusing primarily (if not exclusively) on housework and childcare. With the role of homemaker often came the implicit role of nurturer and caretaker of both husband and children. These traditional roles coincided with and reinforced the traditional female sex-role stereotypes of subordination and submissiveness. Jim and Margaret Anderson, the happily-married couple on the 1950s television program *Father Knows Best,* represented the ideal male and female sex roles of their time. These traditional roles provided few options, but they did provide clear sex-role expectations for men and women in the context of marriage and family.

In the last two decades, however, these roles and their corresponding responsibilities have shifted considerably due to a variety of social factors. As of 1982, 51 percent of married women in the United States worked outside the home (Thornton & Freedman, 1983). As a result of this basic shift in our work force, among other factors, there has been a considerable shift in the traditional roles held by husbands and wives. Husbands no longer hold the exclusive role of provider outside the home; instead, women share that role and may even carry the greatest economic burden associated with that role.

Entrance into the work force has opened a new set of opportunities and challenges for women. Women have been increasingly concerned with education and career development. In many cases, women have postponed marriage and childbearing until well into their thirties and even into their early forties. Once married, women have become concerned with juggling both the traditional expectations of wife and mother and the new role expectation of a member of the work force. This concern over fulfilling dual roles has led to the "super woman" syndrome—society's expectation that women *should* be able to fulfill the expectation of new roles while continuing to fulfill the expectations of traditional roles.

Husbands also are facing a new set of opportunities and challenges with this role shift. Many men are no longer the sole breadwinners in their homes and, as a result, may not carry the control and power they once did. In addition, men are having to adjust to working alongside of and as subordinates to women in the work force. Sharing the work force with a group in society that may have been barred from that work force twenty years earlier creates a new challenge for men. Finally, with women often gaining career opportunities, men increasingly must consider the demands of career development for their wives and the additional burden that places on them for childcare. Househusbands emerged in the late

1970s when women were able to get high-paying jobs and men often lost them. As a result, some women entered the work force to assume the role of sole breadwinner for their families while men stayed at home to assume the role of caretaker.

Unfortunately, husbands still do not perceive themselves as shifting roles in marriage to accommodate social change. In a study of 224 married couples, the majority of husbands did not identify themselves as expressive or nurturant in their roles as husbands (Fitzpatrick & Indvik, 1982). As a result, wives continue to fulfill the traditional role of caretaker within the home as well as being a member of the work force outside the home (Thornton & Freedman, 1983).

Fitzpatrick and Indvik (1982) identify three basic types of couples in marriages: (1) traditional couples, who reflect traditional sex-role stereotyping within the context of marriage; (2) independent couples, who agree to change and redefine their marital relationships over time; and (3) separate couples, who share little contact and few common bonds in their marriage. Of these three types, only independents use communication behaviors to develop roles based on the personal preferences of each spouse. Most husbands perceive their communication as primarily serving an instrumental function (associated with task completion, problem solving, and concern for oneself as an individual); most wives perceive that their communication serves both instrumental and expressive functions (related to nurturance, concern for others, and for relationships with others) in the relationship, depending on the nature of the relationship they have with their husbands in the marriage (Fitzpatrick & Indvik, 1982).

Examination of perceived sex-role congruity in marriages seeks to discover how husbands and wives assess instrumental functions and expressive functions in determining the quality of their relationships. Specifically, marriages perceived to be of the lowest quality are between traditional husbands whose communication serves primarily an instrumental function and modern wives who prefer their husbands to reflect both an instrumental and expressive communication function (Aries, 1982). Dissatisfaction between such husbands and wives most likely stems from a wife's desire to change the role expectations of a traditional husband and the traditional husband's reluctance to change.

Disclosure in Marriage

As they do in mixed-sex friendships, women provide much of the support for disclosure in marriage. Women attempt to initiate considerably more topics into conversations than men do; unfortunately, only about one-third of these topics actually develop into conversations for the couple (Fishman, 1978). The initiation of topics in marital conversations by women eases the flow of conversation. If initiation is abandoned by women, and the conversational flow breaks down, neither husband nor wife may be able to understand *why* the breakdown of disclosure has occurred.

In addition, women ask nearly three times as many questions of men in marital conversations, primarily for the purpose of drawing them out and facilitating interaction. Women use twice as many attention-getters, such as "this is really interesting" or "did you know that . . ." to flag interest in what their husbands are saying. Wives also intersperse the phrase "you know" (commonly considered a filler phrase) throughout conversations about ten times as often as husbands do, apparently to hold their husbands' interest in conversation. In addition, wives use words and phrases like "oh, really" and "uh-huh" to encourage their husbands to keep talking. These cues are common regulators, which serve to maintain the flow of conversation from husbands. Wives continually yield their turns to speak to their husbands.

Another conversational variable in marital communication is the use of idioms and the function they serve in the relationship. Hopper, Knapp, and Scott (1981) note that *idioms* are "the private expressions and gestures shared by a couple that can help define the norms of their relationship and promote its cohesiveness" (p. 23). Idioms stabilize as the couple's communication patterns stabilize over time, and they are generally perceived to have a positive impact on the relationship. Over half the idioms used by couples are restricted to private contexts. Idioms that express affection are the idioms most likely to appear as nonverbal cues, such as holding hands or caressing; teasing insults are primarily expressed in verbal play. Both men and women credit men with originating most of the idioms used in marital relationships, but researchers note that they are unable to determine if husbands initiate more idioms than their wives initiate, or if men's idioms are more likely to become adopted than women's idioms. Men label nicknames they use for their wives as terms of endearment, but wives are more likely to perceive these terms of endearment as insults or criticism (Hopper, Knapp & Scott, 1981).

Nonverbal codes between marriage partners have been found to be a more effective discriminator between distressed and nondistressed couples than verbal codes (Gottman & Porterfield, 1981). For example, when couples are asked to act happy, nonverbal behaviors used between the partners are the only basis for distinguishing between distressed couples and nondistressed couples (Vincent et al., 1979). There is a primary message system rooted in the nonverbal communication between satisfied couples that operates efficiently. Further, there appears to be a deficiency in dissatisfied couples when the husband is unable to discriminate nonverbal behaviors very efficiently or to decode their meaninng very effectively.

The husband's nonverbal decoding ability is extremely important in determining marital satisfaction. In general, there is a positive relationship between marital satisfaction and husbands' nonverbal competence in interpreting their wives' nonverbal cues (Gottman & Porterfield, 1981). A husband's deficiency in decoding nonverbal messages could be the result of differing perceptions of the emotional message contained in the wife's nonverbal messages, or it could be the result of the dissatisfied husband's emotional withdrawal from his wife. Regardless of the reasons, the formation (encoding) and translation (decoding) of nonverbal messages plays an important role in the perception of marital satisfaction. As we noted in Chapter 5, men in general have more difficulty in both encoding and decoding nonverbal messages; the impact of this difficulty is felt most acutely in the interpersonal relationship of marriage.

Communicator Style in Marriage

The communicator style considered effective in other relationships and communication contexts differs from the communicator style considered effective within marriage. While such characteristics as impression formation, dominant, relaxed and attentive communication may predict an effective communicator in other contexts, such characteristics as friendly, attentive, precise, and expressive are the best predictors of an effective communicator in marriage. In fact, such characteristics as relaxed, friendly, open, dramatic, and attentive are most often identified as effective communicator styles by happily married couples, and attentive is considered the best predictor of an effective female communicator in less happily married couples. These characteristics reflect interpersonal dimensions that communicate comfort and sensitivity to a spouse. In addition, dominant is not identified as one of the necessary characteristics of an effective female communicator within marriage, but it does predict an effective communicator in most other communication situations. Overall, happily married couples report a greater number of communicator styles exhibited in maritial communication than less happily married couples report (Honeycutt, Wilson & Parker, 1982).

Communicator styles that reflect dominance and control in marriage also have been examined. The more dominant a husband is compared to his wife, the more likely the wife is to ask questions of him rather than to make definite requests. The more domineering spouse in a relationship, whether it is the husband or the wife, is more likely to interrupt his or her partner (Courtright, Millar & Rogers-Millar, 1979). Hershey and Werner (1975) observed that wives associated with the women's movement were more likely to speak longer and to speak last in conversations with their husbands than wives not associated with the women's movement. However, Hershey and Werner noted no significant differences between groups in the husbands' total speaking time, the number of joint decisions reached, the patterns of talking first, or the measures of conflict.

With the changing roles of men and women in today's society, perhaps no greater area of change can be found than in marriage. Independent couples who are willing to redefine and renegotiate the nature of their relationships are best equipped to cope with changing roles. The communication strategies most married couples use are consistent with traditional sex-role stereotypes—men dictate the topic areas to be discussed, and women facilitate the flow of interaction. Men continue to hold the dominant, power positions, and women continue to maintain a subordinate, facilitative role in the communication process. Perhaps the greatest change reflected in recent communication research is that women increasingly express the desire for their husbands to develop expressive, nurturing skills, both verbal and nonverbal. This desire may stem from the changing roles of husbands and wives; as wives become breadwinners and husbands become caretakers, women are more concerned that men develop skills that will enhance caretaking.

Implications and Consequences of Sex Roles in Friendship and Marriage

In examining both friendship and marriage in this chapter, one observation is apparent: traditional sex-role stereotypes associated with male and female communication in general remain relatively consistent across both types of relationships. In general, females disclose more and use a communicator style that is facilitative and expressive, and males disclose less and use a communicator style that is controlling and instrumental.

Within same-sex friendships, women focus on topics related to people—self, family, and friends. Female friends encourage disclosure in their interactions and provide a supportive communication climate to facilitate such disclosure. Expressive and facilitative behaviors are those typically associated with traditional sex-role stereotypes for women. It is not surprising, then, that these behaviors are prevalent in female interactions and are often the focus for study of communication among women. Men focus on topics related to status, power, and competition. They often avoid rather than facilitate disclosure, often to control the focus and direction of interaction. These functions, too, are consistent with traditional sex-role stereotypes for men. In same-sex friendships, women communicate with the tools they use most effectively, and men communicate with the tools they use most effectively. The ideal communication might be described as a combination of both communication functions; however, communication among women friends and communication among men friends is probably perceived as quite efficient and perhaps even preferable to mixed-sex interactions, even though it does not reflect that blend of both functions.

In our discussion of mixed-sex friendships and marriage, we noted that both men and women continue to maintain traditional sex roles as communicators. The diverse styles that are typically associated with men and women seem to be enhanced in the mixed-sex communication setting. Again, men tend to use communication that reinforces images of power, status, and control, and women tend to use communication that reinforces images of expressivity and facilitation.

In both mixed-sex friendships and marriage, women initiate more topics (facilitation), but men decide which of those topics will actually become conversation (control). In both mixed-sex friendships and marriage, men's topics and language choices are more task-oriented (instrumental), and women's topics and language choices are more personal and emotional (expressive). Men interpret verbs as possessing a control dimension, and women interpret verbs as possessing an emotional dimension.These interpretations reinforce male control and female facilitation during mixed-sex interactions in friendship and marriage. Women encourage disclosure (facilitation), and men avoid disclosure (control). When men and women do disclose, men disclose strengths and conceal weaknesses (superiority), and women disclose weaknesses and conceal strengths (subordination). Again, these communication behaviors reinforce traditional sex-role stereotypes for both men and women.

The quality of communication is important in both friendship and marriage, yet communication in marriage has been analyzed for quality and satisfaction more. In marriage, wives want their husbands to disclose more and actively to serve the expressive and affiliative functions in communication. Husbands do not appear to want their wives to make a similar shift to new communication behaviors; instead, they prefer their wives to continue to serve the expressive and facilitative functions rather than to shift to power and control. As noted by Fitzpatrick and Indvik (1982), however, couples who are open to redefinition and to changes in their relationships (independents) will find perhaps the greatest satisfaction because they explore new communication behaviors rather than remain with traditional ones.

Strategies for Change

With our changing society, change and flux in the basic interpersonal relationships of friendship and marriage are inevitable. With the mobility of our population, it is likely that you will initiate, maintain, and terminate both same-sex and mixed-sex friendships many times throughout your life. Further, with the skyrocketing divorce rate (approximately two out of every three marriages), it is also likely that you will initiate, maintain, and terminate more than one marriage in your lifetime. The statistics reflect the quantity of friendships and marriages you may encounter in a lifetime, but the quality of those relationships is a far more important issue.

The shift away from traditional male and female sex roles in general and from traditional male and female sex roles in marriage has changed the quality of our friendships and marriages by introducing ambiguity and uncertainty. But the answer to increasing quality in these relationships does not lie in creating new, rigid roles to replace the old ones. Instead, we need to create a mechanism for coping with evolving roles in our interpersonal relationships. With the variety of new roles available to men and women because of changing social conditions, we must be open to redefining and renegotiating changes in the roles associated with friendship and marriage. Unfortunately, opportunities for change generate ambiguity; only through effective communication in friendships and marriage can we negotiate role definitions that will enhance relationship satisfaction (Petronio, 1982). Consider the following suggestions to facilitate adaptation and change in friendship and marriage.

Develop a Supportive Climate for Change

Because any change in relationships carries with it an implicit message of dissatisfaction from the one seeking change, it is important that one or both parties in the relationship avoid feeling defensive or threatened by the possibility of change. To view change as an opportunity to create a mutually-satisfying relationship rather than as an attack or a negative assessment of current definitions is essential to the process of change. Using communication techniques that create a supportive climate establishes a positive context for change.

Use communication that encourages others to describe their feelings about the relationship and their role in that relationship. Suggest a willingness to cooperate in a mutual problem-solving orientation that will help establish the communication climate necessary for change. After all, any change requires adaptation from both people in the relationship. To use communication that evaluates feelings rather than communication that describes and understands them, that implies superiority of one person in defining change rather than equality in defining and renegotiating change, and that encourages manipulation and control rather than mutual problem solving is to prevent the communication climate necessary to negotiate new roles and relational change. (Read "Maybe We'll Make It" for another view of this change process.)

Maybe We'll Make It

If I quit hoping he'll show up with flowers, and
He quits hoping I'll squeeze him an orange, and
I quit shaving my legs with his razor, and
He quits wiping his feet with my face towel, and
We avoid discussions like
Is he really smarter than I am, or simply more glib,
Maybe we'll make it.

If I quit looking to prove that he's hostile, and
He quits looking for dust on the tables, and
I quit inviting Louise with the giggle, and
He quits inviting Jerome with the complex, and
We avoid discussions like
Suppose I died, which one of our friends would he
marry,
Maybe we'll make it.

We've fully examined James Reston, the war,
John Updike, religion, the Renaissance, CORE,
And on all major issues we're for and against
The same things.

Yet somehow we've managed to not miss a fight,
He tells me there's nothing to nosh on at night.
I tell him that no one can sleep with a light in her eyes,
Not to mention
He takes too much time in the bathroom. But

If I quit clearing the plates while he's eating, and
He quits clearing his throat while I'm speaking, and
I quit implying I could have done better, and
He quits implying he wishes I had, and
We avoid discussions like
Does his mother really love him, or is she simply one
of those over-possessive, devouring women who
can't let go,
Maybe we'll make it.

Encourage Appropriate Disclosure

In both types of relationships we explored in this chapter, we noted differences in disclosure patterns for males and females. Women traditionally tend to disclose about "self" and about personal topics for the purpose of serving expressive and affiliative needs. Men tend to disclose about task or goal-oriented topics for the purpose of serving instrumental needs. Perhaps one of the greatest frustrations expressed by women in mixed-sex friendships and marriage is that men do not disclose on that expressive level. While men may find it difficult to alter the nature of their disclosure because they are not socialized to do so, men need to practice disclosing about "self" in interpersonal relationships where trust has been established.

Since men appreciate this type of disclosure from women in relationships, men obviously value it. Men should strive to share their feelings more openly with their close friends and spouses. Women should continue to facilitate and positively reinforce this type of disclosure in their relationships. As with any appropriate disclosure, expressive disclosure will vary depending on the type of relationship and the stage of development in that relationship. Ideally, expressive disclosure will occur in small increments over time and will be a reciprocal process in the relationship (Wilmot, 1980).

Husbands and fathers who are willing to explore this range of behaviors will begin to break some of the negative socialization for the next generation of husbands and fathers. Boys who are able to observe this disclosure pattern in adult males and to engage in this disclosure pattern with adult males will be exposed to the most effective form of role-modeling possible. As a result, the quantity of same-sex male intimate friendships may increase without the negative connotations sometimes attached to them, and the quality of mixed-sex relationships will be strengthened by a mutual sharing of expressive, feeling-oriented messages.

Develop Effective Communicator Styles

As we examined both friendship and marriage, we noted some differences between men and women in their communicator styles. These stylistic choices carry with them the intent to control rather than facilitate the relationship. For example, women initiate topics to facilitate conversation, but men are more successful at developing the topic that will be maintained as a form of control. Women use many verbal and nonverbal turn-yielding cues to facilitate the continuation of interaction with males, but men often use interruptions and avoidance to control the continuation or discontinuation of a conversation. Women tend to be more adept at both encoding and decoding nonverbal cues that are related to expressiveness in the relationship. Men tend to use a style that enhances the instrumental functions within the relationship.

Although the traditional male/female relationship in general, and marriage in particular, has reflected male dominance and female subordination, those traditional roles are changing. Any power structure in a relationship may be satisfying to the people involved. Examine the power structures in your relationships and assess your satisfaction with them. Relationships that reflect patterns of communication based on inequality and differences are said to be *complementary* in nature. Much like a parent-child relationship, complementary patterns of communication imply a superior-subordinate relationship. Relationships that reflect patterns of communication based on equality and similarity are said to be *symmetrical* in nature, and are often seen in peers who form friendships based on peer equality. While the complementary pattern of communication may be closer to traditional sex-role stereotypes, where men dominate and women are subordinate, the symmetrical pattern of communication is more closely aligned with the independent, or nontraditional relationships described earlier in the chapter. In these relationships, both people are committed to growth and change in the relationship based on the recognition that there will be equal input into that growth process.

These two patterns of communication provide clear, but dichotomous categories of power in relationships, but the reality is that most relationships probably reflect both of these power structures at various times and on various issues. Rather than using only complementary or only symmetrical patterns of communication in a relationship, consider the benefits of both at given times in the relationship. Consider communication options for your relationship so that no one person is superior or subordinate all the time. For example, a husband may be the primary decision-maker on the purchase of furntiure while the wife may be the primary decision-maker on the purchase of a car. In this instance, both husband and wife serve the instrumental function of decision-maker at different times and concerning different decisions within the relationship. At the same time, symmetrical patterns of communication based on equality in the relationship should become apparent. Relationships that employ a combination of both complementary and symmetrical communication patterns within the relationship are said to be using a *parallel* communication pattern. Again, the key to redefining and changing a relationship is being open to a variety of communication choices—adopting a parallel pattern of communication.

Conclusion

Interpersonal relationships such as friendships and marriage are shaped and maintained through the process of communication. Because of the intimacy that can develop in these relationships, they provide us with the ultimate opportunity for satisfaction in our communication with others. Men and women communicate differently in these relationships. Women tend to be more intimate with their female friends than men are with their male friends. Women share more intimate details of their personal lives and provide more noncritical listening as well as emotional support in their interactions with others.

In mixed-sex friendships, women and men express the same amount of disclosure, but on different topics and in different ways. Men are more likely to enhance their strengths and conceal their weaknesses, while women do just the opposite. Couples who report an egalitarian attitude toward sex roles are the couples who demonstrate more disclosure from both partners. As a result, the modern male sex role of equality may be encouraging more intimacy in relationships than is found in relationships based on traditional sex roles.

When a relationship progresses to marriage, sex differences in communication patterns continue. In fact, marriages perceived to provide the least satisfaction involve a traditional husband whose communication primarily serves an instrumental function and a modern wife who prefers her husband's communication to serve both an instrumental and an expressive function. As in conversations in mixed-sex friendships, women provide much of the support for conversations in marriage. Wives ask more questions, use more attention-getters (for example, "this is really interesting"), and provide encouragement to their husbands to continue talking. This facilitative role of wives in marital communication is crucial for lubricating the communication process.

An examination of communication in interpersonal relationships serves to reinforce the traditional sex roles associated with communication between the sexes in other settings. If we are to provide more satisfaction in our communication and adapt to the shifting roles of men and women in our society, our communication must explore redefining relationships and negotiating change. Men should explore the expressive and facilitative behaviors they can demonstrate, and women should explore the instrumental and control behaviors they can use to facilitate the communication process. A communication climate supportive of change, a commitment to develop appropriate disclosure skills, and a decision to explore alternative communicator styles can enhance the quality of communication in friendship and marriage. The most effective communication in these relationships will not depend on the use of sex-role stereotyped communication behaviors, but will come from both men and women exploring the use of a variety of communication behaviors appropriate to the nature of the relationship and the demands of the situation.

Suggested Activities

1. Think of your best male friend and best female friend. Answer each of the following questsions for each person:

What general topics do you discuss when you are together?
What topics do you discuss in greater depth?
Who most often initiates these topics?
Who most often interrupts the other?
Who asks more questions during a conversation?

Compare your answers to these questions for both of these relationships. What are the similarities and differences between the communication in these two relationships? What is the level of disclosure in each relationship? Does one person tend to disclose more than the other? Why do you think these similarities and differences exist? How do your answers agree with the research presented in this chapter on communication in same-sex and mixed-sex friendships?

2. Watch a re-run of a television program from the 1950s, 1960s, or 1970s that portrays family life (e.g., *The Honeymooners, Leave It to Beaver, I Love Lucy,* or *My Three Sons*). List the behaviors of "mothers," "fathers," and "children" that reflect traditional sex-role stereotyping in families (e.g., father goes to work and mother stays home).

Watch a current television program that portrays the same type of situation (e.g., *Family Ties, The Cosby Show,* or *Silver Spoons*). How have the family structure, roles, role expectations, and behaviors identified with specific roles changed? Did you observe the same types of behaviors that reflect sex-role stereotyping? Why or why not?

3. Select a dating or marital relationship you can observe. This relationship can be one in which you are involved, one that you can observe directly, or one that is portrayed in literature, on television, or in a film. Answer each of the following questions for both people involved in this relationship:

What general topics do they discuss when they are together?
What topics do they discuss in greater depth?
Who most often initiates these topics?
Who most often interrupts the other?
Who asks more questions during a conversation?

From this description, what can you learn about communication in intimate relationships? What is the level of disclosure in this relationship? Does one person tend to disclose more than the other? What communication behaviors does the male in the relationship exhibit that the female does not and vice versa? Why do you think the similarities and differences in communication behavior you observed exist? How do your answers agree with the research presented in this chapter on communication in dating and marriage?

4. In a group of three to five people of the same sex, choose the adjectives from the following list that would best describe the ideal mate:

acts as a leader
adaptable
affectionate
aggressive
ambitious
analytical
assertive
athletic
cheerful
childlike
compassionate
competitive
conceited
conscientious
conventional
defends own beliefs
does not use harsh language
dominant
eager to soothe hurt feelings
feminine
flatterable
forceful
friendly
gentle
gullible
happy
has leadership abilities
helpful
independent
individualistic
inefficient
jealous
likeable
loves children
loyal
makes decisions easily
masculine
moody
reliable
secretive
self-reliant
self-sufficient
sensitive to needs of others
shy
sincere
soft spoken
solemn
strong personality
sympathetic
tactful
tender
theatrical
truthful
understanding
unsystematic
warm
willing to take a stand
willing to take risks
unpredictable
yielding

After you have completed that task, choose the adjectives that you think someone of the opposite sex would choose to describe the ideal mate. Compare your lists with the lists made by other groups. What are the major differences between the male view of an ideal mate and the female view of an ideal mate? What are the major differences between what males think females want as an ideal mate and what females say they want? Which of these perceptions are based on sex-role stereotypes? What are the implications of these differing perceptions for communication between the sexes?

For Further Reading

Bohn, E., and Stutman, R. (1983). Sex-role differences in the relational control dimensions of dyadic interaction. *Women's Studies in Communication, 6,* 96–104.

Briere, J., and Lanktree, C. (1983). Sex-role related effects of sex bias in language. *Sex Roles, 9,* 625-632.

Critelli, J.W., and Waid, L.R. (1980). Physical attractiveness, romantic love, and equity restoration in dating relationships. *Journal of Personality Assessment, 44,* 624–629.

DeForest, C., and Stone, G. L. (1980). Effects of sex and intimacy level on self-disclosure. *Journal of Counseling Psychology, 27,* 93–96.

Hendrick, S. S. (1981). Self-disclosure and marital satisfaction. *Journal of Personality and Social Psychology, 40,* 1150–1159.

Indvik, J., and Fitzpatrick, M. A. (1982). "If you could read my mind, love . . . ," Understanding and misunderstanding in the marital dyad. *Family Relations, 31,* 43–51.

Jorgensen, S. R., and Gaudy, J. C. (1980). Self-disclosure and satisfaction in marriage: The relation examined. *Family Relations, 29,* 281–287.

Montgomery, B. M. (1981). The form and function of quality communication in marriage. *Family Relations, 30,* 21–30.

Rawlins, W. K. (1982). Cross-sex friendship and the communicative management of sex-role expectations. *Communication Quarterly, 30,* 343–352.

Rubin, Z., Peplau, L., and Hill, C. (1981). Loving and leaving: Sex differences in romantic attachments. *Sex Roles, 7,* 821–835.

Communication and Sex Roles in the Educational Environment

7

One of the primary socializing agents in our society is the school. Much of our early life is spent in school; for many children, the school's influence begins by age three, when they enter preschool, and for some this influence continues through graduate school. This socializing agency exerts a great influence in the area of sex-role socialization. Unfortunately, the school, more often than not, has fostered sex-role stereotyping (Jenkins, Gappa & Pearce, 1983; Sadker & Sadker, 1985). Women are marginalized from education by its content and by the classroom interactional processes (Mahony, 1983). Stereotyped behavior for men is reinforced.

Think back to your high-school years. What subjects did young women take? What subjects were primarily reserved for young men? If you took a home economics class like sewing, were many boys in it? If physics was a course you took, how many girls were in the class? If your high school was like many others, science and math classes were the domain of males; home economics, art and office business courses were the domain of females. Regardless of whether we examine the education of females historically, or the differences in male/female occupational choices, or the content of curriculum subjects, we find that the educational system tends to mold the future dominant roles of males and tends to channel females into less dominant roles. Sex-role stereotyping results in what has been termed girls' "below stairs" relationship to education (Mahony, 1983).

The "below stairs" relationship to education, however, is not solely the result of the content of the school curriculum. Male and female teachers communicate differently with male and female students. For example, a common practice for teachers, both male and female, is to *give* male students specific instructions on how to complete a project, but to *show* female students how to do it. Such behavior on the part of teachers may communicate that males are more capable and more important than females, since it takes more time to explain something than to demonstrate it. Despite federal laws and regulations that prohibit sex discrimination in educational institutions, inequities still exist (Hall & Sandler, 1982). In this chapter, we will discuss some of the inequities, the implications and consequences of these inequities, their effect on communication, and strategies for eliminating them.

Inequities in Education

As we noted earlier, sex-role stereotyping exists in both the content of educational materials and in classroom interaction patterns. Often this stereotyping is subtle. In terms of educational content, sex-role stereotyping occurs in textbooks, as well as in other educational materials, such as college catalogs and counseling materials. Sex-role stereotyping exists in classroom communication patterns and, also, as a result of teacher expectancy. In this section, we will examine the extent and types of sex-role stereotyping. Later in this chapter, we will examine the consequences of stereotyping and suggest strategies for change.

Textbooks

Textbooks are an important part of the educational material provided to students. Sex-role stereotyping occurs in textbooks primarily in three areas: numerical differences, stereotyped behavior patterns and characteristics, and sexist language. In this section, we will examine the extent of the stereotyping in each of these areas.

Numerical Differences

In a survey of 134 children's readers (containing a total of 2,750 stories) from fourteen publishers, Women on Words and Images (1972) found the following ratios:

Boy-centered to girl-centered stories	5:2
Adult male to adult female main characters	3:1
Male biographies to female biographies	6:1
Male animal stories to female animal stories	2:1
Male folk or fantasy stories to female folk or fantasy stories	4:1

A 1975 update of this study found similar results. Most ratios remained the same. The only significant changes were that the ratio of male to female biographies improved to 2:1, but the ratio of boy-centered to girl-centered stories decreased to 7:2 (Women on Words and Images, 1975).

Similar results can be found in all subject matter areas. For example, more males than females are pictured in textbook illustrations. Researchers examining the most used elementary textbooks in grades 1 through 6 found disturbing results (Weitzman & Rizzo, 1975). In science textbooks, females are in only 26 percent of the illustrations. In social studies textbooks, 33 percent of the illustrations include females. In one series designed to teach reading, 102 stories are about boys and only 35 are about girls. Math textbooks picture mathematically competent boys and mathematically incompetent girls. In math textbooks, females are pictured as Indian dolls or witches, or participating in activities such as skipping rope and buying balloons. Males are pictured as sailors, kings, bakers, circus performers, band members, and balloon sellers. The ratio of males pictured to females pictured is 15:1 (Mliner, 1977). Such illustrations present negative images of females and present sex-role stereotypes of the behavior considered appropriate for each sex.

In content, as well as in illustrations, numerical discrepancies exist. In the twelve history texts most often used in American public schools, women are almost absent. For example, in one two-volume set of history books, two sentences describe the women's suffrage movement. Another textbook uses five *lines* to describe the role of the frontier woman and five *pages* to describe the six-shooter—a gun (Arlow & Froschel, 1976). Even when women are discussed in history textbooks, passages frequently include misleading words or phrases that detract from the significance of women and their accomplishments. For example, one text informs readers that no women were members of the Senate in 1972 when, in fact, Margaret Chase Smith served as a Senator (Kirby & Julian, 1981).

Discrepancies also exist in the numbers of male and female authors included in textbooks. In a survey of English literature anthologies, the seventeen books that were examined included sections by 147 male authors and selections by only 25 female authors (Arlow & Froschel, 1976). A survey by the same researchers of 400 selections reveals 75 female authors and 306 male authors. Most anthologies dealing with speech communication feature speeches by men (Sprague, 1975).

Stereotyped Behavior Patterns and Characteristics

Although the numerical discrepancies in curriculum materials are disturbing, since the lack of female characters and authors can communicate a lack of importance of females in society, even more problematic is the way in which females are portrayed. They are portrayed as emotional, fearful, and incompetent (relying on others to solve their problems and comfort them). They are constantly concerned with their appearance and spend the majority of their time cooking, sewing, or watching as boys play sports, make things, solve problems, or experience adventures. They often demean themselves and accept ridicule from boys. Boys, on the other hand, are portrayed as clever, adventurous, and brave. According to one study of children's stories (Women on Words and Images, 1975), male characters come from 147 different occupations—architect, hunter, veterinarian, radio reporter, computer operator, news reporter, and museum manager. Women are presented in only 26 different occupations. The major occupation portrayed is that of mother. Others include witch, fat lady, cleaning woman, housekeeper, governess, secretary, nurse, and recreation director.

Generally, stereotypical roles can be found in all types of textbooks. In speech communication textbooks, for example, hypothetical applications of communication skills, such as a man arguing in court and a woman making an announcement at a PTA meeting, perpetuate sex-role stereotypes. (See Randall, 1985; Sprague, 1975). In math texts, men are depicted as active, alert, and scientific. They are more often pictured doing math and most story problems are about males. Women are depicted as dull and insignificant and are rarely involved in career situations. Story problems tend not to be about females unless they involve "feminine" activities such as cooking (Rogers, 1975). In science textbooks, males control the action and females watch the action; boys perform experiments, girls clean up. In addition, adult women are almost never presented in scientific roles (Trecker, 1973).

Sexist Language

As we noted in Chapter 4, one of the problems with textbooks in all subject matter areas is the use of the generic pronoun "he." People have often assumed that when the word "he" is used, children understand that everyone, male and female, is included. Harrison and Passer (1975) attempted to confirm that children automatically include females in traditional generic terms. They presented third-graders with written situations below which were a series of different-sex line drawings. The children were asked to circle the appropriate drawing or drawings. Each situation was presented in two forms: one using a generic term like "men" or "salesmen" and one using a neutral term like "people" and "salesperson." When the traditional generic term was used, 49 to 85 percent of the children circled only the drawings depicting males. When neutral terms were used, only 3 to 31 percent of the pupils circled all the male drawings. Harrison (1975) conducted a similar study with junior high-school students. A similar tendency for students to exclude women from consideration in their interpretation of the situation was found. If a sentence reads "he," students interpret the language literally—it means "male." Thus, language terms such as "he" and "men" are not perceived by children to include women.

Counseling and Guidance Materials

Students use textbooks in the classroom, but they also use materials available through guidance counseling offices. Often these materials contain the same sex-role stereotyping that is found in textbooks in numerical differences, stereotyped roles, and sexist language.

Numerical Differences

Women (compared to their numbers in the labor force) are underrepresented in both the 1972 and the 1974 *Occupational Outlook Handbook,* the vocational guidance materials used in most high schools (Birk, Cooper & Tanney, 1975). Men and women are rarely shown in nontraditional occupations. Similar results are found in the *Vocational Guidance Quarterly*'s career literature bibliography and in two other bibliographies of commercial and noncommercial materials (Vetter, 1975). In all the materials reviewed, 61 percent of all illustrations are of men, 21 percent are of women, and 18 percent are of both men and women. An analysis of the 1974 – 75 *Encyclopedia of Careers and Vocational Guidance* and the *Occupational Outlook Handbook* reveals that 11 percent of the *Encylopedia* illustrations and 17 percent of the *Handbook* illustrations are of women. The women shown are stereotypically represented as helpful, pleasant, and attractive (Harway, 1977).

In an analysis of 100 college catalogs and 19 proprietary school catalogs (which often constitute a portion of the materials high-school counselors use to advise students), Harway (1977) found that a higher percentage of catalog content is devoted to males than to females. This research calculated a percentage of the half-pages in catalogs devoted to males and to females:

	Percent of half-pages devoted to men	**Percent of half-pages devoted to women**
Four-year colleges and universities	23	Less than 1
Two-year institutions	16	2
Proprietary schools	14	9

Stereotyped Roles

Males and females in college catalogs are presented stereotypically. Men are administrators and professors; women are nurses. Men are participating in contact sports; women are exercising alone or in dance classes. One researcher concludes that the limited vistas for women shown in college catalogs may convince many high-school students that the options available to women are also limited in colleges themselves (Harway, 1977).

Sexist Language

Finally, sexist language may appear in material that has an influence on high-school students. For example, in one research study, students rated employment advertisements according to how interested they would be in the jobs (Bem & Bem, 1973). Each student received a list of twelve job advertisements on one of three different forms. Eight of the job opportunities were identical on all of the forms, but four telephone company ads were varied. On one form, the ads were in traditional exclusionary language, for example, "framemen"; on another form, the ads were in inclusionary language, for example, "sales representative"; on the third form, the ads were in sex-reversed exclusionary language, for example, "linewoman." When the wording was exclusionary, men and women expressed interest in the opposite-sex job only 30 percent and 5 percent of the time, respectively. When the wording was inclusionary or sex-reversed exclusionary, students were more willing to show an interest in the job. Thus, sexist language has an impact on how males and females view the appropriateness of occupations for their sex.

Sexism in high-school counseling occurs not only in the materials used, but also in the attitude of the counselors themselves. Four areas of bias have been identified: (1) fostering traditional sex roles; (2) showing bias in expectations and devaluation of women; (3) using sexist theoretical concepts; and (4) responding to women as sex objects (American Psychological Association, 1975).

Thus, sex-role stereotyping in educational materials is a major problem. Males and females are offered limited role models for non-traditional sex roles in textbooks and in counseling and guidance materials. Later in this chapter we will examine the consequences for men and women of limiting role options.

Classroom Interaction

Sex-role stereotyping occurs not only in educational materials, but also in student interactions with teachers, with other students, and with educational personnel, such as guidance counselors.

Teacher Expectancy

In 1968, in a classic study, two researchers examined the expectations teachers have for various students and the effect of these expectations on student achievement. The researchers randomly labeled some elementary-

Are teachers ladies?

school children as high achievers and others as low achievers, then this information was given to teachers. Students who were labeled as high achievers showed a significant increase in their IQ scores from the beginning of the school year to the end (Rosenthal & Jacobson, 1968). This phenomenon is called teacher expectancy. Basically, the process works as follows:

1. Teachers expect certain behaviors from certain students.
2. These expectations influence the teachers' behavior toward these students.
3. The teachers' behavior indicates to the students what the teachers expect of them. These expectations affect the students' self-concepts, motivation to achieve, and achievement.

4. If the teachers' behavior is consistent over time, and the students do not resist it, high expectation students will achieve well and low expectation students will not.

Relating teacher expectancy to sex-role expectations, teachers do not perceive traits that are stereotypically feminine in high-achieving students (Benz, Pfeiffer & Newman, 1981; Fagot, 1977). Both male and female high achievers are perceived as exhibiting androgynous or masculine behaviors. (See Chapter 2 for an explanation of these concepts.) In other words, the feminine sex role is negatively correlated with achievement. This finding does not vary significantly over grade levels or between male and female teachers. Benz and her associates (1981) summarize the implications of these findings when they note that:

> The conclusion of this study, to fit the feminine role is not to achieve, sheds important light on evidence . . . that achievement declines the longer females are in school. Not surprisingly, the evidence implies that females may be fulfilling society's expectations for them. If teachers expect girls to be feminine and boys to be masculine, the results clearly show what playing the roles can mean in terms of academic behavior. (pp. 297–298)

How are these teacher expectancies communicated to students? A review of research at all educational levels suggests six major ways in which teachers communicate sex-role expectations (Hall & Sandler, 1982). In this section we will briefly examine each one.

First, teachers may call on male students more often than on female students. Some female students indicate they feel invisible in the classroom. Female students may raise their hands often; yet, males are continually asked to respond, while females are not. When female students are asked why they believe the teachers call on male students more often, they indicate that the teacher either doesn't expect them to know the answer or doesn't feel the answer would be correct or worthwhile.

Second, teachers often coach male students to help them work toward a fuller answer. Female students are not coached as often. For example, a teacher is more likely to say "What do you mean by that?" or "Why do you believe that to be the appropriate theory of communication?" to male students than to female students. Coaching may communicate to males the expectation that, with a little help, they can succeed. The lack of coaching may communicate to females that their ideas are not important enough to probe further or that they are not intellectually capable of succeeding.

The third way in which teachers communicate sex-role stereotypes, waiting longer for males than they wait for females to answer a question before going on to another student, may subtly communicate to females that they are not expected to know the answer. This behavior on the part of teachers also may communicate to males in the class that they are more intellectually competent than their female counterparts. In addition, a male's silence following a question may be perceived as due to formulating an answer, while a female's may be perceived as due to her lack of knowledge.

Fourth, female students are more likely to be asked questions that require factual answers ("When was television invented?"), male students are more often asked questions that require critical thinking or personal evaluation ("How do you feel the concept of symbolic interaction affects communication?"). Once again, teachers are communicating expectations regarding the intellectual capability of each student—females are capable only of low-level cognitive processes, males are capable of high-level cognitive processes.

Fifth, teachers respond more extensively to male students' comments than to female students' comments. Males, therefore, receive more reinforcement for their intellectual participation than do females. In this way, a teacher may be communicating to female students that their comments are not as worthwhile or interesting as those of male students.

Finally, teachers may inadvertently communicate sex-role stereotypes by their use of sexist language. For example, when a teacher asks, "Why were the fathers of our country so concerned about religious freedom?" or "If a lawyer knows his client is guilty, what should he do?" the teacher may subtly communicate that males have been more important throughout history or that all lawyers are male. Teacher expectations can be a powerful force in the classroom because they can affect a student's sense of intellectual and personal worth. Students may pick up on a teacher's expectations and begin to communicate in the same way with each other. For example, male students are more likely to pay attention and respond more extensively to each other's comments than to comments made by female students.

Expectations are also communicated by other educational personnel. As we have seen earlier in this chapter, one of the major influences on students, in addition to the teacher, is the guidance counselor. Counselors foster sex-role stereotyping by displaying negative reactions toward women entering nontraditional careers (Worell, 1980). For example, counselors may question females who desire to enter nontraditional fields (Thomas & Stewart, 1971). Counselors who hear a female student express a desire to be an engineer, for example, may regard her choice as inappropriate, and may regard the student to be in greater need of counseling than a student who expresses a desire to major in elementary-school teaching. Such probing, of course, influences a student's view of the correct course of action. High-school counselors also recommend occupations for female high-school seniors that are lower paying, more highly supervised, and require less education than those recommended for male high-school seniors (Donahue, 1976).

Male counselors are more biased than female counselors (Hill, Tanney, Leonard & Reiss, 1977; Sherman, Koufacos & Kenworthy, 1978). Although signs of attitude change regarding sex roles on the part of counselors are emerging (Engelhard, Jones & Stiggins, 1976), counselors still tend to view the female career role as incompatible with a more home-oriented role (Ahrons, 1976).

Communication Patterns

Much research has been conducted to determine what kinds of communication patterns exist in the classroom in relation to sex of students and teachers. Generally, we know that differences exist in the areas of initiation, discipline, and dominance (Stake & Katz, 1982). In this section, we will examine each of these.

Initiation

Male students initiate more interactions with teachers than female students initiate (Spender & Sarah, 1980; Sternglanz & Lyberger-Ficek, 1977). In addition, the interactions between male students and teachers last longer (Hall & Sandler, 1982). Perhaps the longer duration of interaction is a result of what teachers and male students discuss. As was suggested earlier in this chapter, teachers explain how to do things to male students and simply do them for female students. Interaction time increases as a teacher explains how to set up lab equipment, work a math problem, or write a thesis sentence. If the teacher is "doing for" the female student, as is often the case, interaction time is decreased.

In several research studies, teachers have suggested that male students are more creative and more fun to teach (Ricks & Pyke, 1973; Sadker & Sadker, 1985). As we discussed in a previous section of this chapter, teachers may communicate this attitude to male students, who, in turn, may be more willing to initiate interactions because they feel more valued in the classroom.

Discipline

Classroom communication patterns differ in how male and female students are disciplined. Criticism of female students focuses on their lack of knowledge or skill; criticism of male students focuses on disruptive behaviors. Male students receive more discipline than female students receive and are likely to be reprimanded in a harsher and more public manner than are female students (Dweck, Davidson, Nelson & Bradley, 1978).

You might be asking, if male students are disciplined more, wouldn't they feel less comfortable in the classroom than female students? To understand why male students would not feel less comfortable than female students, we need to examine the other side of the discipline coin—praise. Although male students receive a larger number of negative messages, their ideas are used by teachers more often (Good, Sikes & Brophy, 1973). For example, a teacher might say, "That's an interesting idea, John. Let's run with that idea for a moment." When male students are praised, they are praised for the intellectual quality of their work. When they are criticized, they are criticized for neatness and form (Dweck et al., 1978). For example, a teacher might say, "Your ideas are very insightful, John, but try to be neater. Your writing is difficult to read." Female students, on the other hand, often are praised for their neatness and form, but not for the intellectual quality of their work ("Your paper is extremely neat, Mary, but you didn't analyze the model of communication well enough.")

High-achieving male students receive more teacher approval and active instruction, and lower-achieving male students receive more criticism. However, high-achieving female students receive less praise than both low- and high-achieving male students (Parson, Heller & Kaczala, 1980). Thus, although male students receive more disciplinary messages, they also receive more praise, in general, than female students receive and more praise of their intellectual ability.

Dominance

Male students dominate classroom talk. They are given more opportunities to respond in the classroom, and teachers direct more responses (both positive and negative) toward them. In addition, teachers ask male students a higher proportion of product-and-choice questions (questions that require synthesis or analysis), thereby encouraging problem solving in male students to a greater extent than in female students (Brophy & Good, 1974).

However, male students dominate more than just the conversation in the classroom, they also dominate nonverbal aspects of classroom communication (Thorne, 1979). In addition to dominating linguistic space, male students dominate the physical space of the classroom. As one researcher suggests:

> What happens in the mixed playground is that boys monopolize almost the total area by playing football, while the girls sit around on benches or

> wander round the periphery. Some, at great risk, pick their way across the football pitch, but few would dare to do so. There are in fact few chances for girls to participate or to be physically active. Even though a number of girls during the course of their interviews expressed a desire to join in, when asked why they did not do so they laughed at the stupidity of the question. It simply was not feasible—they would be howled at by the boys. (Wolpe, 1977, p. 15)

In addition, boys may emphasize their masculine dominance by using girls as a negative reference group. One researcher asked students "Who would you least wish to be like?" All of the boys named girls (and only girls). The characteristic of girls most vehemently rejected by boys was their apparent marginality in classroom encounters. The term "faceless" was used time and time again by the male students (but by none of the females) to describe their female classmates, and seemed to sum up their feeling that silence robs female students of any claim to individual identity and respect (Stanworth, 1981).

Male students use several strategies to achieve dominance in mixed-sex classrooms. They deny female students' academic abilities, make negative remarks about females' appearances, and overtly resist females' adopting of nontraditional roles. The following example from a drama teacher demonstrates the latter strategy:

> The problem of finding roles which girls can identify with became an acute one for me . . . and when I did manage to do so and cast a girl in an important part which might normally have been given to a boy, I found myself feeling *guilty* because I had denied a boy a plum role. Possibly I was also afraid that my choice might cause disruptive behaviour from the boys. Sometimes the boys challenged me, "Airline pilot? A girl can't be an airline pilot Miss!" Each time this happened I saw the girl hesitate, waiting for my judgment, waiting to be sent back to her seat. "Of course she can" I would retort, thinking at the same time, "Can she?" Each time I did this particular lesson, three in all, . . . the girl playing the pilot approached me privately, when the others were busy and whispered was I serious? Could women be pilots? Everytime I reassured the girl that it was perfectly alright and would she please go back to her controls before the plane crashed. (Quoted in Mahony, 1983, p. 113)

Not only do teachers communicate differently with male and female students, but students perceive male and female teachers differently. Women teachers are better liked. Students believe that classes taught by women are more discussion oriented, and that classes taught by men are more structured and emphasize content mastery more (Treichler & Kramarae, 1983). The more student participation female teachers generate in their classroom, the less competent they are perceived to be (Macke

& Richardson, 1980). Evidently, students equate a structured teaching strategy (such as a lecture rather than a discussion) with competence, and male teachers are more likely to use a structured teaching strategy.

Investigating student perceptions of science classes taught by male and female teachers, Lawrenz and Welch (1983) found that students believe that classes taught by females are more diverse and have more instances of teacher favoritism and friction between students than classes taught by male teachers. Students also believe that classes taught by male teachers are more difficult. Cooper, Stewart, and Gudykunst (1982) examined the impact of several variables upon students' evaluation of instructors, including the sex of the instructor. These researchers conclude:

> When evaluating instructors, students give greater significance to the type of interpersonal response they receive from female instructors while giving greater significance to the accuracy of the grade they receive from male instructors. Presumably, female instructors, who are supposed to be sensitive and caring, are evaluated favorably if they confirm this stereotype through their interpersonal response. Male instructors, who are supposed to be competent, are favorably evaluated if they demonstrate their competence by awarding accurate grades. (p. 314)

The perceptions students have of instructors affect student communication in the classroom. Male and female students communicate differently with male and female instructors. When the instructor is male, male student interactions are three times more frequent than female student interactions. When the instructor is female, male and female student interactions are nearly equal (Karp & Yoels, 1976). Perhaps female students feel more comfortable in classes taught by females and are therefore more willing to communicate in an environment they perceive as more supportive.

Classroom communication patterns differ according to the sex of the student and the sex of the teacher. As we noted earlier, regardless of the grade level examined, male students control the communication in the classroom in terms of initiation, discipline, and dominance. Male teachers are regarded as more structured and more concerned with content mastery; female teachers are perceived as less structured and less demanding.

Implications and Consequences of Sex-Role Stereotyping in Education

As the research discussed in this chapter indicates, curriculum materials and classroom interaction patterns influence student sex-role stereotypes and behaviors. The question now becomes, What is the effect of sex-role stereotyping in education? Basically, sex-role stereotyping in education affects three areas: (1) the self-concept of students; (2) the curriculum choices of students; and (3) the occupational choices of students.

Self-Concept

Lenney (1977) reviews the research concerning women's self-confidence in achievement settings and concludes that women's self-confidence is not lower than men's when: (1) the task is appropriate for females; (2) the information available on their ability at a specific task is clear and not ambiguous; and (3) the emphasis placed on comparison to others and evaluation by others is low. Generally, these three criteria are not met in achievement settings. Thus, women's self-confidence in the educational environment is generally low. Low self-confidence affects the self-concept of female students. In a study comparing the self-concept scores of tenth-grade girls with the scores of their male peers, Bohan (1973) found that girls had a significantly lower self-concept rating than did boys. The self-concept scores of tenth-grade girls were also significantly lower than the scores of girls in all other age groups. Bohan posits two interpretations for these findings: (1) that the adolescent years involve a reevaluation of self, and adolescent girls may find themselves wanting in relation to the ideals that they hold or believe to be important; and (2) since adolescence is the period of most intense evaluation of roles, as well as the apex of sex-role development, the adolescent girl may come to recognize that the role she is expected to assume as a female is relatively inferior in status and prestige to the male role. Accordingly, she may decrease her evaluation of herself.

Equally as disconcerting as the decline in the self-concept of adolescent girls are the results of tests that seem to indicate that girls' IQ scores decrease over time while boys' scores increase (Campbell, 1976; Foxley, 1982). In some cases, girls with better grade averages than boys in high school do not believe that they have the ability to do college work (Cano, Solomon & Holmes, 1984; Steinkamp & Maehr, 1984). Seventy-five to 90 percent of the brightest high school graduates who do not go on to college are women (Jacko, Karmos & Karmos, 1980).

Curriculum Choice

The sex-role stereotyping in education also affects the course of study students pursue. Traditionally, female students have perceived math and science courses, spatial ability, and problem solving as male domains (Newcombe & Bandura, 1983; Ware & Steckler, 1983). Males traditionally have viewed home economics, office business courses, and reading as feminine activities (Foxley, 1979). As a result, both sexes generally do not take courses that they perceive to be the domain of the opposite sex—even if they desire to do so.

Of course, male and female students may be equally capable of high achievement in courses traditionally considered the domain of one or the other. For example, the results of one study indicate that among thirteen-year-olds, females' mathematical abilities are comparable and, in some areas, superior to those of males. However, by twelfth grade, males catch up with and then surpass females in certain areas of math achievement (Education Commission of the States, 1978). When women have the same mathematical training as men, they perform equally as well (Pallas & Alexander, 1983; Paulsen & Johnson, 1983). The same is true in science. An analysis of thirteen-year-olds reports no sex differences in science achievement. Yet, females continue to move away from the sciences (Lawrenz & Welch, 1983). Thus, although achievement in science and math may not be different when male and female students are exposed to the same material, female students tend not to take advanced math and science courses.

Occupational Choice

The choice of which curriculum to pursue is directly related to occupational choice. For example, math and science skills are critical in determining educational and occupational choices (Peng & Jaffe, 1979). Thus, when female students avoid science and math training, they preclude themselves from considering a wide range of occupations—not only in engineering and the natural sciences, but also in the social sciences and business administration (Carnegie Commission on Higher Education, 1973).

Even today, large numbers of women are not entering traditionally male-dominated fields. For example, Adkison's (1981) extensive research review suggests that women are underrepresented in educational administration. Other observers have reported similar findings. Only 8 percent of college presidents, 12 percent of academic vice-presidents, and 18 percent of deans are women (Howard, 1980). The picture is no more positive at the high-school and elementary-school levels. For example, less than 1 percent of school superintendents are women (Foxley, 1979). This underrepresentation is explained as a combination of low aspirations, skill deficiencies, and discrimination. (These concepts will be discussed in more detail in Chapter 9.)

In addition to their underrepresentation in educational administration, women are underrepresented in many other areas. Although women are obtaining a growing proportion of college degrees, fields of specialty are still segregated (Wilson & Shin, 1983). Men are disproportionally represented in curricula ranked high on power, income, and prestige dimensions, such as the law, medicine, or management professions. Women are found most often in curricula, such as education and English, which, in general, do not lead to high-paying occupations. In addition, sex inequality exists in the levels of degrees attained by the sexes. Sex inequality, then, exists both in differences in the fields entered by the sexes and in the levels that they achieve within these fields.

Certainly, at every level, women are obtaining an increasing proportion of college degrees (see Chart 7.1). A recent report in *The American Teacher* (1983) analyzed the percentage of women awarded degrees in various professions. The percentage of women graduates in law increased from 2.5 percent in 1960 to 30.2 percent in 1980. The percentage of women graduates in dentistry increased from less than 1 percent in 1960 to 13.3 percent in 1980. From 1950 to 1980, the percentage of women doctors increased from 1 percent to 23.4 percent, while in education the increase was from 46 percent to 71 percent.

Although the percentages seem encouraging, some caution is necessary. For example, in secondary education, approximately two-thirds of the teachers of English, home economics, business education, and foreign languages are female. More than two-thirds of the teachers of industrial arts, agriculture, science, math, social studies, and music are male (Stockard et al., *Sex Equity*, 1980). This differentiation by subject matter closely parallels the occupations of men and women in the labor force (Foxley, 1979). (These differences are discussed in more detail in Chapter 9.)

The majority of women faculty teaching on the college level are at the lower ranks—lecturer, instructor, and assistant professor. Few women are associate professors or full professors (U.S. Dept. of Education, 1981). As the National Advisory Council on Women's Educational Programs (1981) suggests, "the glass remains half empty . . . with much still to be done to fulfill the promise of Title IX." Title IX, enacted in 1972, is the federal law that prohibits sex discrimination in educational programs and activities receiving federal funds.

Chart 7.1 Percentage of degrees earned by women.

	1971–72	**1972–80**
B.A.	44%	49%
M.A.	41%	50%
Ph.D.	16%	30%
First Professional	68%	25%

[*Source:* U.S. Department of Education National Center for Educational Statistics, 1973, 1981.]

At all levels of education, when women and men are portrayed in stereotypical roles and communicated with in stereotypical ways, both sexes are harmed. Women are led to believe their occupational choices are limited, that they are academically inferior, and that they are emotional and dependent. Men are led to believe that their occupational choices are limited to stereotypically male occupations (they should not be nurses or airline flight attendants), that they are academically superior, and that they are unemotional and independent.

Strategies for Change

Teachers are perhaps the primary agents for establishing change in the sex-role stereotyping that exists in American schools and universities. The Department of Health, Education, and Welfare publication, *Taking Sexism Out of Education* (1978), emphasizes the role of the teacher:

> Teacher's behavior is probably the most critical factor in determining whether what happens in the classroom will encourage the development of flexibility or the retention of old stereotyping practices. One of the ways in which teachers can help to eliminate sexism is through their own modeling of nonsexist behaviors. (Quoted in Koblinsky & Sugawara, 1984, p. 365)

In the first major field survey and intervention program for changing sex-role stereotyping in children, Guttentag, Bray, and Amsler (1976) gathered information about several of the major areas that children believe are related to sex roles. They found that children usually tell stories in which women have low status roles, have little opportunity for advancement or pay raises, and are seldom in supervisory positions. Children also believe that although women have jobs, they are not very good at them. Finally, children believe that women are best at being friendly and caring for people, and men are not good at taking care of children or doing household chores. However, when an intervention program of nonsexist curriculum materials and nonsexist teacher-pupil interaction methods was completed, many of these sex-role stereotypes changed.

Teachers can promote interaction between the sexes by integrating teams, lines, seating arrangements, and instructional groups. They can assign classroom tasks on a nonstereotypical basis. For example, girls can help carry chairs and boys can be class secretaries. Perhaps, the most extensive list of behaviors for non-sexist teaching is presented by Hall and Sandler (1982). They suggest that such communication behaviors as asking female *and* male students questions that call for factual knowledge as well as critical thinking skills, coaching female students as well as male students, using language that does not reinforce limited views of male and female role and career choices, and giving female and male students an equal amount of time to respond after asking questions, can begin to communicate the expectations that both males and females are intellectually competent.

To help teachers eliminate their own sexist attitudes, educational trainers need to emphasize the importance of eliminating sexism in education to teachers-in-training. Sadker, Sadker, and Hicks (1980) analyzed teacher education textbooks published between 1973 and 1978. Twenty-three of the twenty-four texts devote less than 1 percent of their space to the issue of sexism in education. None of these texts includes the strategies and resources available for combating sex-role stereotyping in the classroom. As Sprague (1975) notes:

> Teachers can eliminate sexist materials from their curriculum. As long as teachers rely soley on existing teaching materials and linguistic codes, women will be discouraged from exploring the independent, assertive, forceful aspects of their personalities while men will be discouraged from exploring the tenderness, dependence, and compliance that is part of them as human beings. Women will have trouble considering the role of engineer, senator, or laborer, and men will find it difficult to consider seriously how they might fit into roles such as nurse, partner in homes tasks, or elementary teacher. Unless students of both sexes display a variety of individual personality styles and careers, their self-concepts and their human potential will be limited. (p. 45)

Guidance counseling personnel can also strive to eliminate sexist materials. When this is not possible, they can discuss the sexism in the materials with parents and students. They can also model nonsexist behavior and encourage both male and female students to pursue nontraditional careers.

As we discussed earlier, sexist language is a major problem in both educational materials and educational interaction. As several researchers suggest, the generic grammatical structure "cannot fail to suggest to young readers that females are a substandard . . . form of being" (Burr, Dunn & Farquhar, 1972). Certainly, the problem of sexist language in textbooks is improving. Many publishers have recognized the problem. For example, in 1974, Scott, Foresman and Company published guidelines for the elimination of sexism in their textbooks. Since then, other publishers have made similar efforts. All educational personnel should make nonsexist language a major criterion when evaluating educational materials and should eliminate sexist language from their own vocabulary.

Conclusion

Women are marginalized from education by its content and by the classroom interactional processes. Sex-role stereotyping exists in curriculum materials at all educational levels. Textbooks are more likely to portray boys in active roles and girls in passive roles. More stories are about boys or are illustrated with boys' pictures than with girls' pictures. Little space is given to the achievements of women. Sexist language is common.

In addition to curriculum materials, students are exposed to sex-role stereotyped materials and advice in guidance counseling offices. Counselors encourage students to pursue traditional sex-role stereotyped occupations. High school counselors may recommend occupations for female high-school students that pay less, are more highly supervised, and require less education than those recommended for male students.

In the classroom, teachers communicate sex-role expectations to students. Teachers may call on male students more often than on female students. Teachers often coach male students to help them develop fuller answers. Waiting longer for male students than for female students to answer questions may communicate to female students that they are not expected to know the answer. Female students are more likely to be asked questions requiring factual answers while male students are more often asked questions that require critical thinking or personal evaluation. Teachers respond more extensively to male students' comments than to female students' comments. Finally, teachers may communicate sex-role stereotypes by their use of sexist language.

Classroom interactions vary by sex in terms of initiation, discipline, and dominance. Male students initiate more interactions with teachers than female students do. Criticism of female students focuses on their lack of knowledge or skill, whereas criticism of male students focuses on disruptive behaviors. Overall, male students dominate classroom talk and space.

Sexism in the educational environment affects the self-concepts of students, their curriculum choices, and their occupational choices. In the educational environment, women generally lack self-confidence. Males and females do not take courses they perceive to be the domain of the opposite sex. Because of these curriculum choices, women usually do not enter traditionally male-dominated fields, and men usually do not enter traditionally female-dominated fields.

Teachers are perhaps the primary agents for effecting change in the sex-role stereotyping that exists in American education. One of the ways in which teachers can help to eliminate sex-role stereotyping is by modeling nonsexist behaviors. Teachers can promote equality in interaction between the sexes by integrating teams, lines, seating arrangements, and instructional groups. Finally, teachers can eliminate sexist materials from their curricula.

Suggested Activities

1. Use the following categories discussed in this chapter to rate your textbooks on sex-role stereotyping: (1) numerical differences in the portrayal of males and females; (2) stereotyped behavior patterns and characteristics; and (3) sexist language. How would you rate the sex-role stereotyping found in your textbooks? Do some textbooks contain more sex-role stereotyping than others? Is sex-role stereotyping more prevalent in textbooks for some subjects than for others? What messages are being communicated by the authors of these textbooks? If you were the author of one of these textbooks, what changes would you make to avoid sex-role stereotyping?

2. Choose one of your classes to analyze the communication patterns that occur. Answer the following questions:

Who initiates the communication contacts?
Who is criticized by the teacher or other members of the class? For what reasons?
Who is praised? Why?
Who dominates the classroom verbally?
Who dominates the classroom nonverbally?

Analyze your answers in terms of sex differences. Are males praised more than females? Do males or females initiate the most communication? Which sex dominates the classroom? Do you think your observations are influenced by the subject matter? For example, do males tend to dominate engineering classes while females tend to dominate foreign language classes? Compare your results with others in your class. What conclusions can you draw about communication patterns in the classroom? How do these communication patterns create and maintain sex-role stereotypes?

3. Think about the expectancies that are communicated for students in your classrooms. If you were a teacher, how would you communicate that you wanted your students to conform to traditional sex-role stereotypes? Have you observed any of these behaviors in classes that you have attended? How would you communicate that you wanted your students to have a more equal role in classroom interaction? Have you observed any of these behaviors in classes you have attended? How have you been affected by these teacher behaviors?

4. Interview a high school senior female and high school senior male from the same school about their career expectations. Do they plan to continue their education? Where? What subjects do they plan to major in? What are their career goals? How have they been encouraged to pursue

particular careers? Have they been discouraged from pursuing a particular career? What do they think they will be doing in five years? In ten years?

Compare the results you obtain from these two interviews. Are sex-role stereotypes in education and career choice being communicated to high school seniors? How? What is being done by teachers and guidance counselors to change sex-role stereotypes? What else needs to be done by teachers and guidance counselors to change sex-role stereotypes?

For Further Reading

Boileau, D.M. (1982). ERIC report: Gender and communication. *Communication Education, 31*, 368–374.

Brook, V.R. (1982). Sex difference in student dominance behavior in female and male professors' classrooms. *Sex Roles, 8*, 682-690.

Cooper, P. (1984). *Speech communication for the classroom teacher*, 2nd ed. Dubuque, IA: Gorsuch-Scarisbrick.

Frazier, N., & Sadker, M. (1973). *Sexism in school and society*. New York: Harper & Row.

Jenkins, M.M., Gappa, J.M., & Pearce, J. (1983). *Removing bias: Guidelines for student-faculty communication*. Annandale, VA: Speech Communication Association.

Shapiro, J., Kramer, S., and Hunerberg, C. (1981). *Equal their chances: Children's activities for non-sexist learning*. Englewood Cliffs, NJ: Prentice-Hall.

Spender, D. (1982). *Invisible women: The schooling scandal*. London: Writer's and Readers.

Stacey, J., Béreaud, S., and Daniels, J. (Eds.). (1974). *And Jill came tumbling after: Sexism in American education*. New York: Dell.

Stohl, C. (1982). "Sugar or spice: Teachers' perceptions of sex differences in communicative correlates of attraction." In *Communication Yearbook, 6*, ed. M. Burgoon, 811–830. Beverly Hills, CA: Sage.

Travris, C., and Offir, C. (1977). *The longest war: Sex differences in perspective*. New York: Harcourt Brace Jovanovich.

Communication and Sex Roles in the Media

8

The popular media are extremely important influences in our society. The portrayal of males and females in the media affects our image of each other as well as how males and females communicate. Both males and females have been stereotyped in all areas of the media, and these stereotyped images provide poor models of, and for, communication. In this chapter we will focus on seven popular media: film, television, popular music, children's literature, adult literature, cartoons/comic strips, and advertising. We will analyze the images of males and females communicated through these media and the effects of these images, suggest some strategies for changing them, and discuss some changes that have occurred recently.

Media Images

Film[1]

Film critic Parker Taylor (in Malone, 1979, p. 2) claims that movies are "industrialized dreams, the record of our collective unconscious as well as the mass-produced liturgy of our conscious beliefs; just as films express our other ideologies and psychologies, so they express our sexist premise that 'Man's love is of man's life a thing apart; Tis woman's whole existence.' " The image of men and women presented to us in film has changed throughout the years. This section contains a brief summary of some of those changes.

[1] Material for each decade is based on information gathered from Erens (1979), Mellen (1973), and Mellen (1977).

The Twenties

With few exceptions, males on the screen in the 1920s came out of the past. In terms of male roles, the films of this period focused on pioneers, western heroes, thieves, swashbuckling pirates, and war heroes. Men were stereotyped as gallant and macho.

Women, in the films of the 1920s, fit into four predominant stereotypes—flapper, working girl, chorus girl/vamp, and old-fashioned girl. In 1923, Colleen Moore created a revolution in female fashion and behavior with her film *Flaming Youth*. Women across the country bobbed their hair and wore tight dresses like Moore's, and the flapper craze had begun. But we should remember that in films reflecting the flapper image, the goal of being a flapper was to lure a husband, not just to enjoy oneself. Although some of the films of the 1920s portrayed the working girl image, they did so peripherally. A working girl's position was of no real consequence. For example, Louise Brooks ran a drugstore for W. C. Fields in *It's the Old Army Game* in 1926, and Gloria Swanson slung hash in a beanery in the 1924 film *Stage Struck*. As was the case with the flapper image, the chorus girl/vamp image was imitated by females in society. Nightclubs and speakeasies sought out young, naive girls to carry out the chorus girl/vamp role in real life. At the close of the decade, the old-fashioned girl image reappeared—complete with turn-of-the-century values. Actress such as Janet Gaynor in *Seventh Heaven* (1927) and Lillian Gish in *The Wind* (1928) helped revive more nonthreatening heroines.

The Thirties

Sound came to film in the 1930s. Characters suddenly became more real. Stars such as Clark Gable, Gary Cooper, and Cary Grant became popular, and with them came female counterparts who were alert and direct or throaty and provocative. Box office stars of the thirties included Charles Farrell, Clark Gable, Dick Powell, Robert Taylor, Gary Cooper, William Powell, Spencer Tracy, Tyrone Power, and Errol Flynn. These new screen heroes were never seen in mundane occupations such as working on the assembly line. They were the new "sex gods."

The years between 1930 and 1934 began one of the truly liberated periods of cinema. During this time period, women emerged in films as people who could make their own decisions. One of the major screen stars portraying the image of the independent woman was Mae West. In her films, she was a woman who could think faster and more logically than any man. Although Mae West somewhat liberated the scene by portraying a woman of security and independence, this superiority was always portrayed in a humorous vein. The result was that the characters portrayed by Mae West were not taken seriously. Yet, the years from 1930 to 1934 did witness less sex-role stereotyping in films. Stars like Greta Garbo, Jean Harlow, and Marlene Dietrich portrayed characters who initiated sexual encounters, pursued men, and embodied certain male characteristics (such as aggressiveness) without being regarded as unfeminine or predatory.

In 1934, a new Production Code went into effect in the film industry. The code was a response to the "vile and unwholesome" material on the screen—in particular, the explicit sexuality and metaphorical sex scenes (Haskell, 1974). This code suddenly affected women's roles; they became more individualized, stylized, and humanistic. Since the Great Depression, there had been a demand for a more down-to-earth working-woman image in films. Thanks to the new Production Code, this demand was satisfied. After 1934, stars such as Katharine Hepburn, Jean Arthur, and Rosalind Russell played characters who embodied professional and working-class sectors.

The Forties

In the 1940s, many films centered on three main themes dominated by men: sports, westerns, and war stories. In the early 1940s, the average film hero was enthusiastic, full of optimism, and certain of his identity. In films, he committed himself to battle as the only course of action worthy of manhood. Sports stories glorified the masculine, sportsmanlike male in such films as *Knute Rockne: All-American,* in which Ronald Reagan portrayed the all-American boy next door. Westerns, starring actors like John Wayne and Henry Fonda, also helped to glamorize the rough, tough masculine image prevalent throughout the 1920s and 1930s.

Because of the war effort, Hollywood experienced a shortage of male actors during this time period. As a result, a large number of "women's films" were made. Nevertheless, the major preoccupation of these movies was the man's soul and salvation rather than the woman's. Hollywood executives believed (or at least wanted to believe) that women were not fit to handle tough situations; therefore, women in films portrayed war wives and girlfriends who patiently waited for their men to return home safely from war. At the same time, however, stars like Rita Hayworth in *The Lady from Shanghai,* Barbara Stanwyck in *Double Indemnity,* Ava Gardner in *The Killers,* Mary Astor in *The Maltese Falcon,* Maureen O'Hara in *Fallen Sparrow,* Lauren Bacall in *The Big Sleep,* and Bette Davis in *The Letter* were portraying treacherous women, women of dubious ethics or unconventional femininity who were likely to be found on the wrong side of the law. These characters faced tougher, more sexual situations than had previous women on the screen.

The Fifties

Many of the major films of the fifties—*Blackboard Jungle, Rebel Without a Cause,* and *On the Waterfront*—portrayed males as alienated, tormented heroes who, by the end of the film, were forced to conform to the norms of society. For the first time, men were portrayed as thoughtful, understanding of weaknesses (including their own), and perceptive. Traditional toughness and macho personalities were recognized as defense mechanisms as opposed to emblems of masculinity. Yet, there were still a handful of popular films that strongly reinforced the old stereotypes of manhood and masculinity, for example, *High Noon* with Gary Cooper.

In the early fifties, films were still honoring the superwoman and the femme fatale; and, of course, the ultimate female film image of the fifties was Marilyn Monroe. In Monroe's films, audiences saw performances about sex *without* sex. Monroe was the sex goddess of the decade—a vision men dreamed of and women wanted to emulate. So great was her influence that the era of the love goddess virtually ended with her death in 1962 (Kobel, 1973).

The Sixties and Seventies

One of the major male images of this period was James Bond. In the original Bond films, he treated women as disposable sexual objects. Along with the Bond films came a series of Clint Eastwood films, and both instructed us in what was necessary for survival in their worlds (for example, bloodshed, violence, and sexual potency). In the 1970s, Hollywood endorsed the tough cop image in films like *Dirty Harry, Magnum Force, The Enforcer, The French Connection, Walking Tall, Death Wish,* and *Taxi Driver*. A man's survival depended on becoming a violent vigilante who could meet force with force.

The 1960s and 1970s were a confusing time for men in film because as one group of films was glorifying the fantasies of violence and casual sex another group was emphasizing the theme of male friendship. In films like *Deliverance, Longest Yard, The Sting, M*A*S*H, All the President's Men,* and *One Flew Over the Cuckoo's Nest,* men built relationships with each other and did not need to use women to prove their masculinity. In this same time period, masculinity was possible for other men in films only if they excluded women or demonstrated their superiority over women. *Five Easy Pieces, The Godfather,* and *Chinatown* portrayed men achieving a certain masculine ideal through their supposed superiority over women.

The period from 1962 to 1973 was an equally disheartening period for the film images of women. As soon as women in society began to assume a more productive lifestyle than ever before, the film industry stopped reflecting that lifestyle in any constructive or analytical way. Intelligent portrayals of women as productive and emotional beings did not appear in many films (Rosen, 1973). Even the major women's roles of the 1960s and 1970s (Julie Christie in *Darling,* Elizabeth Taylor in *Who's Afraid of Virginia Woolf,* Barbra Streisand in *Funny Girl,* Jane Fonda in *Klute,* Ellen Burstyn in *Alice Doesn't Live Here Anymore,* and Louise Fletcher in *One Flew Over the Cuckoo's Nest*) were, for the most part, jilted wives or mistresses, emotional cripples, drunks, or hookers. Other women portrayed traditional female roles such as housewives, mothers, waitresses, nurses, and models. Although in the late 1970s, Hollywood did portray some liberated women, female liberation usually was presented in sexual rather than intellectual terms. More often than not, a woman's quest for identity led her into the arms of an understanding man (Evans, in *Media Report to Women,* 1983b).

The Eighties

There seems to be a growing movement in films today toward men's liberation, seeking humane treatment of masculinity and identifying the suffering of being male. This suffering can be seen in such films as Alan Alda's *The Four Seasons,* about midlife crisis; *Rocky III,* in which Sylvester Stallone searches for himself much more than he did in previous *Rocky* movies; and *Making Love,* in which a man searches for his true sexual identity. Yet, the All-Powerful-Man, whether he is feminist or macho, is still very much a part of the film image of men.

Films of the 1980s about women have tended to equate being liberated with being tough. One filmmaker indicates the reasons for this image:

> Men like the screen image of the tough woman. It lets them off the hook. How much simpler to deal with a woman who can retaliate with a karate chop; abandon her and she can always find someone else, or go back to college. This is not to say that a woman shouldn't be resilient and seek out alternatives. But the movie version seems to me to be a twisted intrusion of male fantasies onto the female character. (Evans, in *Media Report to Women,* 1983b, p. 5)

In addition to portraying the tough, independent female image, recent films have portrayed women in the stereotyped good woman/martyr and bad woman images. Films of the eighties also have shown women as powerless in their relationships and powerless (or disinterested) in their careers (Dowd, 1983).

Several recent films, however, the so-called farm movies, have presented strong female characters paired with more vulnerable male characters. Films like *Country, The River,* and *Places in the Heart* feature female characters who battle the forces of evil and nature to save their farms. Another popular trend is ensemble movies, such as *The Big Chill*, which present independent roles for both women and men, along with several characters who conform to traditional sex-role stereotypes. At the present time, it is difficult to find films that portray only strong male and female characters. The image of women and men in films has improved over the years but, with the exception of movies such as *Garp* and *Tootsie*, we still do not find many films that overcome the sex-role stereotyping of both males and females.

Television

The U.S. Commission on Civil Rights (1979) maintains that people who are visible on television are considered worthy of attention, and people ignored by television are invisible. Historically, females have been less visible than males in television programming. Perhaps even more important than the invisibility of females is that when females are made visible, they have historically been portrayed in stereotypical roles. In this section, we will discuss the images of males and females in both children's and adult programming and examine some recent changes in these images.

Children's Programming

Many elementary-school children spend more time watching television than they do sitting in a classroom (Brooks-Gunn & Matthews, 1979). For the length of time children watch television, the image they receive of males and females is out of the hands of parents or teachers and into the hands of scriptwriters and advertising agencies. Analyses of popular, commercially produced television programs demonstrate that children's television programs communicate sex-role stereotypes (Brooks-Gunn & Matthews, 1979). Historically, television has stereotyped in three major ways. First, the ratio of males to females was greatly unequal. Male roles exceeded female roles two to one (Sternglanz & Serbin, 1974). Second, behavior differentiated the sexes: males were portrayed as aggressive and constructive (for example, building and planning) and females were portrayed as deferent. Third, the communication patterns of males and females differed—males were more dominant and instrumental.

As we suggested earlier in this chapter, those who are made visible through television become worthy of attention. Based on the numbers of males and females portrayed on television in the past, males are worthy of attention. Females remain somewhat invisible. In both cartoons and in educational television for children, males outnumbered females (Women on Words and Images, 1975). In 1975 cartoon shows, 61 percent of all major characters were male. In adventure cartoons, 85 percent were male. Females not only were less numerous than males (in both leading and supporting roles), but they also spoke fewer lines (Women on Words and Images, 1975). In children's educational television programs, such as *Sesame Street, The Electric Company, Mr. Rogers' Neighborhood,* and *Captain Kangaroo,* 67 percent of all characters were male (65 percent were men, 2 percent were boys). Of course, 100 percent of the lead characters in these shows were men (Dohrmann, 1975).

Behavior patterns also differentiated between the sexes on television. Children's programming portrayed females as less active, less noisy, and as occupying fewer positions of responsibility than males (Streicher, 1974). Females displayed twice as many incompetent behaviors as males (Women on Words and Images, 1975). In addition, males were portrayed in twice as many occupations as females (Women on Words and Images, 1975). Females also were portrayed as younger than males, more likely to be married, and with lower self-esteem (Barcus, 1982).

Finally, the communication interaction of males and females differentiated the sexes. In an analysis of the verbal language in Saturday morning children's programs, McCorkle (1982) found that the main character who appeared most often (the white male adult) also spoke most often. Males spoke more often than females, and adults spoke more often than children. Main characters (primarily male) were twice as likely to be defensive as supportive, and when not giving an opinion, were usually challenging, sarcastic, belittling, blaming, or personally attacking themselves or others. Females were more supportive as a group than males.

A study of the kinds of behavior males and females on television directed to each other when they communicated with one another demonstrated that 13 percent of the males' interactions involved females; 59 percent of the females' interactions were with males. The adult male was the least likely to have a communication partner of the opposite sex; the adult female was the most likely to have a communication partner of the opposite sex. Female children were more likely than male children to enter male/female interactions. When males and females interacted, males were more likely to be on the active, masterful side of the relationship and females on the passive, dependent side (Dohrmann, 1975). Thus, during the past decade, traditional sex-role stereotyping has been reflected in children's television programming.

Adult Programming

In adult prime time television, sex-role stereotypes have been perpetuated in much the same way as in children's programming. In the past, males outnumbered females, sex-role stereotyped behaviors were depicted, and stereotyped female-male relationships were presented. We will examine each of these aspects of sex-role stereotyping briefly and then discuss some recent changes.

An examination of major adult television characters from 1969 to 1972 demonstrated that female characters accounted for only 28 percent of all leading roles (Tedesco, 1974). More recent studies indicate that the percentage has not changed significantly in recent years (cf. Tuchman, Daniels & Benet, 1978). Until recently, one of the most unrealistic aspects of adult programming was the number of female characters who were employed outside the home. When the top twenty-five programs in the Nielsen ratings from 1972 to 1981 were examined only 44 percent of female television characters were portrayed in the work force. In real life, 60 percent of the female population worked outside the home in 1981 (National Commission on Working Women, 1982).

The differentiation in numbers of males and females on television was not the only problem. Many adult television programs depicted stereotypical behaviors. Females were portrayed as more sociable, attractive, happy, warm, youthful, and peaceful, while male characters were more powerful, rational, intelligent, and stable (Downing, 1974; Seggar, 1975). A report by the National Commission on Working Women (1982) indicates that the number of affluent women characters on television increased from less than 1 percent in the early 1970s to 23 percent in 1981 as a result of such prime time television programs as *Dynasty, Dallas, Falcon Crest,* and *Hart to Hart*. However, most of these characters gained their affluence in stereotypical ways—by marriage or inheritance.

In many shows, stereotypical interpersonal relationships existed on television (Downs & Gowan, 1980). For example, an investigation of soap operas found that 22 percent of all conversations were between a man and a woman while only 2 percent were between two men (Fine, 1981). The sex-role stereotype that women talk more about relationships and men talk more about their professions is perpetuated on prime time television (Eakins & Eakins, 1978).

The stereotypical relationships between men and women that were characteristic of television programs in the past are changing somewhat in today's programming. Popular shows such as *The Cosby Show, Cagney and Lacey, St. Elsewhere,* and *Kate and Allie* portray both male and female characters in roles that overcome traditional sex-role stereotypes. For example, in one episode of *The Cosby Show,* Dr. Cliff Huxtable questioned prospective dates for his teenage daughter by asking the young men if they could cook and if they would support their wife's career choice. Huxtable obviously preferred the young man who liked to cook and was supportive of his wife's working outside the home. We hope such shows are setting examples that will help to overcome traditional sex-role stereotyping.

Recent research has shown that the dominant male/submissive female sex-role stereotype is not as prevalent on television today as it was in the past. Male and female characters engage equally in attempts to exert control. Nevertheless, this pattern is not necessarily a sign that sex-role stereotypes no longer exist. Barbatsis, Wong, and Herek (1983) conclude that showing both males and females on television struggling for dominance exemplifies several points:

> First, it exemplifies the idea that traits associated with masculinity are more socially desirable than are those associated with femininity. As represented in the findings of these studies, deviation from a typical stereotypic pattern of male dominance–female submission, was uni-directional. Females took on the stereotypic traits of males, but not the reverse. Second, a preponderance of control asserting messages resulted in a struggle for dominance which has neither been found to be typical of the ways males and females interact normally . . . nor particularly effective. More forthrightly, . . . a constant struggle for control characterizes a "sick" relationship. In short, the portrayal of females according to stereotypic masculine sex-typed communication patterns presents a potentially dysfunctional model for both female self-concept and interpersonal relationships in general. (pp. 154–155).

Music

The literature on sex-role stereotyping in films and television examines the images of both women and men, but the literature on popular music focuses primarily on women. This literature reveals three recurring images of women in popular song: the ideal woman/madonna/saint; the evil or fickle witch/sinner/whore; and the victim (Butruille, 1983). The image of women in popular American songs reflects these stereotypical values and attitudes. In all areas of popular music—pop, country, and rock—the image of females reflects sex-role stereotyping. In her analysis of the top ten popular songs of 1982, Crawford (1983) found that male and female sex-role stereotypes are reflected in the lyrics of most of these songs. Only two of the top ten artists were women, and all but two of the songs reflect stereotypical views of masculine and feminine traits. The views of women reflected in the hit songs of 1982 are largely the same as those found in songs of earlier periods.

In contemporary country music, work outside the home is almost exclusively a male domain. Affairs of political significance center around men. Women are "mothers, wives, barmaids, and truck stop waitresses" (Buckley, 1979, p. 4). Reviewing country songs, Almquist and Freudiger (1978) found that the primary image of women is the ideal-submissive or fickle female. Soul music generally portrays women as hesitant, inconsistent, submissive, and beautiful. Finally, in easy listening music, women generally are portrayed as supportive, inconsistent, and submissive.

Meade (1971) found the witch/sinner/whore image to be the most prevalent image of women in rock music: "Again and again throughout rock lyrics women emerge either as insatiable, sex-crazed animals or all American emasculators. . . . Seldom does one run across a mature, intelligent woman or . . . a woman who is capable enough to hold down a job" (pp. 13–14). Role portrayals are very stereotypical—women are wives, sweethearts, mothers, or wicked witches, men are independent and are the breadwinners.

What happens when women create and sing their own songs? Are the images and themes the same as in popular American songs? Research suggests not. Women's own songs have focused on themes of marriage and family, work and politics (including their own liberation), ambivalence toward culturally-defined roles, pride in their work, and anger at the system (Butruille, 1983). As more and more women enter the mainstream rock charts, sex-role stereotyping in this area may decrease.

Literature

The image of males and females in literature—from a child's first picture book to adult best sellers—can influence the way in which males and females see themselves and can thus influence their communication. In this section, we will examine the sex-role stereotypes of males and females that are communicated in children's literature and adult literature.

Children's Literature

Children's literature, like children's television programming, reflects sex-role stereotypes. Numerical disparities and stereotyped behavior patterns and characteristics reflected in children's literature teach girls to undervalue themselves and teach boys to believe that they always must be stereotypically masculine.

Females are not included in children's books in numbers that reflect their presence in the general population. Three studies have examined how sex roles were treated in books that won the Caldecott Medal or the Newberry Award (Cooper, 1984; Kolbe & LaVoie, 1981; Weitzman, Eifler, Hokada & Ross, 1972). The Caldecott Medal is given by the Children's Service Committee of the American Library Association for the most distinguished picture book of the year. The Newberry Award is given by the American Library Association for the best book for school-age children. The three studies cover the years from 1967 to 1984. From 1967 to 1972, the ratio of male characters to female characters in Caldecott Medal books was 11 to 1. From 1972 to 1979, the ratio of male characters to female characters in Newberry Award books was 1.8 to 1. Finally, from 1980 to 1984, the ratio of male characters to female characters in Caldecott Medal books was 2.3 to 1; the ratio of male to female main characters in Newberry Award books was 3 to 5. Only ten books (out of a total of sixty-four from 1967 to 1984) depicted women working outside the home.

Although numerical disparities seem to be decreasing in children's books, the role models presented for children have not become less stereotyped. The three studies cited above also examined the stereotyped behavior patterns and characteristics depicted in children's books. The 1967 to 1972 study showed that when females were illustrated, traditional sex-role characterizations were reinforced: girls were passive, boys were active; girls followed and served others, boys led and rescued others. Adult men and women in the books surveyed also were stereotyped: women were depicted as wives and mothers; men held a variety of occupations. In the years from 1972 to 1984, sex-role stereotypes were still prevalent. From 1967 to 1971, all eighteen Caldecott Medal books portrayed traditional sex roles; from 1972 to 1979, seventeen out of nineteen did; from 1980 to 1984, fifteen out of twenty did. Out of the nineteen Newberry Award books for 1980 to 1984, fourteen contained traditional sex-role stereotypes.

Sexism in role portrayal does not occur only in Newberry Award and Caldecott Medal books. In his analysis of nursery rhymes and fairy tales (the first literature to which most children are exposed), Donlan (1972) found three recurring types of female characters: the sweet little old lady, the beautiful young heroine, and the aggressive female. The first two types—sweet little old lady and beautiful young heroine—are both depicted as lovable and incompetent. The aggressive female takes many forms—witch, domineering housewife (who functions as wife, mother or stepmother), and shrew (cruel, vain, greedy, demanding). Donlan concludes that in children's literature women are portrayed as ineffectual creatures who need to be dominated by men or as aggressive monsters who must be destroyed by men.

Cooper (1983) examined the sex-role stereotypes in children's books concerning stepfamilies. She examined forty-two books (1975–83) available in libraries in the Chicago metropolitan area and found that for the most part, stereotyped sex roles appeared in these books. Women in the books worked, but in stereotyped occupations, i.e., as receptionists, secretaries, or nurses. When women worked, they neglected their children or became aggressive. They were relatively passive and focused on their appearance. Men were depicted as the lawyers and doctors but were inept at household duties. They were portrayed as caring and sensitive, but only to a point—when problems weren't resolved quickly, they became impatient.

In recent years, several lists of nonstereotyped children's books have been published. One researcher, interested in the sex roles portrayed in a list of nonsexist books entitled *Little Miss Muffet Fights Back,* rated the books in terms of five categories: (1) sex of central characters; (2) sex of figures portrayed on front cover; (3) sex of characters named in titles; (4) numbers of illustrations with males and females; and (5) expressive and instrumental activities (St. Peter, 1979). In addition to analyzing the nonsexist books, this researcher also analyzed titles published prior to the advent of the modern women's movement in the 1970s and titles published after the women's movement. Her analysis of 206 picture books indicates that children are presented with sex-role stereotypes as models. In general, females are underrepresented in titles, central roles, and illustrations; males are overrepresented in instrumental activities and underrepresented in expressive activities. St. Peter (1979) concludes:

> As time passes, . . . and publishers react further to the impact of the women's movement, children's books on conventional lists may begin to reflect changes in female representation. Even now, books on the specialized list, *Little Miss Muffet Fights Back,* contain material that overcomes some stereotypes with females well represented in titles, central roles, and illustrations. These books overcompensate, however, by presenting highly instrumental female models and a minimum of expressive activities. In conclusion, despite the attempted improvement of sex-role models in the Miss Muffet books, the majority of children's picture books today continue to underrepresent women and to stereotype female and male characters. The fact is that, when Jack goes up the hill, Jill stays home. (pp. 259–260)

Much of what has been reviewed in this chapter relates to younger children's literature. However, adolescent literature also has been analyzed for sex-role stereotyping. Magazines for teenagers are very sex-typed according to Kramarae (1981), who notes:

> The journals for adolescent girls appear to concentrate more on advice about appearance, about the interests of males and about what girls should say to males to win their attention and approval. The magazines for boys concentrate (in general) more on athletic skills, and automobile knowledge, and on rough and tough male life apart from females. (p. 89)

Wigutoff (1982) reviewed 300 contemporary realism books published between 1977 and 1980 for adolescents. Traditional sex-role models were depicted—fathers went to work and mothers stayed home. Mothers provided food and clean clothes without expecting gratitude from their husbands or children. Teen romances also promote a stereotypical portrayal of females. As Campion (1983) suggests:

> A new generation is now being subjected to the same nonsense: good looks and the right clothes are a girl's most important attributes; there is no need to take responsibility for your life because a man will do it for you; life ends (at 16 years old, if you're really lucky) when you can walk off into the sunset with the *perfect* boyfriend. (pp. 98–99)

Adult Literature

Literature for adults is often as sexist as teen fiction. For males, the macho image is prevalent. For females, finding a man is of major importance. In this section, we will examine the sex-role portrayal of males and females in popular novels.

Popular novels. In their study of three decades of best-selling books (1949–79), Abramson and Mechanic (1983) examined how sexuality was expressed. They conclude that sex-role stereotypes generally are perpetuated. For males, staying emotionally cool is a major value. Most of the characters are attractive, single, healthy, and young. As you might expect, sexual relations presented in these books changed as society changed. In more recent books, sexual partners know each other for shorter amounts of time and exhibit less romantic love. Across the three decades, sex was initiated by the man (approximately 43 percent of the time) or by mutual consent (approximately 42 percent of the time). When lack of desire was implied, it usually was attributed to the woman.

One of the most popular types of literature is the romance novel. Ruggiero and Weston (1983) suggest there are two types of romance novels: the modern gothic, in which women characters are multi-dimensional and have options, and the historical romance novel, in which women characters have few options and are primarily sexual beings. Three trends are evident in romance fiction for the 1980s: (1) diminished popularity of the modern gothic romance; (2) continued and growing popularity of historical romances; and (3) expansion and extension of Harlequin, Silhouette, Candlelight, and similar lines of romance novels competing with historical romances (Ruggiero & Weston, 1983). The popularity of romance novels is undisputable. According to *Media Report to Women* (1983a), Harlequin Books alone sold four romance novels every second of every day in 1982. Harlequin's consumer relations director, Katherine On, says about 264 million books were sold worldwide last year—retail and through mail order—by Harlequin Enterprises (*Chicago Tribune*, 30 January 1983, Business Section.)

And what is the content of romance novels? The following is a synopsis of a recent Silhouette novel, *Love is Elected:*

> The heroine is Kara Barnett, 21, a public relations specialist for a Washington, D.C., consumer protection group. She's a weak, whiny, whishy-washy wimp . . . The hero is Matt Jordan, 34, a wealthy congressional candidate from Maryland. He's a masterful, muscular, mysterious, macho man . . . They court. She's a chaste beauty; he's a lustful beast . . . . She's a tempestuous child; he's a condescending parent. She's a helpless victim; he's her competent rescuer . . . . After 187 pages of non-stop clashing, they call an unlikely truce, declare their love eternal, and live happily ev . . . . well, you know . . . *(Media Report to Women,* 1983a, p. 12)

Since romance novels are written according to a preset formula, all books of this genre follow the basic synopsis presented above. Eileen Bucholtz, a writer for Silhouette Publishers, explains that there are strict guidelines for writing romance novels. These guidelines are based on what the publisher believes will sell. Bucholtz states, "If you're a writer and you want to write in a certain genre, then you have to follow the general guidelines or else they're not going to buy it" *(Media Report to Women,* 1983a, p. 12). Asked why women (the major authors of romance novels) would write such material, Caroly Males, another romance writer, explained, "It was a business decision. That's how I look at it. We wrote to a particular market, so we did it the way they wanted" (*Media Report to Women,* 1983a, p. 12).

Cartoons and Comic Strips

Both males and females are victims of sex-role stereotyping in cartoons. Numerically, females do not fare well in cartoons and comic strips. A recent survey of the cartoons in a major newspaper found twenty-one comic strips with male names and/or lead characters, including two double-named strips. The total is twenty-eight if you include the three boy's names and the four male animals. There are six cartoons with female names and/or leading characters; if you include two strips with girl's names, the total is eight. Thus, male-oriented comic strips outnumber female-oriented comic strips by a ratio of 3.6 to 1 (Thaler, 1983).

Several sex-role stereotyped messages about male/female roles are communicated in the comics (Braman, 1977). First, females serve males: they tidy up after males, they serve food, and they do the housework. In fact, the most important thing in life for most females in the comics is a male. Second, when females are portrayed in an occupation, it is generally a stereotypical one—women are nurses; men are doctors. Third,

What *is* a man's job?

powerful females are dangerous. Only males should be leaders since females make poor leaders. Females should assist with, but not initiate, action. Finally, females are usually portrayed as one of three images—sex symbol, slave (in the sense that their major purpose is to serve males), or goddess. Although women are often portrayed as passive, quiet, gentle, and nurturing, they often get their way through devious means.

Men, on the other hand, are often dominated, in much the same way as women, by their bosses, friends, family, and circumstances. As a result, men are just as oppressed by their stereotypical portrayal in the comics as are women (Thaler, 1983).

Male and female speech also is stereotyped in cartoons. An examination of the speech of women in the cartoons of the *New Yorker, Playboy, Cosmopolitan,* and *Ladies' Home Journal* reveals:

> The speech of women in these captions is ineffective and restrictive. It cannot deal forthrightly with a number of topics, such as finance and politics, which have great importance in our culture. It cannot be spoken in as many different places as men's speech. Women's speech is weaker than men's speech in emphasis; there are fewer uses of exclamations and curse words. (Kramer, 1974, p. 628)

And how many men, in reality, speak with exclamation marks at the end of every sentence? Thus, stereotypical depictions of males and females exist in cartoons and comics. The speech, as well as the behaviors, of both sexes are portrayed according to sex-role stereotypes.

Some recent cartoons, however, are beginning to break through these stereotypes. Comic strips such as *Doonesbury* and *Sally Forth* focus on the trials and tribulations of both career women and career men. We hope that these comic strips will be successful enough to turn the public's attention away from the sex-role stereotyping of comic strips such as *Blondie, Snuffy Smith,* and *The Lockhorns.*

Advertisements

We are bombarded by advertisements every day in the magazines we read, in between and during the television shows we watch, and on the billboards we see as we drive along the highway. The sex-role stereotypes communicated in these advertisements can affect our views on appropriate behavior for each sex. For example, children who believe television commercials are real (and most young children do), change their attitudes toward women to reflect the traditional role models they view (Pingree, 1978). In this section, we will examine advertisements in the popular media—magazines and television.

Magazines

Generally, advertisements in magazines promote sex-role stereotyping by communicating that: (1) a woman's place is in the home; (2) women do not make important decisions or do important things; (3) women are dependent on men and are isolated from their own sex; and (4) men regard women as sex objects (Pingree, 1978; Poe, 1976). Men have also been affected by sex-role stereotyping in magazine advertisements. Skelly and Lundstrom (1981) compared male sex roles in advertisements in 1959, 1969, and 1979, in general-interest magazines *(Reader's Digest, Time,* and the *New Yorker),* in magazines marketed primarily to men

(Esquire, Field and Stream, and *Sports Illustrated),* and in magazines marketed primarily to women *(Cosmopolitan, House Beautiful,* and *Redbook).* Ads were rated on five levels of sexism toward men. The following percentages were obtained for the three years studied:

Percentage of sexism toward men in magazine ads.

		1959	**1969**	**1979**
Level 1	Man as sex object [decorative]	21.9%	29.3%	42.8%
Level 2	Man's place is at work [traditional]	78.7	69.2	53.7
Level 3	Man may help in home but his first place is at work	0.0	1.4	1.4
Level 4	Man and woman as equals	0.0	0.0	2.1
Level 5	Man and woman as individuals	0.0	0.0	0.0

As we progress from Level 1 to Level 5, males are shown less stereotypically. In Level 1, advertisements involving the macho man image are prevalent. The male shown is desirable not because of his personal qualities, but because of his body. Level 2 ads depict males struggling with roles that are beyond their capabilities, such as caring for children or performing household duties. In Level 3 ads, males are capable of more than one role: they can be effective fathers and effective in their chosen profession. Unlike Level 3 ads, Level 4 advertisements do not remind us that certain roles are considered men's work or women's work. In other words, when we see a male functioning well as a father and as a professional, we do not find that unusual. Childrearing is viewed as both a male and a female role. Level 5 is completely nonstereotypic. Males and females are judged not on the basis of their sex, but on the basis of their individuality. Individual males and females are superior to one another in some areas, inferior in others.

In general, men in advertisements were shown in less-stereotypical roles from 1959 to 1979. The smallest decrease of use of Level 2 was found in magazines marketed to men, from 77.5 percent in 1959 to 66.2 percent in 1979. Advertisements in magazines marketed to women have shown men in a mixed light. They show the highest increase in advertisements of Level 3 and Level 4, but also in Level 1. Men have been increasingly used as sex objects in these magazines. Advertisers believe that women, as they achieve more sexual equality and buying power, will be increasingly attracted to ads that use men as sex objects and will buy their products. Though Level 3 and 4 advertisements are shown in 1979, when none were shown in 1959, the discouraging truth is that only 13 of the 660 advertisements were coded at the higher levels. In general, the male sex role, as portrayed in magazine advertisements, has been slow to change.

Television

Research on sex-role portrayal in television advertisements consistently finds that voice-overs are almost exclusively male. In television advertisements shown in the afternoon, 92 percent of the voice-overs are male (Knill et al., 1981). Women are portrayed predominantly as housewives or mothers, are more frequently used as representatives for domestic products, and are most often located in the home (O'Donnell & O'Donnell, 1978). Women have few opportunities to demonstrate their expertise, and, when they do, it is largely restricted to the traditional areas of homemaking and personal care (Marecek et al., 1978).

Children's commercials on television fare no better. Verna (1975) coded 173 commercials and found that 101 commercials were directed toward males, 24 were directed toward females, and 48 were neutral. Loudness of sound track, activity levels, cooperativeness, independence, and aggressiveness were significantly higher in ads directed toward males than in ads directed toward females. Quietness and passivity characterized ads directed toward females. Finally, all ads directed toward males had a male actor or a male voice-over. Twelve of the twenty-four ads directed toward females had a male actor or a male voice-over. Another study examined the level of action, the pace, visual and camera techniques,and auditory techniques in children's commercials (Welch et al., 1979). Commercials aimed at males contained active toys, varied scenes, high rates of camera cuts, high levels of sound effects, and loud music.

Implications and Consequences of Media Images

If there were no effects of the media images portrayed, there would be little need for concern. However, research demonstrates that the images presented in the media do affect the sex roles men and women consider appropriate. In part, because of the traditional sex roles perpetuated by the media, males and females believe they have only limited options for their careers and relationships. In this section, we will examine some of the consequences of the media images of males and females.

What effect does the portrayal of traditional sex roles have on children's sex-role development? Television promotes sex-role stereotypes (Gross & Jeffries-Fox, 1978; Katz, 1980). Children of both sexes identify more with same-sex television models than with opposite-sex ones (Sprafkin & Liebert, 1978). Children who frequently watch television tend to accept more sex-role stereotypes than children who seldom watch television (Frueh & McGhee, 1975). Katz (1980) found that the traditional content of children's television preferences is a more reliable predictor of their future sex-role expectations than the socialization practices of their parents. Children use television characters as models for adult roles (Avery, 1979; Mayes & Valentine, 1979). They also model their problem-solving behavior on the behavior of their favorite television characters (Roloff & Greenberg, 1979).

Several researchers have investigated the effects of viewing programs with nontraditional sex-role content. McArthur and Eisen (1976) found that after viewing televised counterstereotypical role portrayals, preschoolers recall and imitate more of the activities of an adult same-sex model than an opposite-sex model—even when the same-sex model displays sex-inappropriate behavior. Eisenstock (1984) found similar results with preadolescent boys and girls. Commercials in which females are depicted in nontraditional roles elicit fewer traditional beliefs about females (Atkin & Miller, 1975). In a recent study, Eisenstock (1984) examined the effects of television in promoting nonsexist role learning among children with different sex-role orientations. Her results suggest that androgynous and feminine children identify with nontraditional televised models more often than masculine children do. (See Chapter 2 for a further discussion of these concepts.)

Two points are important to remember. First, although study after study confirms the stereotypical portrayal of males and females on television, there is less agreement concerning the effects of such stereotypical portrayal. Certainly, children are exposed to a variety of stereotyped sources—books, school, parents, and peers. However, if Henderson, Greenberg, and Atkin (1980) are correct when they say that sex-role stereotypes are "woven deeply into the fabric" of television, then we should examine this medium and its effects more extensively.

Second, the major focus of research on sex-role stereotypes on television has been on the negative effects these stereotypes have on females. However, the effects are no doubt as devastating for males. The stereotype of the macho, unemotional male portrayed in the media perpetuates the sex-role stereotype that males must not allow their emotions to show—that big boys don't cry. This restriction on behavior may have physical consequences. As Katz (1980) suggests, "The limitations placed upon what is allowable as 'appropriate' masculine behavior may well have implications for why males develop more stress-related diseases" (p. 4).

Adult television programming also communicates sex-role stereotypes (Tan, 1982). The more people watch television, the more they tend to believe in social stereotypes. Sex-role stereotypes are learned more easily by people who watch television a significant portion of time than by those who don't (McGhee & Frueh, 1980). Therefore, the influence of television on the formation and perpetuation of sex-role stereotypes suggests that television could play a very influential role in changing sex-role stereotypes.

What effect does the communication of the stereotypical images in music have? Before answering this question, we need to ascertain how much time people spend listening to music. Both teenagers and adults spend a significant amount of time listening to music on the radio. For example, one study of 500 respondents in Santa Barbara, California, found that "Top 40" listeners spend an average of 124 minutes per day listening to music. Members of the rock music listening audience spend an average of 188 minutes per day listening to music (Lull, Johnson & Edmond, 1981). When such a large portion of time is spent listening to music, music serves as a socialization agent by explicitly or implicitly communicating societal norms. One such norm involves the appropriate behavior for each sex. In fact, when university students were asked to comment on the role of music in their social conditioning, 66 percent of those responding felt that the lyrics of popular songs had influenced their standards for dating behavior (Toohey, 1982). As we have already seen, most of these standards are based on sex-role stereotypes.

The concern with sexism in children's literature results from the belief that books influence children's behavior. What effect does sex-role stereotyping in children's books have on children? Book content does influence children's sex-role stereotypes (Campbell & Wirtenberg, 1980). Several studies reveal the effects on children of traditional sex-role stereotypes in children's books. Koblinsky, Cruse, and Sugawara (1978) tested children's recall after listening to stories with males and females in traditional roles and found that boys recall the masculine characteristics of males, and girls remember the feminine characteristics of females. When preschool children read stories with traditional and nontraditional behaviors of boys and girls, they prefer stories in which the characters display traditional behavior for their sex (Jennings, 1975; Kropp & Halverson, 1983).

Research also demonstrates the effect nonbiased stories can have on children. Children who were asked their career preferences after hearing stories with characters in nontraditional roles made more nontraditional choices than children who only heard about traditional characters (Lutes-Dunckley, 1978). Girls who hear nontraditional stories rate male jobs and characteristics as more appropriate for females than girls who hear traditional stories (Ashby & Wittmaier, 1976). Nursery school girls exhibit more achievement behavior after listening to a story about an achieving girl than after listening to a story about an achieving boy (McArthur & Eisen, 1976). Female sex-role stereotypes can be modified through the use of books that depict egalitarian sex roles (Flerx, Fidler & Rogers, 1976). When females are portrayed in roles traditionally assumed by males, both boys and girls increase their perceptions of the number of girls who can engage in these traditionally male activities (Scott & Feldman-Summers, 1979).

Television's stereotyped portrayal of men and women—both in programming and in advertising—affects men's and women's self-perceptions. For example, women often define their ideal self according to the traits emphasized in the television programs they view (Lull, 1980). Results of studies examining the effects of repeated viewing of nontraditional commericals suggest that such commercials may help to reverse sex-role norms (Brown, 1979).Although male and female portrayals in advertisements have been slow to change, both males and females desire change (Alreck, Settle & Belch, 1982; Courtney & Whipple, 1980). Perhaps when the general public makes its dissatisfaction with current sex-role images in advertisements known to advertisers, more changes will be forthcoming. Until changes are made, occupational choices for males and females will be limited, females will feel inferior because of underrepresentation in the media, and the roles depicted will perpetuate the traditional roles of males and females. As we have seen in previous chapters, sex-role stereotyping resulting from the portrayal of traditional roles affects communication between the sexes.

Strategies for Change

The major roadblock to changing the media images of men and women is that much of the media is controlled by people unwilling to change the stereotypes. For example, the limited images of women in films is attributable, in part, to the makeup of the film industry itself. Filmmaker Barbara Evans (in *Media Report to Women,* 1983b) summarizes the problem:

> The established film industry presents serious problems for a woman filmmaker. Even women directors find the films they make not wholly within their control, being dependent, as they are, on a large crew composed mainly of men, who are still seen as the chief bearers of technical knowledge and skills. And women's voices are far too often stifled by those who control the purse-strings. Unfortunately for the cause of women's self-expression, these are usually men. (p. 5)

The majority of writers of romance novels are women, and the publishing industry is male-controlled (Stern, 1983; West, 1978). As a result, men dictate what will be published, who will have access to it, and which publications will be promoted as significant. One researcher explains the problem of male-dominated publishing and its effect on women:

> The commercial publishing industry is controlled by men and under the guise of rational and objective decision-making, it manages to produce and disseminate material that it claims to be "universal" and representative of all humanity. In fact, through gatekeeping, the publishing industry selects and promotes the ideas and knowledge that effectively maintain and support the dominant male view of the world. This constitutes a rarely acknowledged "political" dimension in the production of knowledge and in the publishing industry. Alternative views, such as those presented by feminists, are contained at a level where they inevitably remain marginal and without the legitimacy that the sheer volume of production and expensive promotion accord to masculine ideals and practices. (Spender, 1983, p. 469)

Given the economic realities of the media, change will not be easy; yet, change is occurring—slowly. For example, advertisements are beginning to portray women in more out-of-the-home roles. Women characters in romance novels increasingly are being portrayed as in control of their lives and fully responsible for all their actions (Hubbard, 1985). Television programs are featuring male and female characters in more equal roles.

But what can you, as an individual, do to overcome some of the sex-role stereotyping that is portrayed in the media? Perhaps the simplest answer is to expose yourself to a variety of media sources. For example, watch some of the television shows that feature men and women in a variety of nonstereotyped roles, seek out films that include both strong female and strong male characters, and listen to the music of some of the newer female rock stars instead of just to well-established male groups. In addition, you might want to write letters to companies whose advertising tries to make women feel guilty for having kitchens that are less than spotless or uses men as decorative sex objects. If men and women truly want the media images of males and females to change, perhaps the media will begin to depict people in complex, ever-changing roles instead of in stereotyped roles.

Conclusion

In this chapter, we have analyzed sex-role stereotypes communicated through the media of film, television, music, children's literature, adult literature, cartoon/comic strips, and advertising. Generally, the sex-roles communicated in the media are stereotypical. Males are independent, active professionals. Females are dependent, passive wives and mothers. Recently, some media images have begun to change in response to changing sex roles in society. Since the communication of sex-role stereotypes in the media serves to perpetuate stereotypes in society, we should work to support productive changes in the media portrayal of both men and women.

Suggested Activities

1. Watch an hour of children's programming on television such as *Sesame Street, Mister Rogers,* or *The Electric Company*. In addition, watch an hour of children's cartoon shows such as *He-Man and Masters of the Universe, She-Ra: Princess of Power,* or *Smurfs*. Compare and contrast the sex-role stereotypes portrayed on these programs. What types of messages about the roles of males and females in society are being communicated by these shows? What are these shows doing to overcome sex-role stereotyping? How are these shows creating and maintaining sex-role stereotyped images for children?
2. Choose a popular fairy tale such as "Snow White," "Cinderella," "Jack and the Beanstalk," or "Rapunzel." Identify the sex-role stereotypes contained in the story. Rewrite the story to eliminate these stereotypes. (For example, a rich princess could save Cinder-fella from his wicked banker.) What sex-role stereotypes did the original fairy tale contain? How does your re-written story avoid these stereotypes? Did you add any new sex-role stereotypes in your version? How difficult is it to write a children's story that eliminates sex-role stereotypes?
3. Obtain a copy of a magazine that is marketed primarily to women (e.g., *Woman's Day, Cosmopolitan, Good Housekeeping*) and a magazine that is marketed primarily to men (e.g., *Sports Illustrated, Popular Mechanics, Esquire*). Examine advertisements in each magazine that are for similar products (e.g., perfume and cologne ads, liquor ads, cigarette ads). How do ads designed to sell products to women differ from those designed to sell similar products to men? Describe the sex-role stereotyping contained in the ads. What sex-role stereotypes are communicated through these ads? Do any of the ads avoid sex-role stereotypes (e.g., picturing a father taking care of an infant, showing a woman business executive)? In your opinion, which of these ads is most effective? Why?
4. Watch a re-run of a television situation comedy from the 1950s, 1960s, or 1970s (e.g., *The Honeymooners, Brady Bunch, I Love Lucy, Bewitched, Make Room for Daddy*) and a similar show that is currently on television (e.g., *Kate and Allie, Family Ties, Who's the Boss?*). Compare and contrast the sex-role stereotypes contained in these shows. Compare the portrayal of men and women. How has the portrayal of families changed on these shows? How have the sex-role messages contained in these shows influenced our perceptions of communication between the sexes?

5. Locate a group devoted to networking (e.g., a chapter of a Business and Professional Women's Club, the Jaycees, Women in Communications, or similar organization). Attend several meetings. (You may have to get permission from the group's leader to attend meetings. Make sure that you tell the leader that you want to observe the meeting and describe it to your class.) Answer the following questions:

What is the purpose of the network?
How old are the members?
What other personal characteristics of members seem to be significant (e.g., all members are bankers, all members are personnel directors)?
How are the meetings conducted?
What kinds of things do participants discuss at meetings?

During a class discussion, compare networks that are primarily male, primarily female, and mixed-sex. How are they similar? How do they differ? In your opinion, which of the networks are most effective in overcoming barriers to effective upward communication? Why?

For Further Reading

Busby, L.J. (1975). Sex-role research on the mass media. *Journal of Communication, 25*(4), 107–131.

Butler, M., and Paisley, W. (1980). *Women and the mass media: Sourcebook for research and action*. New York: Human Sciences Press.

Harrison, R.P. (1981). *The cartoon: Communication to the quick*. Beverly Hills, CA: Sage.

Haskell, D. (1979). The depiction of women in leading roles in prime time television. *Journal of Broadcasting, 23,* 191–196.

Johnston, J., and Ettema, J.S. (1982). *Positive images: Breaking stereotypes with children's television*. Beverly Hills, CA: Sage.

Potkay, C.R., and Potkay, C.E. (1982). Perceptions of female and male comic strip characters II: Favorability and identification and different dimensions. *Sex Roles, 10,* 119–128.

Tuchman, G., Daniels, A.K., and Benet, J. (Eds.). (1978). *Hearth and home: Images of women in the mass media*. New York: Oxford University Press.

Turner, K.J. (1977). Comic strips: A rhetorical perspective. *Central States Speech Journal, 28,* 24–35.

Weibel, K. (1977). *Mirror, mirror: Images of women reflected in popular culture*. Garden City, NY: Anchor Books.

Williams, F., La Rose, R., and Frost, F. (1981). *Children, television, and sex-role stereotyping*. New York: Praeger.

Communication and Sex Roles in the Organization

9

In Chapter 1, we described how men and women may be treated differently or communicate differently because of their sex. We noted that one of the contexts in which differences are most apparent is at work in organizations. Most of you probably intend to pursue a career once you graduate from college. Many of these careers will be in organizations such as banks, insurance companies, public relations agencies, computer firms, or television stations. If you work a forty-hour week outside the home (and many of you will work much longer hours than that) for the next thirty years, you will have spent approximately sixty-thousand hours in various formal organizations. We know that at work men and women sometimes are treated differently based on sex-role stereotypes and, in some ways, communicate differently.

When you think of your future career, do you see yourself in a managerial position? How do you think your co-workers will view your actions? What type of leader or manager will you be? From a great deal of research evidence, we know that if you pursue a managerial career, sex-role stereotypes will affect how you are viewed as a manager.

Dr. Samuel Johnson, an eighteenth-century lexicographer, is reported to have said, "A woman preaching is like a dog walking on his hind legs. It is not done well; but you are surprised to find it done at all" (quoted in Jacobson & Effertz, 1974, p. 393). Although women in leadership positions today are more common than Dr. Johnson's dogs walking on their hind legs, female managers are still perceived differently than men. For example, common wisdom holds that a female manager has to work twice as hard as a man to prove herself (Woods, 1975). As a female banking executive said: "If I were a male, I could probably make at least one small mistake without disrupting my career. As a woman, I know there's not room for even one. I exhaust every possibility before I make a loan because I'm putting my career on the line every time" (Up the ladder, 1975, p. 67). Women think they have to work harder and make fewer mistakes than men to survive in the corporate world.

The years from 1960 to 2000 are a period of transition for women in leadership and managerial positions. One author claims that by the year 2000 there will be no reason to study women leaders apart from men leaders (Bass, 1981). We hope that this will be the case. Until then, however, there a number of sex differences and sex-role issues in communication behavior within organizations that need to be examined. This chapter will examine how women and men in organizations are perceived, how they communicate, and how their attitudes are shaped by their experiences. In addition, since many of you may plan to pursue managerial careers, this chapter will focus on sex-role issues in managerial communication.

What Are the Stereotypes?

As discussed in Chapters 1 and 2, sex-role stereotyping is the "belief that a set of traits and abilities is more likely to be found among one sex than the other" (Schein, 1978, p. 259). These beliefs also include what is considered appropriate male and female behavior (Terborg, 1977). Take a minute to read "Impressions from An Office." Although this list is a somewhat humorous look at sex-role stereotypes, these stereotypes do have profound effects on workers. For example, "sex-role stereotypes include far more than oversimplified distinctions between the characteristics of males and females. For much of this society, these distinctions have been translated into rigid expectations regarding the appropriate roles that members of each sex are to play" (Garland & Price, 1977, p. 29). Often, in our society, women are expected to play low-status or submissive roles, while men are expected to assume high status or dominant roles (Remland, Jacobson & Jones, 1983). The business world reflects the expectations traditionally ascribed to these sex roles (Heinen et al., 1975).

Impressions From An Office

The family picture is on HIS desk:
Ah, a solid, responsible family man.

The family picture is on HER desk:
Umm, her family will come before her career.

HIS desk is cluttered:
He's obviously a hard worker and a busy man.

HER Desk is cluttered:
She's obviously a disorganized scatterbrain.

HE's not at his desk:
He must be at a meeting.

SHE's not at her desk:
She must be in the ladies' room.

Impressions From An Office (continued)

HE is talking with his co-workers:
He must be discussing the latest deal.

SHE is talking with her co-workers:
She must be gossiping.

HE's not in the office:
He's meeting customers.

SHE's not in the office:
She must be out shopping.

HE's having lunch with the boss:
He's on his way up.

SHE's having lunch with the boss:
They must be having an affair.

The boss criticized HIM:
He'll improve his performance.

The boss criticized HER:
She'll be very upset.

HE got an unfair deal:
Did he get angry?

SHE got an unfair deal:
Did she cry?

HE's getting married:
He'll get more settled.

SHE's getting married:
She'll get pregnant and leave.

HE's having a baby:
He'll need a raise.

SHE's having a baby:
She'll cost the company money in maternity benefits.

HE's going on a business trip:
It's good for his career.

SHE's going on a business trip:
What does her husband say?

HE's leaving for a better job:
He knows how to recognize a good opportunity.

SHE's leaving for a better job:
Women are undependable.

[Natasha Josefowitz, *Paths to Power*, © 1980, Addison–Wesley, Reading, MA, p. 60. Reprinted with permission.]

In 1971, Orth and Jacobs listed the typical male view of women workers:

1. Women will get married and leave.
2. Women will not work while they have young children.
3. Women are uncomfortable in a man's world and make men uncomfortable when they intrude on it.
4. Women are not dependable—they are too emotional and fall apart in a crisis.
5. Women managers are not transferable when their husbands have equal or better jobs. (pp. 141–142)

These sex-role stereotypes are changing, but not as quickly as we might like.

In the business world, many people still assume that only men have careers (Rosenfeld, 1979). Women may work outside the home, but traditional sex roles dictate that their primary commitment is to their role within the home. This sex-role stereotype is reflected in the observation that the behavior of males is perceived as basically active, aggressive, and instrumental, while the behavior of females is perceived as passive, nurturant, and expressive (Cowan & Koziej, 1979). In addition, a higher social value is generally ascribed to masculine behaviors.

Traditional sex-role stereotypes hold that men are more competent at task accomplishment than women. As a result of this stereotype, when men and women perform with equal competence, males are rated more positively than females (Nieva & Gutek, 1980). In contrast, when men and women perform incompetently, the incompetent men are rated even lower than the equally incompetent women. Researchers conclude that since success at demanding jobs is expected of men but not of women, unsuccessful women are not penalized as severely for doing a poor job as unsuccessful men are. On the other hand, women are not rewarded as highly for their success, either. Thus, when women's behavior is congruent with sex-role stereotypes, they are viewed relatively positively even if they fail to complete a task. If their behavior is not congruent with sex-role stereotypes and they succeed at a task, they are not likely to be rewarded as highly as men who succeed at the same task.

In general, the female sex role is more consistent with "followership" than the male sex role. Both males and females expect females to be effective in the role of follower and males to perform well as leaders. When they do not live up to these ideals, they are judged harshly. Jacobson and Effertz (1974) set up a situation in which male and female leaders directed groups to reproduce a pattern of dominoes. The situation was designed so that no group could succeed at the task in the time allotted. Although the groups did not differ in actual performance, leaders rated the performance of female followers lower than the performance of male followers. Followers, on the other hand, rated the performance of male leaders lower than the performance of female leaders. The highest degree of failure was perceived in groups with a male leader and all female followers. Since their task roles were consistent with their sex roles, they should have had the highest expectation of success and, consequently, felt the worst when they did not succeed. Male leaders were highly critical of themselves when the group did not perform well. Thus, they accepted the blame for the poor performance of the group even when it was not their fault.

As we can see from this discussion, sex-role stereotyping leads to the differential treatment of men and women at work. Although women increasingly are being accepted into positions of authority in business, some people still question women's abilities to do an effective job. In many cases, women who do a good job, in contrast to sex-role stereotypes, are not rewarded as highly for their performance as men whose work is of the same quality.

Sex-Role Stereotypes of Managers

In 1973, Schein noted that management could be classified as a masculine occupation because of the high ratio of men to women and because of the belief that this is how it should be. When asked to rate women in general, men in general, and successful middle managers on ninety-two descriptive terms, both men and women judged successful middle managers to possess characteristics, attitudes, and temperaments more commonly ascribed to men in general than to women in general (Schein, 1973). Successful managers *and* men were perceived to possess leadership ability, competitiveness, objectivity, aggressiveness, forcefulness, and ambition, and to desire responsibility. A few managerial behaviors were ascribed to women—employee-centeredness, understanding, helpfulness, and intuition. Thus, as Schein concludes, "all else being equal, the perceived similarity between the characteristics of successful middle managers and men in general increases the likelihood of a male rather than a female being selected for or promoted to a managerial position" (p. 99).

The "masculine is best in management" ethic continues to be held by both men and women. Both sexes tend to believe management is man's business since leadership is usually defined in masculine terms (Koehn, 1976). This same attitude has been traced over the years.

In 1965, a *Harvard Business Review* study asked the question, "Are Women Executives People?" (Bowman, Worthy & Greyser, 1965). This survey of two thousand male and female executives indicated that women executives may be people, but they are not particularly popular people. Attitudes did differ by sex, though. Only 9 percent of the male respondents, but 48 percent of the female respondents, were "strongly favorable" toward women in management. Forty-one percent of the men and only 7 percent of the women were either "mildly" or "strongly unfavorable" to women in management. Male and female respondents (61 percent of the males and 47 percent of the females) agreed that the business community would never wholly accept women business executives. And male and female respondents agreed that "a woman has to be exceptional, indeed overqualified, to succeed in management today" (p. 15).

According to a 1971 study, managers felt that other men *and* women would prefer a male supervisor and would be uncomfortable with a female supervisor (Bass, Krusell & Alexander, 1971). This finding supports

Bowman, Worthy, and Greyser's (1965) earlier finding that relatively few men felt they would be comfortable as a subordinate to a woman, and that most men believed men in general would not be comfortable. Bass and his colleagues concluded in 1971 that "societal norms do not sanction the placement of women in dominant positions" in organizations (p. 223).

A more recent study found that male middle managers and top-level executives overwhelmingly reject stereotypical statements that treat women as a "lower species" (Baron & Abrahamsen, 1981). Even though 80 percent of their respondents agreed that "In time, women executives will become commonplace," 49 percent still believed, "People are reluctant to work for females." The authors concluded that men still question women's capabilities as managers. Overall, managers agreed that men are better suited to handling executive responsibilities than women are and that male subordinates feel inferior when their supervisor is female.

As women become more active participants in the labor force, the experience of working with competent women may reduce the relationship between sex-role stereotypes and the use of masculine characteristics to define the managerial role (Schein, 1973). There is some evidence to support the idea that familiarity with a woman in a typically male job increases the likelihood of another woman filling that job (Smith, 1979). In addition, men who work for and with women managers generally have a higher acceptance of women in management roles than men who do not work with or for women managers (Baron & Abrahamsen, 1981; Wheeless & Berryman-Fink, 1985).

Other variables also affect men's acceptance of women as leaders. For example, the higher the level of a man's education, the greater his acceptance of women in management roles (Baron & Abrahamsen, 1981). Younger men tend to be less in favor of the idea of women executives than older men (Bowman et al., 1965), perhaps because older managers have had more experience working with women in management roles and, therefore, have modified some of their stereotypical perceptions of women (Schein, 1973). In addition, husbands whose wives are working in what the husbands describe as "career positions" rather than "just a job" agree that women make good executives and, consequently, have a higher acceptance of women in nontraditional roles.

Interpretations of a female manager's success are strongly related to general attitudes toward women in managerial roles. People with a positive attitude toward women in management associate women managers' success with ability and hard work (Garland & Price, 1977). People with negative attitudes toward women in management think that successful women managers succeed because of good luck or an easy job.

Nevertheless, in the presence of external pressure, such as Equal Employment Opportunity (EEO) legislation, the promotion of men is attributed to task-related ability significantly more frequently than the promotion of women (Wiley & Eskilson, 1983). In addition, men promoted for task-irrelevant reasons are seen as having a greater chance for promotion, being better liked by their subordinates, and able to get more cooperation from their subordinates than women promoted to fill EEO requirements. Thus, if the promotion of women is seen as resulting from outside pressures and not their own task competence, their ability to handle the job is seriously questioned no matter what their qualifications are.

Managerial Communication Style

As we discussed earlier, a manager's success is judged according to sex-role stereotypes. In addition, sex-role stereotypes influence the perception of a manager's communication style. Evaluators believe that the employees of managers who use sex-role appropriate behaviors will be more productive and more satisfied, and that such managers will be more effective and will be evaluated better by their superiors. This situation is indeed the case. Female managers are evaluated more favorably when they use consideration behaviors, such as thanking subordinates for their suggestions or allowing someone time off to visit the dentist; male managers are evaluated more favorably when they use structuring behaviors, such as taking charge of reorganizing a department or giving employees new job descriptions (Bartol & Butterfield, 1976). Such evaluations indicate that strong sex-role stereotypes exist for male and female managers' communication behavior.

Evaluations of the effectiveness of supervisory communication styles are influenced both by sex of the supervisor and by sex of the subordinate. A rewarding communication style—telling subordinates that salary increases depend on performance—is rated more effective for male supervisors; and a friendly, dependent communication style—approaching subordinates in a friendly way and asking them to help out by improving their performance—is rated more effective for supervisors of either sex when the subordinate is of the opposite sex (Rosen & Jerdee, 1973). In general, a threatening supervisory style is rated low, and a helping style is rated high. The similar ratings of supervisory communication style by both sexes "provides evidence that men and women share common perceptions and expectations regarding what constitutes appropriate behavior for males and females in supervisory positions" (Rosen & Jerdee, 1973, p. 47). In general, the stereotype of the aggressive, threatening role for males and the compassionate, helping role for females is not supported when the subordinate's sex is taken into account.

Sex composition of the work group may affect perceptions of the leader or manager. For example, groups with an equal number of males and females who hold a positive attitude toward female leadership, in general, are the most satisfied with female leadership. Groups composed of an equal number of males and females who hold a generally negative attitude toward female leaders are the least satisfied with female leadership. This dissatisfaction is also true of groups composed of only one female member and three male members, even if the males have a generally positive attitude toward female leadership (Yerby, 1975). Thus, as Yerby somewhat flippantly suggests, if employees are generally hostile toward female leadership, the female manager should have all male subordinates since they will reinforce the female leader "as a way of expressing deference to her." In a climate that is receptive to female leadership, subordinates will be more satisfied if there are subordinates of both sexes.

Sex Differences in Organizational Communication

The above discussion examined how sex-role stereotypes influence people's perceptions of men and women in organizations. In some organizational situations, sex-role stereotypes may affect how men and women communicate. Studies of the actual communication behavior of managers, however, provide contradictory results. Although Birdsall (1980) found that male and female managers use the same communication style in weekly staff meetings, Alderton and Jurma (1980) found that, in discussions, female leaders communicate significantly more agreement than male leaders, regardless of the sex of the followers. Although followers tend to disagree more with same-sex leaders than with opposite-sex leaders, overall they disagree the most with female leaders. Nevertheless, male and female leaders do not differ in their task-oriented communication behavior, so group members are equally satisfied with their leadership.

Lockheed and Hall (1976) draw three generalizations about the behavior of men and women in mixed-sex groups. First, men are more active than women; the average man initiates more speech than the average woman. This pattern appears as early as age 7. Second, men are more influential than women. A woman is more likely to yield to a man's opinion. Third, men initiate more task-oriented behavior, and women initiate more socioemotional behavior. In other words, men spend more time making suggestions and giving opinions to a group than women do. Women spend a greater percentage of their interaction time agreeing with or praising others.

In a situation where the solution is not supplied to the leader, females play a less dominant role than in situations where the solution is supplied to the leader. If female leaders are given a management-oriented solution to a problem facing a work group, they will be as persuasive and tactful as male leaders in getting the group to adopt the solution (Maier, 1970). On the other hand, when a solution has not been supplied, female leaders are less likely than males to have their groups adopt a management-oriented solution, even if it is fairly obvious. Female leaders tend to become more permissive in this situation.

Sex composition of work groups also influences how members decide to accomplish their tasks. With an unstructured task, all-male groups are more likely to have a differentiated division of labor than all-female groups (Fennell et al., 1978). That is, to prevent constant struggles for authority, all-male groups are likely to divide up the task because all

Just who *is* the breadwinner today?

group members are equally legitimate incumbents of authority. In all-female groups, no one is perceived as the legitimate authority, so a highly differentiated division of labor is unlikely to develop. Without a highly differentiated division of labor, all-female groups come up with superior decisions.

There is increasing evidence that, viewed objectively, women managers perform as credibly as their male counterparts (Larwood, Wood & Inderlied, 1978). In the military, male and female leaders exhibit similar patterns of leadership behavior and have similar effectiveness (Day & Stogdill, 1972). Male and female supervisors consider themselves similar in management values, except that females are higher in tolerance for ambiguity and consideration (Bartol & Wortman, 1976). Donnell and Hall (1980) studied a large group of managers and found no difference in managerial style or philosophy between male and female managers. Both male and female managers approach motivating their subordinates in the same way and employ participative practices in a similar manner. Donnell and Hall conclude that "women, in general, do not differ from men, in general, in the ways in which they administer the management process" (p. 76). Under stress, however, some differences do arise. Male managers are more likely to become dictatorial, while female managers are more likely to become conciliatory.

These findings contradict several studies discussed previously that indicated that subordinates notice different behaviors from male and female supervisors. This discrepancy many occur because, in actual organizations, organizational authorities may react differently to male and female managers and, thus, cause different reactions from the managers' subordinates. Organizational authorities are less likely to back up the authority of a woman in a leadership role (Fennell et al., 1978). If this is the case, "subordinates, whether male or female, would be less likely to accept directives and evaluations from a female . . . in an authority position because, unless shown otherwise, they would assume she does not have the legitimacy necessary for these acts" (p. 601). As a consequence, a woman supervisor would be perceived differently than a man because of her lack of actual authority in the organization.

Downward Communication

Another important type of communication in organizations is sharing information with subordinates. Female supervisors may be less willing than male supervisors to share relevant information with their colleagues. Subordinates of female managers solicit less feedback from their managers and relate differently to their managers than subordinates of male managers (Donnell & Hall, 1980). Male managers are more open and candid with their colleagues. As noted earlier in this chapter, female managers may be less open with their subordinates because they do not get as much support from organizational authorities and, therefore, do not have as much information to share.

If female supervisors are supported by upper management, however, their communication behaviors may be quite different from male supervisors' behavior. Baird and Bradley (1979) found that subordinates feel female supervisors give them more information about other departments, place greater emphasis on happy interpersonal relations, are more receptive to subordinates' ideas, and encourage subordinates' efforts more than male supervisors. Male supervisors are considered more dominant, more directive, and quicker to challenge others than female supervisors. Thus, male and female supervisors differ in both communication content and communication style.

Baird and Bradley conclude that female managers actually may be more effective supervisors than male managers because their communication behaviors are closer to those prescribed by classic management theorists.

Upward Communication

Upward communication in an organization reduces the psychological distance between status levels and helps subordinates be closer to and identify more with their supervisors (Mulder, 1960). Upward communication is especially important for women in organizations because it may serve to decrease sex-role stereotyping. As an indication of this situation, female subordinates are more likely than male subordinates to believe that seeking and giving information strategies for upward communication are important for advancement (Sussman et al., 1980). Because of sex-role stereotyping in industry, women may feel far removed from the information mainstream and, therefore, may place a high value on behaviors that are designed to get this necessary information. In one study, 65 percent of the women surveyed believed that conversation between superiors and subordinates was their primary source of information about the organization (Shockley & Staley, 1980). In fact, women who often engage in upward communication with their supervisors advance in the organizational hierarchy faster than women who do not spend as much time communicating upward (Stewart & Gudykunst, 1982). (Later in this chapter we will discuss how mentors can be used as another type of upward communication strategy to overcome barriers to effective communication in organizations.)

Women also seem to be less selective than men in the information they choose to communicate upward. Female subordinates perceive disclosure of potentially negative information as more appropriate, have less fear that harmful consequences will result, and report greater willingness to disclose such information to their managers than do male subordinates (Young, 1978). This may be because female subordinates tend to distort upward communication more than males do (Athanassiades, 1974), so that even though they intend to send accurate, but potentially negative, messages to their superiors, the messages that are actually communicated verbally may be less negative than intended. Glauser (1982) contends that females may be more accurate upward communicators of relevant task information than males, but less accurate upward communicators of personal problems, attributes, and needs.

Informal Communication Networks

Women are at a disadvantage when managers choose subordinates on the basis of shared values since most managers are male and, therefore, likely to select males for advancement and promotion (Riger & Galligan, 1980). Rosen and Jerdee (1974) note, "When the information is scant and the position ambiguous, managers tend to fall back on traditional concepts of male and female roles" (p. 58). If a supervisor believes that a woman is less likely than a man to be aggressive, competitive, or ambitious, the supervisor may be less likely to provide job assignments calling for these skills. Differential task assignments can prevent a woman from developing abilities necessary for future advancement (Schein, 1978). Larwood, Wood, and Inderlied (1978) argue:

> The informal work groups surrounding male supervisors are more likely to contain other men than women, and male subordinates are consequently more likely to gain the confidence of their superiors. With less interaction and communication, women have less opportunity to engage in the training needed for advancement. . . . As a result, the woman is less likely to be chosen for important responsibility in her organization irrespective of her original abilities—but because of her sex. (p. 53)

Women tend to wait to be chosen for promotion instead of actively promoting themselves as men do. In a classic study, Hennig and Jardim (1977) interviewed women at all levels of management—corporate vice presidents and presidents, chief executive officers, middle managers, Harvard Business School M.B.A. students, and undergraduate business majors. Among these women, they found an overwhelming sense of "waiting to be chosen." The women interviewed believed that if they were competent and performed their jobs well, they would be rewarded. Hennig and Jardim conclude that women rely on the formal structure of the organization—its rules, policies, and procedures—to sustain their careers. They discount the "informal system of relationships and information sharing, ties of loyalty and of dependence, of favors granted and owed, of mutual benefit, of protection—which men unfailingly and invariably take into account" (p. 31).

Developing a career within an organization depends on accumulating the power necessary to influence other people (Zaleznik, 1970). But, as Schein (1978) notes, "Even if a woman is aware of the necessity to be strategic and to acquire power and influence, she may be excluded from one of the most significant components of successful power acquisition—the development of informal/influence relationships" (p. 265). From the previous discussion, we can conclude that women may be excluded from informal communication networks or may not even perceive that informal networks are important sources of the power necessary for corporate advancement.

There is some evidence that women and men use different communication strategies when expressing their desire for promotion to their supervisors. Sussman and his colleagues (1980) found that women use more task-facilitative-seeking strategies than men. In other words, women who desire promotion are more likely than men who desire promotion to ask for their superiors' opinions and suggestions. Women consider providing information to supervisors to be more important than men do, and women more strongly believe they should show positive support to their male supervisors than men subordinates do. In contrast, men think it is more advantageous for them to show positive support to a female supervisor than to show positive support to a male supervisor. Overall, both men and women believe it is more important to use social facilitative strategies—such as, agreement, tension release, and solidarity—with female supervisors than with male supervisors.

Implications and Consequences of Sex-Role Stereotyping in Organizations

As we noted earlier, you are probably planning on a career. When you think of your future career, what do you picture? Managing a large office? Inventing a new product? Planning a multi-million-dollar advertising campaign? If you are a woman, you probably view the career process from a different perspective than you would if you were a man. Men tend to use a plan-ahead strategy (Veiga, 1977). They stress the need for planning career goals and methods to obtain them. Women emphasize the value of proving their ability through hard work. Women tend to take a more short-term perspective than men, who plan for the long-term future.

Women also tend to need more encouragement from others in order to set high career goals for themselves (Stake & Levitz, 1979). Men set high career goals for themselves regardless of the amount of encouragement they receive from others. This difference may result because men react to the general societal expectation that they become high achievers, while women may need support to overcome their sex-role expectation of nonachievement. Or women achievers just may choose to associate with people who encourage their ambitious careers. As one author notes, "Females are less likely to strive for high occupational achievement because it has been less central to fulfillment of the traditional female role, and a women's anticipated rewards for doing so are therefore lower" (Marini, 1980). Supportive associates can provide some of the necessary rewards. One study has shown that undergraduate women with low levels of fear of success and more nontraditional sex-role attitudes have the highest levels of career salience (Illfelder, 1980). In other words, a career has a more central position in their lives than it does for women with more traditional sex-role attitudes.

Among high-school seniors, women's occupational aspirations are not lower than men's, just different. High-school senior women desire professional and technical occupations slightly *more* than high-school men do and managerial occupations slightly *less* than men do (Fottler & Bain, 1980). Approximately 70 percent of all high-school students aspire to either a professional or managerial position. Yet, males are more likely to aspire to management, crafts, or laborer positions, while females indicate a desire for clerical or service positions or positions in the teaching or nursing professions. Women may be not choosing higher-paying managerial positions for several reasons (Allison & Allen, 1978; Fottler & Bain, 1980). First, female students may not meet practicing managers who could serve as role models. Second, as we saw in Chapter 7, since women's career choices are often made in high school, high-school programs and guidance counselors may steer women away from the higher-paying professions, such as those in science. Third, as discussed in Chapter 8, students may be reacting to the negative portrayal of managers, and especially women managers, by the mass media. Finally, discrimination in promotion and hiring may be pervasive or perceived as pervasive by women. In other words, women may be not entering higher-paid fields because they believe either that they will not be hired or that they will not be promoted once they are hired.

Entering the Organization

Women's perceptions that there are barriers to their entry into organizations may be correct. Fortunately, although women may not be the first choice for managerial jobs, they are not considered the least desirable choice either. In one study, business school students were asked to rate applicants for two managerial jobs on the basis of their résumés. When job qualifications of all "applicants" were basically the same (only the applicant's sex, marital status, undergraduate major, and graduate degree varied), the applicant most desired by the raters was a married male with two children, an undergraduate degree in business administration, and an M.B.A. (Renwick & Tosi, 1978). The least desirable applicant was a divorced male with an undergraduate major in history and a master's degree in administration. Female applicants were rated somewhere between the two extremes.

Nevertheless, women are less likely than men to be offered interviews on the basis of their résumés. Researchers sent unsolicited résumés and cover letters to various employers to apply for entry-level jobs (McIntyre, Moberg & Posner, 1980). The résumés were equivalent except for the sex of the applicant. The researchers found that female applicants were less likely to be offered interviews by the companies than male applicants. In addition, the companies took an average of 2.6 days longer to reply to the female applicants' letters.

Although women fare more poorly than men when judged on the basis of their résumés, when recruiters view videotapes of job applicants, female applicants fare better than males. In one study, sixty-six recruiters watched videotapes of male and female job applicants who behaved either passively or aggressively. Sex of the applicant did not affect the recruiters' decisions to invite the applicant for an interview. The researchers concluded that "a woman who clearly demonstrates the 'masculine' traits of moderate aggressiveness, self-confidence, and ambition will be received no less favorably by raters than a man demonstrating the same traits" (Dipboye & Wiley, 1977, p. 10).

When business school students evaluate employees for placement in either a highly challenging task or one involving little challenge, they are more likely to see females as more suitable for the unchallenging position (Taylor & Ilgen, 1981). This is a potentially devasting form of discrimination since early placement decisions affect later career chances for advancement. There is some evidence, though, that initial stereotyping may be overcome. When the same business students had a simulated working experience with a competent female, they were less likely to place subsequent women in low-challenge positions.

Although the research discussed above found that male and female business students assign females to unchallenging tasks, other researchers have found that male bankers prefer men for a challenging task, and women bankers prefer women (Mai-Dalton & Sullivan, 1981). Males prefer to assign a male subordinate to a challenging task because of his competence on the job and because the supervisor expects little conflict with the male subordinate on the job. Females prefer female subordinates because they feel they can supervise female subordinates more comfortably than male subordinates. Thus, men and women choose same-sex subordinates for a challenging job because they expect a more rewarding relationship with the subordinates. They also think there will be less conflict while working with subordinates of the same sex. Men justify their choices on the basis of sex-role stereotyping. Men indicate that the male subordinate is more competent at the challenging task. They conclude that a female would be more competent at the dull tasks because a female would be more interested in getting the job done. Female supervisors, on the other hand, may be compensating for the sex-role stereotyping by their male colleagues by placing other women in challenging tasks.

Overall, the more an evaluator has to infer about a job applicant, the more likely the evaluation will be biased (Nieva & Gutek, 1980). If there is a great deal of task-relevant information provided about the applicant and the criteria to be used in the evaluation situation are explicit, less bias results. As one researcher notes, "Unless there are clear and valid predictors of performance potential, selection procedures may become particularistic" (Smith, 1979, p. 368). This situation is especially dangerous for women because, when there is no background given on job applicants, evaluators rely on sex-role stereotypes that assume women do not have the appropriate educational background for managerial careers (Renwick & Tosi, 1978). Evaluators may use sex-role stereotypes to fill in for any missing information (Bartol, 1978).

Moving Up the Hierarchy

If you are planning to start a career, you probably also are concerned about advancement opportunities. Yet, as discussed earlier, women are often at a disadvantage in moving up an organizational hierarchy. Men are often rewarded for effective work by rapid advancement, while women are not. When slow advancement "occurs on the part of women supervisors [it] is not a result of ineffectiveness or lack of such factors as influence, predictive accuracy, or reconciliation of conflict demands, but as a result of their being female" (Day & Stogdill, 1972, p. 356). Read "What is a male chauvinist in the office?" for another look at this problem.

What is a male chauvinist in the office?

A man who, through his cultural background, brings prejudices about women to work with him. He believes that women are emotionally, physically, and mentally weaker than men. That they are best qualified to look nice, bear children, tend to the home, and take care of him. His attitude is, "She takes care of the inside—I do the outside work. It's all very simple."

Some office male chauvinists are tricky. They spout equality all over the place and mouth all the reasons in the book why you should get to the top. They make grand claims about how proud they are of your performance. Deep down, they think that you have a nerve trying to make a career for yourself. You'd be better off if you stuck to female-role things like typing, keeping their appointment books, and choosing gifts for their women. Their deepest convictions concern money and authority, the areas people at the top deal with. They believe that women cannot be trusted to handle either successfully, and therefore they do not belong in top management.

What are women's chances of getting into top management?

Not terrific. A recent survey shows that 78 percent of all managerial jobs are held by men. The reasons are that we are new to the territory. We lack training. And there are enough male chauvinists around whose visions are blurred by stereotypes that keep them from helping us get ahead.

What are some of the male-minded stereotypes that hold us back?

A male chauvinist thinks it is natural for all women to place home and personal life above career. Therefore, he reasons, if there should ever be a conflict between your family and work obligations, you'd quit your job or give it short shrift. So, since you probably won't be around very long, he thinks he'd better keep the big responsibilities away from you and give them to a man. Men, after all, can be counted on to assign top priority to their careers.

Another belief chauvinists have is that any man has more business sense than a woman. If there's a choice between you and a man for a managerial job, or if he has to pick one of you for managerial training, he is bound to select the man and leave you behind.

A third chauvinist point of view that can hurt you is that it's OK for a man to play around, but taboo for a woman. It's not so much that he wants to protect your virtue: it's his belief that men are more valuable than women and when push comes to shove, he will favor the man. For instance, if you get involved in an affair that upsets the office and one of you has to be let go, you can be sure that the male chauvinist will hang onto your lover and get rid of expendable you.

Is male chauvinism disappearing?

It's beginning to. The Victorian gentlemen who were reared to believe that a woman's function is to make a home are dying off of old age or retirement. Some of them are being replaced, however, by the kind of young man who is determined to hang onto the *status quo*. To him, you are a threat to the established system. You get in his way. You may even take over his territory. This is why women today have to work extra hard to prove their worth, and must be extra cooperative to keep resentment from growing. You have to bear with the fact that it is hard for people to overcome longtime prejudices.

The good news is that we are on the threshold of real integration. It is my feeling that within the next very few years the most diehard, conservative, all-male company is going to open up for us. All it will take is a few hardworking women who are smart enough to take advantage of the fact that they can still be bought cheaper than men, at first. They will get their foot in the door and then work their way up to top management, opening the door wider for the rest of us. It is a bottom-line fact of life that in today's market you pay less for a woman to do an executive job. There is nothing the president of any company likes better than a bargain that makes his bottom-line figures look better.

[From *Women and Work* by Carole Hyatt. Copyright © 1980 by Carole Hyatt and Patricia Linden. Reprinted by permission of the publisher, M. Evans and Co., Inc., New York, NY 10017.]

To make matters even more complicated for women at work, promotion may not mean advancement. On the average, women need 1.8 promotions to reach the same level in an organizational hierarchy that men reach in one promotion. This phenomenon has been called "pacification by promotion" (Flanders & Anderson, 1973). In other words, women are getting promoted, but their promotions do not move them up the organizational hierarchy as fast as men. For example, in one study, older women who had received more promotions in an organization were at a lower level in the hierarchy than younger women with more education who had been in the organization for a shorter length of time (Stewart & Gudykunst, 1982).

Thus, women either may not be promoted or, if they are promoted, they still may not be moving up the organizational hierarchy at the same rate as men. One important reason for this may be biased decisions based on sex-role stereotyping. An unbiased decision can be made when a candidate for promotion's qualifications are clearly acceptable or clearly unacceptable (Rosen & Jerdee, 1974), which is rarely the case. Often, candidates' qualifications are quite similar, and there is no clear-cut, objective way of predicting who will be the most successful person on the next job. In this case, if information is missing or imprecise, a manager may make promotion choices on the basis of personal values, and these values may not be work related. Managers prefer subordinates with similar values and reject those with dissimilar values. One researcher (Senger, 1971) concludes that this situation might be functional for an organization because there could be better communication and less message distortion between persons with similar value structures. But, there may be increased conformity in organizations where people of similar values are promoted and retained. An organization such as this might have more effective communication and higher morale but less creativity than an organization where diversity is valued.

Sexual Harassment

Another consequence of the sex-role stereotyping of men and women within organizations is sexual harassment. Sexual harassment has been defined by the Equal Employment Opportunity Commission as:

> Unwelcome sexual advances, requests for sexual favors, and other verbal and physical conduct of a sexual nature . . . when (1) submission to such conduct is made either explicitly or implicitly a term or condition of an individual's employment, (2) submission to or rejection of such conduct by an individual is used as the basis for employment decisions affecting such individuals, (3) or such conduct has the purpose or effect of unreasonably interfering with an individual's work performance or creating an intimidating, hostile, or offensive work environment. (Mastalli, 1981, p. 94)

Thus, sexual harassment includes any behavior of a sexual nature that adversely affects a person's job performance. These behaviors can range from off-color jokes to unwanted touching or even sexual assault.

Sexual harassment often occurs in private without witnesses and, therefore, is often unreported. Nevertheless, some surveys have found startling results. In a 1976 survey conducted by *Redbook* magazine (Safran, 1981), nine out of ten of the female respondents said they had experienced some form of sexual harassment on the job; most, however, had experienced subtle forms of harassment, such as sexual jokes. Forty-five percent of the respondents indicated that either they or a woman they knew had quit or been fired from a job because of sexual harassment. In another survey, 70 percent of the respondents had experienced at least one instance of sexual harassment on the job (Silverman, 1976–77). The Center for Women Policy Studies estimates that at least eighteen million women were sexually harassed on the job in 1979 and 1980 (Mid-revolutionary mores, 1981). A survey of over twenty thousand federal employees indicated that 42 percent of the women and 15 percent of the men had been sexually harassed in the previous two years (U.S. Merit Systems Protection Board, 1981). In other surveys, up to 100 percent of the respondents reported experiencing some type of sexual harassment at work (see Neugarten & Shafritz, 1980, for a discussion of other surveys). Even taking the most conservative estimates into account, sexual harassment is clearly a problem at work.

Women are more often the victims of harassment than men, and harassers are more likely to be male than female. Twenty percent of the male respondents to the U.S Merit Systems Protection Board's survey reported that their harassers were male; while only 3 percent of the female respondents reported female harassers.

Sexual harassment has profoundly negative consequences for its victims. People who have experienced sexual harassment on the job report both personal and professional consequences (Loy & Stewart, 1984). On a personal level, victims report symptoms such as nervousness, irritability, loss of motivation, sleeplessness, and even weight loss. On a professional level, the victims of sexual harassment may be ignored by their harasser (who is often their superior and, therefore, can negatively influence their career), transferred to a different department, or even fired.

Numerous suggestions have been offered on ways to respond to sexual harassment. Suggested strategies include ignoring the harassment, jokingly or bluntly asking the harasser to stop, and, at the most extreme level, taking legal action (Backhouse & Cohen, 1978). Although ignoring sexual harassment generally is the most prevalent response, it is an ineffective response. In a Working Women United survey, for the 76 percent of the respondents who used this strategy, the harassment continued in the same form or worsened (Collins & Blodgett, 1981). Yet, women who ignore their harassers tend to receive fewer negative organizational outcomes than women who speak out (Loy & Stewart, 1984).

Strategies for Change

In the previous sections of this chapter we have discussed the prevalent sex-role stereotypes of men and women in organizations and some of the consequences of these stereotypes. In this section, we discuss some communication strategies that have been suggested to overcome the negative consequences of sex-role stereotypes in organizations.

Assertiveness

To overcome the sex-role stereotypes associated with their behavior in organizations, women have been encouraged to be more assertive. Since the late 1950s, the use of assertiveness training as a counseling technique to increase self-expression has been encouraged (Bate, 1976). Yet, one of the most striking examples of how the communication styles of men and women are perceived differently is in the area of assertive communication.

There are three interpersonal communication styles that are important to consider when examining your own communication behavior—assertive, nonassertive, and aggressive communication. Bloom, Coburn, and Pearlman (1975) delineated these three interpersonal communication styles by identifying the underlying motivation and resulting verbal and nonverbal behaviors for each style. Table 9.1 contains a summary of these styles.

Table 9.1 Verbal and nonverbal components of behaviors.

	Non-Assertive (Passive)	Assertive	Aggressive
1. Verbal	apologetic words veiled meanings hedging, failure to come to the point failure to say what you mean at a loss for words	statement of wants honest statement of feelings objective words direct statements which say what you mean "I" messages	loaded words accusations descriptive, subjective terms imperious, superior "you" statements which blame and label
2. Nonverbal			
a. General	actions instead of words hoping someone will guess what you want looking as if you don't mean what you say	attentive listening behavior general assured manner communicating caring and strength	exaggerated show of strength flippant, sarcastic style, air of superiority
b. Specific			
1. voice	weak, hesitant, soft, wavering	firm, warm, relaxed, well-modulated	tense, shrill, loud shaky, cold, deadly quiet, demanding, superior
2. eyes	averted, downcast, teary, pleading	open, frank, direct eye contact, but not staring	superior, authoritarian, expressionless, narrowed cold staring, not really seeing you
3. posture	lean for support, stooped, excessive head nodding	well-balanced, erect, relaxed	
4. hands	fidgety, fluttery, clammy	relaxed motions	clenched, abrupt gesture, finger-pointing, fist pounding

Adapted from Bloom, L.Z., Coburn, K., and Pearlman, J. (1975). *The new assertive woman*. New York: Dell.

Passive communication is a communication style denying or restricting an individual's rights because he or she fails to express needs and desires. As a result, the passive, or nonassertive, individual will feel misunderstood or used; these feelings are often compounded by the additional feelings of guilt, depression, anxiety, and lowered self-esteem. The recipient of nonassertive behavior is constantly forced to infer what the other person is really thinking and feeling, which can lead to frustration, annoyance, and anger by the recipient.

Aggressive communication is a communication style in which a person expresses feelings and opinions in a punishing, threatening, assaultive, demanding, or hostile manner. Since the aggressive individual chooses to infringe on the rights of others, aggressive behavior reflects little or no consideration for the rights and feelings of others. Aggressive behavior often results in immediate and more forceful counteraggression, which often produces long-term strain in the relationship. The recipient of aggressive behavior may experience feelings that range from humiliation and abuse to resentment and anger.

In contrast to nonassertive communication and aggressive communication, the goal of *assertive communication* is to express feelings and opinions directly and honestly; by doing so, the assertive communicator hopes to negotiate reasonable changes to solve interpersonal problems. An assertive communicator can express feelings in a manner that is both personally satisfying and socially effective. Aggressive and nonassertive communication control the outcome of a given situation by "shutting off" the other person; assertive communication is the only style of the three that opens the possibility for increased dialogue.

The rationale for assertive communication rather than nonassertive or aggressive communication is based on the social learning theory that early training rather than anatomy determines personality. (These concepts were discussed more fully in Chapter 2.) Increased assertion leads to increased self-esteem and self-confidence, especially among women.

Nevertheless, the impact of the assertive communication style may vary with the sex of the communicator (Jakubowski-Spector, 1973). Specifically, the same assertive act will be evaluated in more favorable terms if the person exhibiting the behavior is a male rather than a female. For example, Hull and Schroeder (1979) measured the responses of males and females during role plays with a female confederate who behaved assertively, nonassertively, or aggressively. The nonassertive female's behavior was perceived as positive, the aggressive female's behavior was perceived as negative, and the assertive female's behavior was perceived as fair but unsympathetic, aggressive, and dominant. In another study, people completed an interpersonal attraction inventory after viewing videotaped interactions involving nonassertive, assertive, and aggressive behavior (Kelly, Kem, Kirkley & Patterson, 1981). While assertive people were evaluated more positively on competence, ability, and achievement, they also were seen more negatively in terms of likeability, warmth, flexibility, and friendliness. Further, both men and women devalued the assertive behavior of the female compared to the male on measures of likeability, attractiveness, ability, and competence.

These findings reinforce the impact of traditional sex-role stereotypes that have historically devalued assertive behavior for females and have reinforced such behavior for males. Kelly and his colleagues conclude that females learn to inhibit their expressions of assertiveness during real-life interactions in anticipation of being disliked—even if they are clearly faced with unreasonable behavior (Kelly et al., 1981). For women, the traditional nonassertive role is still the communication style most universally perceived as positive; if women select assertive or aggressive styles, they run the risk of being perceived negatively by both both males and females.

Implications of Assertiveness

Of the three communication styles presented in this section, assertive communication offers both the greatest growth potential and the greatest risk for women in organizations. While assertive communication may be the key to making needs and desires known, it also may be the key to rejection and alienation from both male and female co-workers. Women need to assess the risks involved when they choose an assertive communication style (Bloom et al., 1975).

If you are thinking about adopting an assertive communication style, you should keep the following questions in mind:

1. What do I gain from staying nonassertive?
   a. Protection from others
   b. Praise for conforming to others' expectations
   c. Maintenance of a familiar behavior pattern
   d. Avoidance of taking the responsibility for initiating or carrying out plans
   e. Avoidance of possible conflict/anger/rejection/acceptance of responsibility for my feelings
2. Would I be willing to give up any of the above? Which one(s)?
3. What do I lose by being nonassertive?
   a. Independence
   b. The power to make decisions
   c. Honesty in human relationships

d. Others' respect for my rights and wishes
e. My ability to control my emotions (I can deny my own rights for only so long and then I blow up)
f. Relaxation, inner tranquility
g. My ability to influence others' decisions, demands, expectations —particularly with regard to myself and what they expect me to do for or with them
h. The satisfaction of initiating and carrying out plans

4. Do the gains of staying nonassertive outweigh the losses?
   a. If so, why?
   b. If not, am I willing to make the change by acting assertively?
   c. Can I enlist the support, understanding, and cooperation of others involved either in the situation or in my life?
5. What are my short-term goals (in my relationships and in my activities)?
6. What are my long-term goals?
7. How can assertive behavior help me achieve these goals? (Bloom et al., 1975, pp. 80–81)

Although these questions are general in nature, they can provide the basis for a framework from which the appropriateness of all three communication styles may be assessed.

Mentors

One of the many communication strategies men and women use to overcome sex-role stereotyping in organizations is to acquire a *mentor*—someone who gives advice on appropriate career strategies and who may even help you gain a desired promotion by influencing decisions affecting your future in an organization. Since more women are obtaining mentors, there is a growing interest in the effect of mentors on women's careers in organizations. Although the desperate search for a mentor can be overdone, mentorship does appear to be related to success and mobility for both males and females (Hunt & Michael, 1983; Shapiro, Haseltine & Rowe, 1978). As Kanter (1977) notes:

> If sponsors are important for the success of men in organizations, they seem absolutely essential for women. If men function more effectively as leaders when they appear to have influence upward and outward in the organization, women need even more the signs of such influence and the access to real power provided by sponsors. (p. 66)

The classic model of mentorship claims that young men choose a career, search for their identity and for an important patron or friend to be a mentor in their twenties and thirties, and become the mentors of others in their forties (Levinson et al., 1978). Today, women are starting to follow this model (Hunt & Michael, 1983). For both men and women, mentors are especially useful at two career junctures: (1) in the early phase of a career when the idea to move up in an organization crystallizes; and (2) when it is time for the final push to the top rungs of the organizational ladder (Halcomb, 1980).

Besides helping out at these critical periods, a mentor's stamp of approval gives legitimacy to a woman in an organization (Fitt & Newton, 1981). This approval enables the protégé to gain the respect of people both inside and outside the organization (Halcomb, 1980). As Halcomb (1980) dramatically notes, "to have a mentor is to be among the blessed. Not to have one is to be damned to eternal oblivion, or at least to a mid-level status" (p. 13). This may be an exaggeration, but there is evidence that women with male mentors at least are better paid than those without mentors (Fitt & Newton, 1981).

Having the guidance of a mentor is especially important for a woman if there are few other women in her organization and, thus, fewer role models. Mentors are also useful in large organizations, which may be impersonal or remote, and in organizations without formal career planning programs (Fitt & Newton, 1981). Most mentors are male (Halcomb, 1980) because most of the high-status people in organizations are male. At the early stages of women's careers, male mentors counsel them about managerial style, the organizational culture, and personal style. Once the protégés have learned the ropes, the emphasis shifts to building their careers (Fitt & Newton, 1981).

There are four stages in a mentor relationship: initiation, cultivation, separation, and redefinition (Kram, 1983). In the initiation stage, the relationship is started. The mentor is admired and respected for his or her competence or ability to provide guidance. The protégé feels cared for and admired by the mentor, who has superior status in the organization. This stage lasts approximately a year. In the second stage, cultivation, the relationship between the mentor and protégé develops. The mentor coaches or challenges the protégé. The protégé develops a growing self-confidence. This stage may last two to five years. In the separation stage, the protégé experiences more independence and autonomy, causing both participants to reassess their relationship. The protégé may be physically separated from the mentor by a promotion to a new location or psychologically separated by a growing feeling of independence. As the separation increases, the participants redefine their relationship. If the redefinition stage is successful, the mentor and protégé become primarily friends. They may continue to see each other and to support each other's careers, but the mentor is no longer involved in the day-to-day guidance of the protégé's career.

Casbolt and DeWine (1982) identified the communication behaviors associated with mentors. Mentors have effective interpersonal skills; they are good listeners who are reflective and nonjudgmental. Mentors are trusting and take their protégés into their confidence. They exhibit openness by not being dogmatic and by allowing protégés to argue without fear of losing trust in the relationship. Mentors share valuable organizational information that protégés would not hear otherwise. They give verbal recognition and rewards for their protégé's achievements. They serve as a sounding board for new or controversial ideas and give counsel, not opinions. Mentors link protégés with other influential members of the organization or profession. Finally, mentors verbally encourage their protégés to continue the relationship.

As we said earlier, women often have men as their mentors, but there are significant limitations in male/female mentor relationships (Kram, 1983). Since the male mentor cannot provide a totally adequate role model, female protégés must seek guidance and support from female peers. The women in these relationships may maintain feelings of dependency and incompetence. Also, women may avoid important interactions with their mentor because of concerns about increasing intimacy or about their public image. Remember the case of Mary Cunningham and William Agee a few years ago. She was forced to resign from her job as executive vice president for strategic planning at Bendix Corporation after rumors of a sexual relationship with William Agee, the chief executive officer of the company, were circulated. Because of problems such as this one, for women, having a women as a mentor would be ideal if she were in a highly influential position in an organization (Halcomb, 1980).

Networking

Having a mentor allows you access to an *internal* organizational communication system that you otherwise would be excluded from. Networking gives you an *external* organizational communication system that helps you to gain valuable information for planning your career.

Networking is "the process of developing and using your contacts for information, advice, and moral support as you pursue your career" (Welch, 1980, p. 15). Men have traditionally had their "old boys' networks" to help them find jobs, make stock deals, or get the best seats at sporting events. Women are beginning to form networks of their own or to join some of the established male networks.

Networks may be developed for specific purposes or they may result from casual friendships. For example, a group of photographers may decide to meet once a month to share ideas and discuss potential opportunities for jobs. In some cities, people in prominent positions in organizations are invited to meet each other. Some networks are formally run:

there may be membership requirements and dues, and meetings may be scheduled in advance.

If you cannot find a formal network that supports people in your particular field, you can obtain valuable career-related information by establishing a networking pattern of your own. Think about the people you know and what they know. Do you know someone who knows someone who works for a company you are interested in? Ask that person to put you in contact with their contact. You will be surprised at how helpful people are if you explain your desire for information and are able to demonstrate your qualifications for a particular career.

Welch (1980) offers the following do's and don'ts for successful networking:

Do try to give as much as you get from your network. The more people you can be useful to, the more will be useful to you.

Don't be afraid to ask for what you need. . . . Trust the other person to decide for herself whether she wants to do what you ask; don't decide for her by not asking.

Do report back to anyone who ever gives you a lead, telling her what happened and repeating your thanks.

Do follow up on any leads and names you're given.

Don't tell everything to everybody. Be selective in both your choice of listeners and the material you impart. . . A good rule is to tell only what the other person needs to know in order to understand and help you on your project.

Do be businesslike in your approach to your network. Keep your conversation on track and your phone calls short.

Don't pass up any opportunities to network. (pp. 98–99)

Conclusion

As we have seen in this chapter, the work environment faced by men and women is different and has a differential effect on their behavior. Management is perceived as a stereotypically male occupation. Although the acceptance of women in leadership roles is growing, there is still some doubt about the willingness of men to work for female supervisors. Evidence suggests, however, that men are more willing to support women in managerial roles once they have had experience working with and for women supervisors.

Perceptions of male and female managerial styles differ. Managers who use sex-role-appropriate behaviors are thought to have more productive and satisfied employees. Sex of subordinate also influences the evaluation of a leader's communication style. A rewarding communication style is rated as more effective for male managers and a friendly, dependent style is rated more effective for female managers if the subordinate is of the opposite sex. In addition, perceptions of a leader's effectiveness may be affected by the sex composition of the group of subordinates, as well as by the subordinates' general attitudes toward women in management roles. Although women managers perform as credibly as their male counterparts and hold similar management values, male and female managers may be perceived differently by subordinates if they are not supported equally strongly by organizational authorities.

As a consequence of these stereotypes, women view the career process from a different perspective than men and need more encouragement than men to set high career goals for themselves. Their goals may be blocked, however, by barriers to successful communication in organizations. For example, women job applicants, on the basis of their résumés, are less likely to be offered employment interviews than are equally qualified men. Women are also more likley than men to be given less challenging assignments, although this tendency can be overcome if the evaluator has worked with competent women previously. Overall, women are more likely to be judged on the basis of sex-role stereotypes if the criteria for the position are not explicit and there is little task-revelant information on the applicant. Discrimination against women is more likely to exist in the absence of objective performance data.

Women are also at a disadvantage in moving up the organizational hierarchy. Men are generally rewarded for effective performance by rapid advancement; women are not. This phenomenon may be due to sex-role stereotyping. If a supervisor believes a woman is less likely than a man to be aggressive, competitive, or ambitious, the supervisor may be less likely to give the woman assignments calling for these skills. Thus, the woman is denied opportunities to develop necessary managerial skills. Women also use different communication strategies than men when demonstrating their desire for promotion. Women use more task-facilitative-seeking strategies—asking for their supervisors' opinions and suggestions—than men. These strategies may be an expression of women's general tendency to passively wait for promotion and to rely on the formal organizational communication system to recognize and reward their good performance.

Although women have been encouraged to overcome sex-role stereotyping through the use of an assertive communication style, being assertive presents some risks. Women using an assertive communication style are perceived as less attractive, less flexible, and less friendly than nonassertive women. Unfortunately, the sex-role stereotypes of women as passive, nonassertive comunicators still exists. We hope, however, that as one author (Bass, 1981) contends, by the year 2000, such sex-role stereotypes will no longer exist, and there will be no need to study the communication behavior of women leaders apart from the communication behavior of men in leadership positions.

Suggested Activities

1. Re-read the excerpt from "Impressions from an Office" contained in this chapter. Add as many sex-role stereotypes that occur in the workplace as you can. What is the effect of each of these stereotypes on men and women at work? Which stereotypes have negative consequences for men? Which stereotypes have negative consequences for women? What can be done to overcome each of these sex-role stereotypes?

2. Find two student groups on campus—one with a female leader and one with a male leader. Interview each leader. Try to determine the leaders' communication styles. Ask them how they conduct meetings, how they deal with particular problems in their groups, how they make decisions. In addition, attend a meeting conducted by each leader. Did you find any sex differences in communication style between the two leaders? Compare and contrast their communication styles? Which style was most effective? Why? What advice would you give the leaders for improving their leadership behavior?

3. Keep a log of your communication behavior for a week. Note any instances of non-assertive, assertive, or aggressive communication behavior. Rate the effectiveness of these behaviors when they occurred. Using the questions presented in this chapter as guidelines, for the next week try to use more assertive communication behaviors when appropriate. Keep a communication log for the week during which you actively try to use appropriate assertive communication. Did you find it difficult to modify your communication behavior? Why? How effective were these behaviors? In which communication contexts is assertive communication most effective? Do you plan to continue to use them? Why or why not?

4. Imagine yourself in the following situation:

> You are a personnel analyst in a large insurance company. Your company is considering starting a flextime program in which employees could work during different hours of the day depending on their preference. For example, instead of working from 9:00 AM until 5:00 PM, a person could work from 6:00 AM until 2:00 PM or from noon to 8:00 PM. Your boss, Pat Simmons, is opposed to the idea. Pat thinks everyone should work from 9 to 5. You think, however, that Pat's boss, Chris Carpenter, likes the idea. You are asked to write a report on flextime and give your recommendation on whether it should be implemented.

How are you going to present your report? List several strategies you could use when you write your recommendations. Compare your strategies with your classmates' strategies. Are there any sex differences in the strategies chosen? If you assumed that Pat and Chris were men, were your strategies different from the strategies chosen by people who assumed Pat and Chris were women? How do the results you obtained reflect the material in this chapter on upward communication?

For Further Reading

Bass, B.M. (1981). "Women and leadership." In *Stogdill's handbook of leadership*, ed. B.M. Bass, 481–507. New York: Free Press.

Farley, L. (1978). *Sexual shakedown: The sexual harassment of women on the job*. New York: Warner Books.

Harragan, B.L. (1977). *Games mother never taught you: Corporate gamesmanship for women*. New York: Warner Books.

Hennig, M., and Jardim, A. (1977). *The managerial woman*. New York: Pocket Books.

Josefowitz, N. (1980). *Paths to power: A woman's guide from first job to top executive*. Reading, MA: Addison-Wesley.

Kanter, R.M. (1977). *Men and women of the corporation*. New York: Basic Books.

MacKinnon, C.A. (1979). *Sexual harassment of working women: A case of sex discrimination*. New Haven: Yale University Press.

Pilotta, J.J. (Ed.). (1983). *Women in organizations: Barriers and breakthroughs*. Prospect Heights, IL: Waveland Press.

Schein, V.E. (1978). Sex role stereotyping, ability and performance: Prior research and new directions. *Personnel Psychology, 31*, 259–268.

Welch, M.S. (1980). *Networking: The great new way for women to get ahead*. New York: Harcourt Brace Jovanovich.

References

Abramson, P., and Mechanic, M. (1983). Sex and the media: Three decades of best-selling books and major motion pictures. *Archives of Sexual Behavior, 12,* 185–206.

Addington, D.W. (1968). The relationship of selected vocal characteristics to personality perceptions. *Speech Monographs, 35,* 492–503.

Adkison, J.A. (1981). Women in school administration: A review of the research. *Review of Educational Research, 51,* 311–343.

Ahrons, C.R. (1976). Counselors' perceptions of career images of women. *Journal of Vocational Behavior, 8,* 197–207.

Alderton, S.M., and Jurma, W.E. (1980). Genderless/gender related task leader communition and group satisfaction: A test of two hypotheses. *Southern Speech Communication Journal, 46,* 48–60.

Allen, R.R., and Brown, K.L. (1976). *Developing communication competence in children.* Skokie, IL: National Textbook.

Allison, E., and Allen, P. (1978). Male-female professionals: A model of career choice. *Industrial Relations, 17,* 333–337.

Almquist, E.M., and Freudiger, P. (1978). Male and female roles in the lyrics of three genres of contemporary music. *Sex Roles, 4,* 51–65.

Alreck, P.L., Settle, R.B., and Belch, M.A. (1982). Who responds to "gendered" ads, and how? *Journal of Advertising Research,* 22(2), 25–32.

American Psychological Association. (1975). Report of the task force on sex bias and sex-role stereotyping in psychotherapeutic practice. *American Psychologist, 30,* 1169–1175.

The American Teacher. (1983). Washington, DC: Fiestritzer Publications.

Aries, E.J. (1982). Verbal and nonverbal behavior in single-sex and mixed-sex groups: Are traditional sex roles changing? *Psychological Reports, 51,* 127–134.

Aries, E.J., and Johnson, F.L. (1983). Close friendship in adulthood: Conversational content between same-sex friends. *Sex Roles, 9,* 1183–1196.

Arlow, P., and Froschel, M. (1976). "Women in the high school curriculum: A review of U.S. history and English literature texts." In *High school feminist studies,* ed. C. Ahlum, J. Fralley, and F. Howe, xi–xxviii. Old Westbury, NY: Feminist Press.

Ashby, M.S., and Wittmaier, B.C. (1978). Attitude changes in children after exposure to stories about women in traditional and nontraditional occupations. *Journal of Educational Psychology, 70,* 945–949.

Athanassiades, J.C. (1974). An investigation of some communication patterns of female subordinates in hierarchical organizations. *Human Relations, 27,* 195–209.

Atkin, C., and Miller, M. (1975). The effects of television advertising on children: Experimental evidence. Paper presented at the meeting of the International Communication Association, Chicago.

Avery, R.K. (1979). Adolescents' use of the mass media. *American Behavioral Scientist, 23,* 53–70.

Ayres, J. (1980). Relationship stages and sex as factors in topic dwell time. *Western Journal of Speech Communication, 44,* 253–260.

Backhouse, C., and Cohen, L. (1978). *Sexual harassment on the job.* Englewood Cliffs, NJ: Prentice-Hall.

Baird, J.E., Jr., and Bradley, P.H. (1979). Styles of management and communication: A comparative study of men and women. *Communication Monographs, 46,* 101–111.

Bandura, A. (1969). "Social-learning theory and identification processes." In *Handbook of socialization theory and research,* ed. D.A. Goslin, 213–262. Chicago: Rand McNally.

Barbatsis, G.S., Wong, M.R, and Herek, G.M. (1983). A struggle for dominance: Relational communication patterns in television drama. *Communication Quarterly, 31,* 148–155.

Barcus, E. (1982, July 14). Kids programs biased: TV study. *Chicago Sun Times,* p. 23.

Barfield, A. (1976). "Biological influences on sex differences in behavior." In *Sex differences: Social and biological perspectives,* ed. M.S. Teitelbaum, 62–121. Garden City, NY: Anchor Books.

Barnlund, D.C. (1970). "A transactional model of comunication." In *Foundations of communication theory,* ed. K.K. Sereno and C.D. Mortensen, 83–102. New York: Harper & Row.

Baron, A.S., and Abrahamsen, K. (1981, November). Will he—or won't he—work with a female manager? *Management Review,* pp. 48–53.

Bartol, K.M. (1978). The sex structuring of organizations: A search for possible causes. *Academy of Management Review, 3,* 805–815.

Bartol, K.M., and Butterfield, D.A. (1976). Sex effects in evaluating leaders. *Journal of Applied Psychology, 61,* 446–454.

Bartol, K.M., and Wortman, M.S., Jr. (1976). Sex effects in leader behavior self-descriptions and job satisfaction. *Journal of Psychology, 94,* 177–183.

Bass, B.M. (1981). *Stogdill's handbook of leadership.* New York: Free Press.

Bass, B.M., Krusell, J., and Alexander, R.A. (1971). Male managers' attitudes toward working women. *American Behavioral Scientist, 15,* 221–236.

Bate, B. (1976). Assertive speaking: An approach to communication education for the future. *Communication Education, 25,* 53–59.

Bate, B. (1978). Nonsexist language use in transition. *Journal of Communication, 28*(1), 139–149.

Baxter, L.A. (1984). An investigation of compliance-gaining as politeness. *Human Communication Research, 10,* 427–456.

Beach, D.R., and Sokoloff, M.J. (1974). Spatially dominated nonverbal communication of children: A methodological study. *Perceptual and Motor Skills, 38,* 1303–1310.

Beckwith, L. (1972). Relationships between infants' social behavior and their mothers' behavior. *Child Development, 43,* 397–411.

Bell, R.Q., Weller, G.M., and Waldrop, M.F. (1971). Newborn and preschooler: Organization of behavior and relations between periods. *Monographs of the Society for Research in Child Development, 36* (1–2), Serial No. 142.

Bem, S.L. (1974). The measurement of psychological androgyny. *Journal of Counseling and Clinical Psychology, 42,* 155–162.

Bem, S.L., and Bem, D. (1973). Does sex-biased job advertising "aid and abet" sex discrimination? *Journal of Applied Social Psychology, 3,* 6–18.

Bennetts, L. (1979, October 14). Women: New opportunity, old reality. *New York Times, Section 12, p. 58.*

Benz, C.R., Pfeiffer, I., and Newman, I. (1981). Sex role expectations of classroom teachers, grades 1-12. *American Educational Research Journal, 18,* 289–302.

Berger, J., Rosenholtz, S.J., and Zelditch, M., Jr. (1980). "Status organizing processes." In *Annual Review of Sociology,* ed. A. Inkeles et al., 479–508. Palo Alto, CA: Annual Reviews.

Berlo, D.K. (1960). *The process of communication: An introduction to theory and practice.* New York: Holt, Rinehart and Winston.

Berryman, C.L., and Wilcox, J.R. (1980). Attitudes toward male and female speech: Experiments on the effects of sex-typical language. *Western Journal of Speech Communication, 44,* 50–59.

Berryman-Fink, C., and Wilcox, J.R. (1983). A multivariate investigation of perceptual attributions concerning gender appropriateness in language. *Sex Roles, 9,* 663–681.

Berscheid, E., Walster, E., and Bohrnstedt, G. (1973, November). Body image. *Psychology Today,* p. 119.

Beuf, A. (1974). Doctor, lawyer, household drudge. *Journal of Communication, 24*(2), 142–145.

Birdsall, P. (1980). A comparative analysis of male and female managerial communication style in two organizations. *Journal of Vocational Behavior, 16,* 183–196.

Birdwhistell, R.L. (1970). *Kinesics and context.* Philadelphia: University of Pennsylvania Press.

Birk, J.M., Cooper, J., and Tanney, M.F. (1973). Racial and sex-role stereotyping in career illustrations. Paper presented at the meeting of the American Psychological Association, Montreal.

Birk, J.M., Cooper, J., and Tanney, M.F. (1975). Stereotyping in "Occupational Outlook Handbook" illustrations: Follow-up study. Paper presented at the meeting of the American Psychological Association, Chicago.

Blakesmore, J.E.O., LaRue, A.A., and Okejnik, A.B. (1979). Sex-appropriate toy preference and the ability to conceptualize toys as sex-role related. *Developmental Psychology, 15,* 339–340.

Bloom, L.Z., Coburn, K., and Pearlman, J. (1975). *The new assertive woman.* New York: Dell.

Blumer, H. (1969). *Symbolic interactionism: Perspective and method.* Englewood Cliffs, NJ: Prentice-Hall.

Bohan, J.S. (1973). Age and sex differences in self-concept. *Adolescence, 8,* 379-384.

Bowman, G.W., Worthy, N.B., and Greyser, S.A. (1965). Are women executives people? *Harvard Business Review, 43*(4), 14–28, 164–178.

Bradley, P.H. (1981). The folk-linguistics of women's speech: An empirical examination. *Communication Monographs, 48,* 73–90.

Braman, O. (1977). "Comics." In *Is this your life? Images of women in the media,* ed. J. King and M. Stott, 83–92. London: Virago.

Brooks, J., and Lewis, M. (1974). Attachment behavior in thirteen-month-old opposite sex twins. *Child Development, 45,* 243–247.

Brooks-Gunn, J., and Matthews, W.S. (1979). *He and she: How children develop their sex role identity*. Englewood Cliffs, NJ: Prentice–Hall.

Brophy, J.E., and Good, T.L. (1974). "The influence of the sex of the teacher and student on classroom interaction." In *Teacher-student relationships: Causes and consequences*, ed. J. Brophy and T. Good, 199–239. New York: Holt, Rinehart and Winston.

Brown, V. (1979, September). *Media Report to Women* (p. 6). (Available from 3306 Ross Place NW, Washington, DC).

Buck, R. (1976). A test of nonverbal receiving ability: Preliminary studies. *Human Communication Research, 2,* 162–171.

Buckley, J. (1979). Country music and American values. *Popular Music and Society, 4,* 295.

Burr, E., Dunn, S., and Farquhar, N. (1972). Women and the language of inequality. *Social Education, 36,* 841–845.

Butruille, S. (1983, October). Women in American popular song: The historic image and the reality. Paper presented at the Sixth Annual Communication, Language, and Gender Conference, New Brunswick, NJ.

Campbell, P. B. (1976). Adolescent intellectual decline. *Adolesence, 11,* 629–635.

Campbell, P. B., and Wirtenberg, J. (1980). How books influence children: What the research shows. *Interracial Books for Children Bulletin, 11*(6), 3–6.

Campion, K. L. (1983, February). Intimate strangers: The readers, the writers, and the experts. *Ms. Magazine,* pp. 98–99.

Candor, M. G. (1979). Our days and our nights on T.V. *Journal of Communication, 29*(4), 66–72.

Cano, L., Solomon, S., and Holmes, D. (1984). Fear of success: The influence of sex, sex-role identity, and components of masculinity. *Sex Roles, 10,* 341–346.

Carnegie Commission on Higher Education. (1973). *Opportunities for women in higher education*. New York: McGraw-Hill.

Casbolt, D., and DeWine, S. (1982). How do women use mentors? A field research study. Paper presented at the Fifth Annual Communication, Language, and Gender Conference, Athens, OH.

Cherry, L., and Lewis, M. (1976). Mothers and two-year-olds: A study of sex differential aspects of verbal interaction. *Developmental Psychology, 12,* 278–282.

Cherry, L., and Lewis, M. (1978). "Differential socialization of girls and boys: Implications for sex differences in language development." In *The development of communication*, ed. N. Waterson and C. Snow, 189–197. New York: John Wiley and Sons.

Cheyne, J. A. (1976). Development of forms and functions of smiling in preschoolers. *Child Development, 47,* 820–823.

Chicago Tribune. (1983, January 30). Business section, p. 1.

Clarke-Stewart, K.A. (1973). Interactions between mothers and their young children: Characteristics and consequences. *Monographs of the Society for Research in Child Development, 38*(6-7), Serial No. 153.

Cohen, L. J., and Campos, J. J. (1974). Father, mother, stranger as elicitors of attachment behaviors in infancy. *Developmental Psychology, 10,* 146–154.

Collins, E. G. C., and Blodgett, T. B. (1981). Sexual harassment . . . Some see it . . . Some won't. *Harvard Business Review, 59*(2), 76–94.

Condry, J., and Condry, S. (1976). Sex differences: A study of the eye of the beholder. *Child Development, 47,* 812–819.

Cooper, P. (1983, October). The communication of sex role stereotypes: The image of stepparents in children's literature. Paper presented at the Sixth Annual Communication, Language, and Gender Conference, New Brunswick, NJ.

Cooper, P. (1984, November). Sexism in children's literature: Extent and impact on adult behavior. Paper presented at the meeting of the Speech Communication Association, Chicago.

Cooper, P. J., Stewart, L. P., and Gudykunst, W. B. (1982). Relationship with instructor and other variables influencing student evaluations of instruction. *Communication Quarterly, 30,* 308–315.

Courtney, A. E., and Whipple, T. W. (1974). Women in TV commercials. *Journal of Communication, 24*(2), 110–118.

Courtney, A. E., and Whipple, T. W. (1980). How to portray women in TV commercials. *Journal of Advertising Research, 20*(2), 53–59.

Courtright, J. A., Millar, F. E., and Rogers-Millar, E. L. (1979). Domineeringness and dominance: Replication and expansion. *Communication Monographs, 46,* 179–192.

Cowan, G., and Koziej, J. (1979). The perception of sex-inconsistent behavior. *Sex Roles, 5,* 1–10.

Crawford, S. (1983, October). A view of the top ten hits of 1982: The stereotypes live on. Paper presented at the Sixth Annual Communication, Language, and Gender Conference, New Brunswick, NJ.

Culley, J. D., and Bennett, R. (1976). Selling women, selling blacks. *Journal of Communication, 26*(4), 160–174.

Dance, F. E. X., and Larson, C. E. (1976). *The functions of human communication.* New York: Holt, Rinehart and Winston.

Day, D. R., and Stogdill, R. M. (1972). Leader behavior of male and female supervisors: A comparative study. *Personnel Psychology, 25,* 353–360.

Densmore, D. (1970). *Speech is the form of thought* (10 pp). (Reprint available from KNOW, Inc., P. O. Box 86031, Pittsburgh, PA 15221.)

Dipboye, R. L., and Wiley, J. W. (1977). Reactions of college recruiters to interviewee sex and self-presentation style. *Journal of Vocational Behavior, 10,* 1–12.

Dohrmann, R. (1975). A gender profile of children's educational TV. *Journal of Communication, 25*(1), 56–65.

Donahue, T. J. (1976). Discrimination against young women in career selection by high school counselors. Ph.D. diss., Michigan State University.

Donlan, D. (1972). The negative image of women in children's literature. *Elementary English, 49,* 604–611.

Donnell, S. M., and Hall, J. (1980). Men and women as managers: A significant case of no significant difference. *Organizational Dynamics, 8*(4), 60–77.

Douglass, R. (1984). Her life as a man. *Chicago Tribune TV Week.*

Dowd, J. (1983). Images of American women in American films: A method of analysis. *Women and Performance, 1,* 49–50.

Downing, M. (1974). Heroine of the daytime serial. *Journal of Communication, 24*(2), 130–137.

Downs, A. C., and Gowan, D. C. (1980). Sex differences in reinforcement and punishment on prime time television. *Sex Roles, 6,* 683–693.

DuBois, B. L., and Crouch, I. (1975). The question of tag questions in women's speech: They don't really use more of them, do they? *Language in Society, 4,* 289–294.

Dweck, C. S., Davidson, W., Nelson, S., and Bradley, E. (1978). I. Sex differences in learned helplessness; II. The contingencies of evaluative feedback in the classroom; III. An experimental analysis. *Developmental Psychology, 14,* 268–276.

Eakins, B. W., and Eakins, R. G. (1976). "Verbal turn-taking and exchanges in faculty dialogue." In *Papers in southwest English IV: Proceedings of the conference on the sociology of the languages of American women,* ed. B. L. DuBois and I. Crouch, 53–62. San Antonio: Trinity University Press.

Eakins, B. W., and Eakins, R. G. (1978). *Sex differences in human communication.* Boston: Houghton Mifflin.

Eberts, E. H., and Lepper, M. R. (1975). Individual consistency in the proxemic behavior of preschool children. *Journal of Personality and Social Psychology, 32,* 841–848.

Education Commission of the States. (1978). Grant from the National Institute for Education.

Eisenberg, N., Murray, E., and Hite, T. (1982). Children's reasoning regarding sex-typed toy choices. *Child Development, 53,* 81–86.

Eisenberg-Berg, N., Boothby, R., and Matson, T. (1979). Correlates of preschool girls' feminine and masculine toy preferences. *Developmental Psychology, 15,* 354–355.

Eisenstock, B. (1979). Television as a source of career awareness for children: Effects of sex and sex role preferences. Ph.D. diss., Annenberg School of Communication, University of Southern California.

Eisenstock, B. (1984). Sex role differences in children's identification with counterstereotypical televised portrayals. *Sex Roles, 10,* 417–430.

Engelhard, P. A., Jones, K. O., and Stiggins, R. J. (1976). Trends in counselor attitude about women's roles. *Journal of Counseling Psychology, 23,* 365–372.

Entwisle, D., and Baker, D. (1983). Gender and young children's expectations for performance in arithmetic. *Developmental Psychology, 19,* 200–209.

Erens, P. (1979). *Sexual strategems: The world of women in film.* New York: Horizon Press.

Erkut, S. (1983). Exploring sex differences in expectancy, attribution, and academic achievement. *Sex Roles, 9,* 217–232.

Esposito, A. (1979). Sex differences in children's conversation. *Language and Speech, 22,* 213–220.

Evans, G. W., and Howard, R. B. (1973). Personal space. *Psychological Bulletin, 80,* 334–344.

Fagot, B. I. (1977). Preschool sex stereotyping: Effect of sex of teachers vs. training of teacher. Paper presented at the meeting of the Society for Research in Child Development, New Orleans.

Fagot, B. I. (1978). The influence of sex of child on parental reactions to toddler children. *Child Development, 49,* 459–465.

Falbo, T. (1977). Relationships between sex, and sex role, and social influence. *Psychology of Women Quarterly, 2,* 62–72.

Falbo, T., and Peplau, L. A. (1980). Power strategies in intimate relationships. *Journal of Personality and Social Psychology, 38,* 618–628.

Feldman, R. S., and White, J. B. (1980). Detecting deception in children. *Journal of Communication, 30*(2), 121–128.

Fennell, M. L., Barchas, P. R., Cohen, E. G., McMahon, A. M., and Hildebrand, P. (1978). An alternative perspective on sex differences in organizational settings: The process of legitimation. *Sex Roles, 4,* 589–604.

Fillmer, H. T., and Haswell, L. (1977). Sex-role stereotyping in English usage. *Sex Roles, 3,* 257–263.

Fine, M. G. (1981). Soap opera conversations: The talk that binds. *Journal of Communication, 31*(3), 97–107.

Firester, L., and Firester, J. (1974). Wanted: A new deal for boys. *Elementary School Journal, 75,* 28–36.

Fisher, J. D., and Byrne, D. (1975). Too close for comfort: Sex differences in response to invasion of personal space. *Journal of Personality and Social Psychology, 32,* 15–21.

Fishman, P. M. (1978). Interaction: The work women do. *Social Problems, 25,* 397–406.

Fiske, J. (1983). The discourses of TV quiz shows or, school + luck = success + sex. *Central States Speech Journal, 34,* 139–150.

Fitt, L. W., and Newton, D. A. (1981). When the mentor is a man and the protegé is a woman. *Harvard Business Review, 59*(2), 56–60.

Fitzpatrick, M. A., and Indvik, J. (1982). The instrumental and expressive domains of marital communication. *Human Communication Research, 8,* 195–213.

Fitzpatrick, M.A., and Winke, J. (1979). You always hurt the one you love: Strategies and tactics in interpersonal conflict. *Communication Quarterly, 27,* 3–11.

Flanders, D. P., and Anderson, P.E. (1973). Sex discrimination in employment: Theory and practice. *Industrial and Labor Relations Review, 26,* 938–955.

Flerx, V. C., Fidler, D. S., and Rogers, R. W. (1976). Sex role stereotypes: Developmental aspects and early intervention. *Child Development, 47,* 998–1007.

Fottler, M. D., and Bain, T. (1980). Sex differences in occupational aspirations. *Academy of Management Journal, 23,* 144–149.

Foxley, C. H. (1979). *Nonsexist counseling: Helping women and men redefine their roles.* Dubuque, IA: Kendall/Hunt.

Foxley, C. H. (1982). Sex equity in education: Some gains, problems, and future needs. *Journal of Teacher Education, 33,* 6–9.

Freedman, N., O'Hanlon, J., Oltman, P., and Witkin, H. A. (1972). The imprint of psychological differentiation on kinetic behavior in varying communicative contexts. *Journal of Abnormal Psychology, 79,* 239–258.

Frueh, T., and McGhee, P. E. (1975). Traditional sex role development and amount of time spent watching television. *Developmental Psychology, 11,* 109.

Garland, H., and Price, K. H. (1977). Attitudes toward women in management and attributions for their success and failure in a managerial position. *Journal of Applied Psychology, 62,* 29–33.

Gelman, D., Carey, J., Gelman, E., Lubenow, G.C., and Contreras, J. (1981, May 18). Just how the sexes differ. *Newsweek,* pp. 72–75, 78–83.

Glauser, M. J. (1982). Factors which facilitate or impede upward communication in organizations. Paper presented at the meeting of the Academy of Management, New York City.

Goleman, D. (1978, November). Special abilities of the sexes: Do they begin in the brain? *Psychology Today,* pp. 48–59, 120.

Golinkoff, R. M., and Ames, G. J. (1979). A comparison of fathers' and mothers' speech with their young children. *Child Development, 50,* 28–32.

Good, T. L., Sikes, J. N., and Brophy, J. E. (1973). Effects of teacher sex and student sex on classroom interaction. *Journal of Educational Psychology, 65,* 74–87.

Gottman, J. M., and Porterfield, A. L. (1981). Communicative acceptance in the nonverbal behavior of married couples. *Journal of Marriage and the Family, 43,* 817–824.

Graziano, W., Brothen, T., and Berscheid, E. (1978). Height and attraction: Do men and women see eye to eye? *Journal of Personality, 46,* 128–145.

Greenblatt, L., Hasenauer, J. E., and Freimuth, V. S. (1980). Psychological sex type and androgyny in the study of communication variables: Self-disclosure and communication apprehension. *Human Communication Research, 6,* 117–129.

Gross, L., and Jeffries-Fox, S. (1978). "What do you want to be when you grow up, little girl?" In *Hearth and home: Images of women in the mass media,* ed. G. Tuchman, A.K. Daniels and J. Benet, 240–265. New York: Oxford University Press.

Guardo, C. J. (1976). Personal space, sex differences, and interpersonal attraction. *Journal of Psychology, 92,* 9–14.

Gunnar, M. R., and Donahue, M. (1980). Sex differences in social responsiveness between six months and twelve months. *Child Development, 51,* 262–265.

Guttentag, M., Bray, H., and Amsler, J. (1976). *Undoing sex stereotypes: Research and resources for educators.* New York: McGraw-Hill.

Haas, A., and Sherman, M.A. (1982). Reported topics of conversation among same-sex adults. *Communication Quarterly, 30,* 332–342.

Hacker, H.M. (1981). Blabbermouths and clams: Sex differences in self-disclosure in same-sex and cross-sex friendship dyads. *Psychology of Women Quarterly, 5,* 385–401.

Haertel, G.D., Walberg, H.J., Junker, L., and Pascarella, E.T. (1981). Early adolescent sex differences in science learning: Evidence from the national assessment of educational progress. *American Educational Research Journal, 18,* 329–341.

Halcomb, R. (1980, February). Mentors and the successful woman. *Across the Board,* pp. 13–18.

Hall, J.A. (1978). Gender effects in decoding nonverbal cues. *Psychological Bulletin, 85,* 845–857.

Hall, J.A. (1979). "Gender, gender-roles, and nonverbal communication skills." In *Skill in nonverbal communication: Individual differences,* ed. R. Rosenthal, 32–67. Cambridge, MA: Oelgeschlager, Gunn and Hain.

Hall, R.M., and Sandler, B.R. (1982). *The classroom climate: A chilly one for women?* (Available from Project on the Status and Education of Women, Association of American Colleges, 1818 R Street NW, Washington, DC 20009.)

Harper, L., and Sanders, K.M. (1975). Preschool children's use of space: Sex differences in outdoor play. *Developmental Psychology, 11,* 119.

Harris, M.B. (1977). The effects of gender, masculinity-femininity and trait favorability on evaluations of students. *Contemporary Educational Psychology, 2,* 353–363.

Harrison, L. (1975). For CroMagnon: Women-in eclipse. *The Science Teacher, 42*(4), 8–11.

Harrison, L., and Passer, R.N. (1975). Sexism in the language of elementary school textbooks. *Science and Children, 12*(4), 22–25.

Harway, M. (1977). Sex bias in counseling materials. *Journal of College Student Personnel, 18,* 57–64.

Haskell, M. (1974). *From reverence to rape: The treatment of women in the movies.* New York: Holt, Rinehart and Winston.

Haslett, B.J. (1983). Communicative functions and strategies in children's conversations. *Human Communication Research, 9,* 114–129.

Haviland, J.M. (1977). Sex-related pragmatics in infants' nonverbal communication. *Journal of Communication, 27*(2), 80–84.

Hawkins, J.L., Weisberg, C., and Ray, D.W. (1980). Spouse differences in communication style: Preference, perception and behavior. *Journal of Marriage and the Family, 42,* 585–593.

Heinen, J.S., McGlauchin, D., Legeros, C., and Freeman, J. (1975). Developing the woman manager. *Personnel Journal, 54,* 282–286, 297.

Henderson, L., Greenberg, B.S., and Atkin, C.K. (1980). "Sexual differences in giving orders, making plans and needing support on television." In *Life on television: Content analyses of U.S. TV drama,* ed. B.S. Greenberg, 49–63. Norwood, NJ: Ablex.

Henley, N.M. (1977). *Body politics: Power, sex, and nonverbal communication.* Englewood Cliffs, NJ: Prentice-Hall.

Hennig, M., and Jardim, A. (1977). *The managerial woman.* New York: Pocket Books.

Hershey, S., and Werner, E. (1975). Dominance in marital decision making in women's liberation and non-women's liberation families. *Family Process, 14,* 223–233.

Hetherington, E.M., and Parke, R.D. (1979). *Child psychology: A contemporary viewpoint,* 2nd ed. New York: McGraw-Hill.

Hill, C.E., Tanney, M.F., Leonard, M.M., and Reiss, J.A. (1977). Counselor reactions to female clients: Type of problem, age of client, and sex of counselor. *Journal of Counseling Psychology, 24,* 60–65.

Hoffman, M.L. (1977). Sex differences in empathy and related behaviors. *Psychological Bulletin, 84,* 712–722.

Honeycutt, J. M., Wilson, C., and Parker, C. (1982). Effects of sex and degrees of happiness on perceived styles of communicating in and out of the marital relationship. *Journal of Marriage and the Family, 44,* 395–406.

Hopper, R., Knapp, M. L., and Scott, L. (1981). Couples' personal idioms: Exploring intimate talk. *Journal of Communication, 31*(1), 23–33.

Howard, S. (1980). *Fact sheet on women in educational administration.* Arlington, VA: American Association of School Administrators.

Howell, W. S. (1981). *The empathic communicator.* Belmont, CA: Wadsworth.

Hubbard, R. C. (1985). Relationship styles in popular romance novels, 1950–1983. *Communication Quarterly, 33,* 113–125.

Hull, D. B., and Schroeder, H. E. (1979). Some interpersonal effects of assertion, nonassertion and aggression. *Behavior Therapy, 10,* 20–28.

Hunt, D. M., and Michael, C. (1983). Mentorship: A career training and development tool. *Academy of Management Review, 8,* 475–485.

Illfelder, J. K. (1980). Fear of success, sex role attitudes, and career salience and anxiety levels of college women. *Journal of Vocational Behavior, 16,* 7–17.

Isenhart, M. W. (1980). An investigation of the relationship of sex and sex role to the ability to decode nonverbal cues. *Human Communication Research, 6,* 309–318.

Jacklin, C. N., and Maccoby, E. E. (1978). Spatial behavior at 33 months in same-sex and mixed-sex dyads. *Child Development, 43,* 557–569.

Jacko, C. M., Karmos, A. H., and Karmos, J. S. (1980). Classroom teachers and sex-role stereotyping: Awareness, attitudes, and behaviors. *Journal of Instructional Psychology, 7*(2), 43–49.

Jacobson, M. B., and Effertz, J. (1974). Sex roles and leadership: Perceptions of the leaders and the led. *Organizational Behavior and Human Performance, 12,* 383–396.

Jakubowski-Spector, P. (1973). Facilitating the growth of women through assertive training. *The Counseling Psychologist, 4,* 75–86.

Jenkins, M. M., Gappa, J. M., and Pearce, J. (1983). *Removing bias: Guidelines for student-faculty communication.* Annandale, VA: Speech Communication Association.

Jenni, D. A., and Jenni, M. A. (1976, November 19). Carrying behavior in humans: Analysis of sex differences. *Science,* pp. 859–860.

Jennings, S. A. (1975). Effects of sex typing in children's stories on preference and recall. *Child Development, 46,* 220–223.

Johnson, F. L., and Aries, E. J. (1983). The talk of women friends. *Women's Studies International Forum, 6,* 353–361.

Jourard, S. M., and Secord, P. F. (1955). Body cathexis and personality. *British Journal of Psychology, 46,* 130–138.

Kanter, R. M. (1977). *Men and women of the corporation.* New York: Basic Books.

Karp, D. A., and Yoels, W. C. (1976). The college classroom: Some observations on the meanings of student participation. *Sociology and Social Research, 60,* 421–439.

Katz, P. (1980). *Correlates of sexual flexibility in children.* NIMH Final Report, Contract MH 29417.

Kelck, R. E., Richardson, S. A., and Ronald, L. (1974). Physical appearance cues and interpersonal attraction in children. *Child Development, 45,* 305–310.

Kelly, J. A., Kem, J. M., Kirkley, B. G., and Patterson, J. N. (1981). Reactions to assertive versus unassertive behavior: Differential effects for males and females and implications for assertive training. *Educational Resources Information Center,* ED 193 424.

Kelly, J. A., O'Brien, G. G., and Hosford, R. (1981). Sex roles and social skills in considerations for interpersonal adjustment. *Psychology of Women Quarterly, 5,* 758–766.

Kemper, S. (1984). When to speak like a lady. *Sex Roles, 10,* 435–443.

Kennedy, C. W., and Camden, C. T. (1983). A new look at interruptions. *Western Journal of Speech Communication, 47,* 45–58.

Kerin, R. A., Lundstrom, W. J., and Sciglimpaglia, D. (1979). Women in advertisements: Retrospect and prospect. *Journal of Advertising, 8,* 37–42.

Key, M.R. (1972). Linguistic behavior of male and female. *Linguistics, 88,* 15–31.

Kimlicka, T., Cross, H., and Tarnai, J. (1983). A comparison of androgynous, feminine, masculine, and undifferentiated women on self-esteem, body satisfaction, and sexual satisfaction. *Psychology of Women Quarterly, 7,* 291–294.

Kirby, D. F., and Julian, N. B. (1981). Treatment of women in high school U. S. history textbooks. *Social Studies, 72,* 203–207.

Klein, R. P., and Durfee, J. T. (1978). Effects of sex and birth order on infant social behavior. *Infant Behavior and Development, 1,* 106–117.

Kleinke, C. L., Desaultels, M., and Knapp, B. (1977). Adult gaze and affective and visual responses of preschool children. *Journal of Genetic Psychology, 131,* 321–322.

Knill, B.J., Pesch, M., Pursey, G., Gilpin, P., and Perloff, R. (1981). Still typecast after all these years? Sex role portrayals in television advertising. *International Journal of Women's Studies, 4,* 497–506.

Kobel, J. (1973). *Romance and the cinema.* London: Roxby Press Production.

Koblinsky, S.G., Cruse, D.F., and Sugawara, A.I. (1978). Sex role stereotypes and children's memory for story content. *Child Development, 49,* 452–458.

Koblinsky, S.G., and Sugawara, A.I., (1984). Nonsexist curricula, sex of teacher, and children's sex role learning. *Sex Roles, 10,* 357–367.

Koehn, H.E. (1976). Attitude: The success element for women in business. *Journal of Systems Management, 27*(3), 12–15.

Kolbe, R., and LaVoie, J.C. (1981). Sex-role stereotyping in preschool children's picture books. *Social Psychology Quarterly, 44,* 369–374.

Kon, I. (1975). Women at work: Equality with a difference. *International Social Science Journal, 27,* 655–665.

Konsky, C. (1978). Male-female language attributions in the resolution of conflict.Paper presented at the meeting of the Speech Communication Association, Minneapolis. Cited in Murdock, J.I., and Konsky, C.W. (1982). An investigation of verbosity and sex-role expectations. *Women's Studies in Communication, 5,* 65–76.

Kram, K.E. (1983). Phases of the mentor relationship. *Academy of Management Journal, 26,* 608–625.

Kramarae, C. (1981). *Women and men speaking.* Rowley, MA: Newbury House.

Kramer, C. (1974). Stereotypes of women's speech: The word from the cartoons. *Journal of Popular Culture, 8,* 624–630.

Kropp, J., and Halverson, C. (1983). Preschool children's preferences and recall for stereotyped versus nonstereotyped stories. *Sex Roles, 9,* 261–273.

Kumin, L., and Lazar, M. (1974). Gestural communication and preschool children. *Perceptual and Motor Skills, 38,* 708–710.

Lakoff, R. (1975). *Language and woman's place.* New York: Harper & Row.

Lamb, M.E., and Roopnarine, J.L. (1979). Peer influences on sex-role development in preschoolers. *Child Development, 50,* 1219–1222.

Lambert, H.H. (1978). Biology and equality: A perspective on sex differences. *Signs, 4,* 97–117.

Langlois, J.H., and Downs, A.C. (1979). Peer relations as a function of physical attractiveness: The eye of the beholder or behavioral reality? *Child Development, 50,* 409–418.

Langlois, J.H., Gottfried, N.W., Barnes, B.M., and Hendricks, D.E. (1978). The effect of peer age on the social behavior of preschool children. *Journal of Genetic Psychology, 132,* 11–19.

Larwood, L., Wood, M.M., and Inderlied, S.D. (1978). Training women for management: New problems, new solutions. *Academy of Management Review, 3,* 584–593.

Lau, S. (1982). The effect of smiling as person perception. *Journal of Social Psychology, 117,* 63–67.

Lavrakas, P.J. (1975). Female preferences for male physiques. *Journal of Research in Personality, 9,* 324–334.

Lawrenz, F.P., and Welch, W.W. (1983). Student perceptions of science classes taught by males and females. *Journal of Research in Science Teaching, 20,* 655–662.

Lazar, C., and Dier, S. (1978). The labor force in fiction. *Journal of Communication, 28*(1), 174–182.

Lee, A.M., Hall, E.G., and Carter, J.A. (1983). Age and sex differences in expectancy for success among American children. *Journal of Psychology, 113,* 35–39.

Lemon, J. (1977). Women and blacks on prime-time television. *Journal of Communication, 27*(4), 70–79.

Lenney, E. (1977). Women's self-confidence in achievement settings. *Psychological Bulletin, 84,* 1–13.

Lerner, R.M. (1969). The development of stereotyped expectancies of body build–behavior relations. *Child Development, 40,* 137–141.

Lerner, R.M., Venning, J., and Knapp, J.R. (1974). Age and sex effects of personal space schemata toward body build in late childhood. *Developmental Psychology, 11,* 855–856.

Levinson, D.J., Darrow, C.M., Klein, E.B., Levinson, M.A., and McKee, B. (1978). *The seasons of a man's life.* New York: Alfred A. Knopf.

Lewis, M. (1972, May). Culture and gender roles—there's no unisex in the nursery. *Psychology Today,* pp. 54–57.

Lewis, M., and Freedle, R. (1973). "Mother-infant dyad: The cradle of meaning." In *Communication and affect: Language and thought,* ed. P. Pliner, L. Krames, and T. Alloway, 127–155. New York: Academic Press.

Lewis, R.A. (1978). Emotional intimacy among men. *Journal of Social Issues, 34,* 108–121.

Liska, J., Mechling, E.W., and Stathas, S. (1981). Differences in subjects' perceptions of gender and believability between users of deferential and nondeferential language. *Communication Quarterly, 29,* 40–48.

Lockheed, M.E., and Hall, K.P. (1976). Conceptualizing sex as a status characteristic: Applications to leadership training strategies. *Journal of Social Issues, 32,* 111–124.

Lombardo, W.K., Cretser, G.A., Lombardo, B., and Mathis, S.L. (1983). Fer cryin' out loud—there is a sex difference. *Sex Roles, 9,* 987–1003.

Loy, P.H., and Stewart, L.P. (1984). The extent and effects of the sexual harassment of working women. *Sociological Focus, 17,* 31–43.

Lull, J. (1980). Girls' favorite TV females. *Journalism Quarterly, 57,* 146–150.

Lull, J., Johnson, L.M., and Edmond, D. (1981). Radio listeners' electronic media habits. *Journal of Broadcasting, 25,* 25–36.

Lutes-Dunckley, C.J. (1978). Sex role preferences as function of sex of storyteller and story context. *Journal of Psychology, 100,* 151–158.

Maccoby, E.E., and Jacklin, C.N. (1974). *The psychology of sex differences.* Stanford, CA: Stanford University Press.

Macke, A.S., and Richardson, L.W. (1980). *Sex-typed teaching styles of university professors and student reactions.* Columbus: Ohio State University Research Foundation.

Mahony, P. (1983). How Alice's chin really came to be pressed against her foot: Sexist processes of interaction in mixed-sex classrooms. *Women's Studies International Forum, 6,* 107–115.

Mai-Dalton, R.R., and Sullivan, J.J. (1981). The effects of manager's sex on the assignment to a challenging or a dull task and reasons for the choice. *Academy of Management Journal, 24,* 603–612.

Maier, N.R.F. (1970). Male versus female discussion leaders. *Personnel Psychology, 23,* 455–461.

Malone, M. (1979). *Heroes of Eros: Male sexuality in the movies.* New York: E.P. Dutton.

Maltz, D.N., and Borker, R.A. (1982). "A cultural approach to male-female miscommunication." In *Language and social identity,* ed. J.J. Gumperz, 196–216. New York: Cambridge University Press.

Marecek, J., Piliavin, J.A., Fitzsimmons, E., Krogh, E.C., Leader, E., and Trudell, B. (1978). Women as TV experts: The voice of authority? *Journal of Communication, 28* (1), 159–168.

Marini, M.M. (1980). Sex differences in the process of occupational attainment: A closer look. *Social Science Research, 9,* 307–361.

Marecek, J., Piliavin, J.A., Fitzsimmons, E., Krogh, E.C., Leader, E., and Trudell, B. (1978). Women as TV experts: The voice of authority? *Journal of Communication, 28*(1), 159–168.

Markel, N.N., Long, J.F., and Saine, T.J. (1976). Sex effects in conversational interaction: Another look at male dominance. *Human Communication Research, 2,* 356–364.

Martin, J.N., and Craig, R.T. (1983). Selected linguistic sex differences during initial social interactions of same-sex and mixed-sex student dyads. *Western Journal of Speech Communication, 47,* 16–28.

Mastalli, G.L. (1981). Appendix: The legal context. *Harvard Business Review, 59*(2), 94–95.

Mayes, S.L., and Valentine, K.B. (1979). Sex-role stereotyping in Saturday morning cartoon shows. *Journal of Broadcasting, 23,* 41–50.

McArthur, L.Z., and Eisen, S.V. (1976). Achievements of male and female storybook characters as determinants of achievement behavior by boys and girls. *Journal of Personality and Social Psychology, 33,* 467–473.

McCorkle, S. (1982). An analysis of verbal language in Saturday morning children's programs. *Communication Quarterly, 30,* 210–216.

McGhee, P., and Frueh, T. (1980). Television viewing and the learning of sex role stereotypes. *Sex Roles, 6,* 179–188.

McIntyre, S., Moberg, D.J., and Posner, B.Z. (1980). Preferential treatment in preselection decisions according to sex and race. *Academy of Management Journal, 23,* 738–749.

McMillan, J.R., Clifton, A.K., McGrath, D., and Gale, W.S. (1977). Women's language: Uncertainty or interpersonal sensitivity and emotionality? *Sex Roles, 3,* 545–559.

Mead, G.H. (1934). *Mind, self and society.* Chicago: University of Chicago Press.

Meade, M. (1971, March 17). Does rock degrade women? *New York Times,* pp. 13, 22.

Media Report to Women. (1983a, March–April). (Available from 3306 Ross Place NW, Washington, DC.)

Media Report to Women. (1983b, August–September). (Available from 3306 Ross Place NW, Washington, DC.)

Mehrabian, A. (1972). *Nonverbal communication.* Chicago: Aldine-Atherton.

Mehrabian, A. (1981). *Silent messages: Implicit communication of emotion and attitudes,* 2nd ed. Belmont, CA: Wadsworth.

Meisels, M., and Guardo, C.J. (1969). Development of personal space schemata. *Child Development, 40,* 1167–1178.

Mellen, J. (1973). *Women and their sexuality in the new film*. New York: Horizon Press.

Mellen, J. (1977). *Big bad wolves: Masculinity in the American film*. New York: Pantheon Books.

Melson, G.F. (1976). Determinants of personal space in young children: Perception of distance cues. *Perceptual and Motor Skills, 43,* 107–114.

Metts, S. (1984). A reinterpretation of conversational dominance. Paper presented at the meeting of the Speech Communication Association, Chicago.

Mid-revolutionary mores. (1981, July). *Ms. Magazine,* p. 18.

Millett, K., and Swift, C. (1972, Spring). De-sexing the English language. *Ms. Magazine,* p. 7.

Mliner, J. (1977). *Sex stereotypes in mathematics and science textbooks for elementary and junior high schools: Report of sex bias in the public schools*. New York: National Organization for Women.

Montgomery, B.M., and Norton, R.W. (1981). Sex differences and similarities in communicator style. *Communication Monographs, 48,* 121–132.

Morse, B.W., and Eman, V.A. (1980). "The construct of androgyny: An overview and implications for research." In *Communication, language and sex,* ed. C.L. Berryman and V.A. Eman, 76–90. Rowley, MA: Newbury House.

Mulder, M. (1960). The power variable in communication experiments. *Human Relations, 13,* 241–256.

Natale, M., Entin, E., and Jaffe, J. (1979). Vocal interruptions in dyadic communication as a function of speech and social anxiety. *Journal of Personality and Social Psychology, 37,* 865–878.

National Advisory Council on Women's Educational Programs, U.S. Department of Education. (1981). *Title IX: The half-full, half-empty glass*. Washington, DC: U.S. Government Printing Office.

National Commission on Working Women. (1982). *What's wrong with this picture? A look at working women on television*. Washington, DC: National Commission on Working Women.

Neugarten, D.A., and Shafritz, J.M. (eds.). (1980). *Sexuality in organizations: Romantic and coercive behaviors at work*. Oak Park, IL: Moore.

Newcombe, N., and Bandura, M. (1983). Effect of age at puberty on spatial ability in girls: A question of mechanism. *Developmental Psychology, 19,* 215–224.

Nguyen, T., Heslin, R., and Nguyen, M.L. (1975). The meanings of touch: Sex differences. *Journal of Communication, 25*(3), 92–103.

Nieva, V.F., and Gutek, B.A. (1980). Sex effects on evaluation. *Academy of Management Review, 5,* 267–276.

Norton, R.W. (1978). Foundation of a communicator style construct. *Human Communication Research, 4,* 99–112.

O'Barr, W.M., and Atkins, B.K. (1980). " 'Women's language' or 'powerless language'?" In *Women and language in literature and society,* ed. S. McConnell-Ginet, R. Borker and N. Furman, 93–110. New York: Praeger.

Octigan, M., and Niederman, S. (1979). Male dominance in conversations. *Frontiers: A Journal of Woman's Studies, 4,* 50–54.

O'Donnell, W.J., and O'Donnell, K.J. (1978). Update: Sex-role message in T.V. commercials. *Journal of Communication, 28*(1), 156–158.

Orth, C.D., and Jacobs, F. (1971). Women in management: Pattern for change. *Harvard Business Review, 49*(4), 139–147.

Pallas, A.M., and Alexander, K.L. (1983). Sex differences in quantitative SAT performance: New evidence on the differential coursework hypothesis. *American Educational Research Journal, 20,* 165–182.

Parlee, M.B. (1979a, March). Women smile less for success. *Psychology Today,* p. 16.

Parlee, M.B. (1979b, May). Conversational politics. *Psychology Today,* pp. 48–56.

Parson, J.E., Heller, K.A., and Kaczala, C. (1980). "The effects of teachers' expectancies and attributions on students' expectancies for success in mathematics." In *Women's lives: New theory, research and policy,* ed. D.G. McGuigan, 373–380. Ann Arbor: University of Michigan Center for Continuing Education of Women.

Parsons, T. (1964). *Social structure and personality.* New York: Free Press.

Parsons, T., and Bales, R. (1955). *Family, socialization and interaction process.* New York: Free Press.

Paulsen, K., and Johnson, M. (1983). Sex role attitudes and mathematical ability in 4th, 8th, and 11th grade students from a high socioeconomic area. *Developmental Psychology, 19,* 210–214.

Pearce, W.B., and Sharp, S.M. (1973). Self-disclosing communication. *Journal of Communication, 23*(4), 409–425.

Pearson, J.C., Miller, G.R., and Senter, M.M. (1983). Sexism and sexual humor: A research note. *Central States Speech Journal, 34,* 257–259.

Peng, S.S., and Jaffe, J. (1979). Women who enter male-dominated fields of study in higher education. *American Educational Research Journal, 16,* 285–293.

Peterson, P. (1976). "An investigation of sex differences in regard to nonverbal body gestures." In *Siscom '75: Women's (and men's) communication,* ed. B. Eakins, G. Eakins, and B. Lieb-Brilhart, 20–27. Falls Church, VA: Speech Communication Association.

Petronio, S.S. (1982). The effect of interpersonal communication on women's family role satisfaction. *Western Journal of Speech Communication, 46,* 208–222.

Pingree, S. (1978). The effects of nonsexist television commercials and perceptions of reality on children's attitudes about women. *Psychology of Women Quarterly, 2,* 262–277.

Pingree, S., Hawkins, R.P., Butler, M., and Paisley, W. (1976). A scale for sexism. *Journal of Communication, 26*(1), 193–200.

Pleck, J.H. (1977). The psychology of sex roles: Traditional and new views. In *Women and men: Changing roles, relationships and perceptions,* ed. L.A. Cater and A.F. Scott, with W. Martyna, 181–199. New York: Praeger.

Poe, A. (1976). Active women in ads. *Journal of Communication, 26*(4), 185–192.

Randall, P.R. (1985). Sexist language and speech communication texts: Another case of benign neglect. *Communication Education, 34,* 128–134.

Rawlins, W.K. (1982). Cross-sex friendship and the communicative management of sex-role expectations. *Communication Quarterly, 30,* 343–352.

Reeves, B., and Miller, M.M. (1978). A multidimensional measure of children's identification with television characters. *Journal of Broadcasting, 22,* 71–86.

Rekers, G.A., Amoro-Plotkin, H.D., and Low, B.P. (1977). Sex-typed mannerisms in normal boys and girls as a function of sex and age. *Child Development, 48,* 275–278.

Rekers, G.A., and Rudy, J.P. (1978). Differentiation of childhood body gestures. *Perceptual and Motor Skills, 46,* 839–845.

Remland, M.S., Jacobson, C.M., and Jones, T.S. (1983). Evaluations of sex-incongruent nonverbal communication for male and female managers. *Women's Studies in Communication, 6,* 24–33.

Renwick, P.A., and Tosi, H. (1978). The effects of sex, marital status, and educational background on selection decisions. *Academy of Management Journal, 21,* 93–103.

Rheingold, H.L., and Cook, K.V. (1975). The contents of boys' and girls' rooms as an index of parents' behavior. *Child Development, 46,* 459–463.

Richmond, V.P., and Dyba, P. (1982). The roots of sexual stereotyping: The teacher as model. *Communication Education, 31,* 265–273.

Ricks, F.A., and Pyke, S.W. (1973). Teacher perceptions and attitudes that foster or maintain sex-role differences. *Interchange, 4,* 26–33.

Riger, S., and Galligan, P. (1980). Women in management: An exploration of competing paradigms. *American Psychologist, 35,* 902–910.

Rogers, M.A. (1975). A different look at word problems. *Mathematics Teacher, 68,* 285–288.

Roloff, M.E., and Greenberg, B.S. (1979). Resolving conflict: Methods used by T.V. characters and teenage viewers. *Journal of Broadcasting, 23,* 285–300.

Rosen, B., and Jerdee, T.H. (1973). The influence of sex-role stereotypes on evaluations of male and female supervisory behavior. *Journal of Applied Psychology, 57,* 44–48.

Rosen, B., and Jerdee, T.H. (1974). Sex stereotyping in the executive suite. *Harvard Business Review, 52*(2), 45–58.

Rosen, M. (1973). *Popcorn Venus: Women, movies and the American dream.* New York: Coward, McCann and Geoghegan.

Rosenfeld, L.B. (1979). Self-disclosure avoidance: Why am I afraid to tell you who I am? *Communication Monographs, 46,* 63–74.

Rosenfeld, L.B., Kartus, S., and Ray, C. (1976). Body accessibility revisited. *Journal of Communication, 26*(3), 27–30.

Rosenfeld, R.A. (1979). Women's occupational careers: Individual and structural explanations. *Sociology of Work and Occupations, 6,* 283–311.

Rosenthal, R., and DePaulo, B.M. (1979). "Sex differences in accommodation in nonverbal communication." In *Skill in nonverbal communication: Individual differences,* ed. R. Rosenthal, 68–103. Cambridge, MA: Oelgeschlager, Gunn and Hain.

Rosenthal, R. et al. (1979). *Sensitivity to nonverbal communication: The PONS test.* Baltimore: Johns Hopkins University Press.

Rosenthal, R., and Jacobson, L. (1968). *Pygmalion in the classroom.* New York: Holt, Rinehart & Winston.

Rubin, Z., Hill, C.T., Peplau, L.A., and Dunkel-Schettes, C. (1980). Self-disclosure in dating couples: Sex roles and the ethic of openness. *Journal of Marriage and the Family, 42,* 305–316.

Ruble, D.N., Balaban, T., and Cooper, J. (1981). Gender constancy and the effects of sex-typed televised toy commercials. *Child Development, 52,* 667-673.

Rudman, M.K. (1984). *Children's literature: An issues approach,* 2nd ed. New York: Longman.

Ruggiero, J.A., and Weston, L.C. (1983). Conflicting images of women in romance novels. *International Journal of Women's Studies, 6,* 18–25.

Sadker, M.P., and Sadker, D.M. (1977). *Now upon a time: A contemporary view of children's literature*. New York: Harper & Row.

Sadker, M.P., and Sadker, D.M. (1979). Between teacher and student: Overcoming sex bias in the classroom. Non-Sexist Teacher Education Project, Women's Educational Equity Act Program, U.S. Department of Health, Education, and Welfare, Office of Education.

Sadker, M.P., and Sadker, D.M. (1985, March). Sexism in the schoolroom of the '80s. *Psychology Today*, pp. 54–57.

Sadker, M.P., Sadker, D.M., and Hicks, T. (1980). The one percent solution? Sexism in teacher education texts. *Phi Delta Kappan, 61*, 550–553.

Safran, C. (1981), March). Sexual harassment: A view from the top. *Redbook*, pp. 1–7.

Schau, C.G., Kahn, L., Diepold, J.H., and Cherry, F. (1980). The relationships of parental expectations and preschool children's verbal sex typing to their sex-typed toy play behavior. *Child Development, 51*, 266–270.

Schein, V.E. (1973). The relationship between sex role stereotypes and requisite management characteristics. *Journal of Applied Psychology, 57*, 95–100.

Schein, V.E. (1978). Sex role stereotyping, ability and performance: Prior research and new directions. *Personnel Psychology, 31*, 259–268.

Schwichtenberg, C. (1983). *Dynasty:* The dialectic of feminine power. *Central States Speech Journal, 34*, 151–161.

Scott, Foresman and Company. (1974). Guidelines for improving the image of women in textbooks. Glenview, IL.

Scott, K.P., and Feldman-Summers, S. (1979). Children's reactions to textbook stories in which females are portrayed in traditionally male roles. *Journal of Educational Psychology, 71*, 369–403.

Seggar, J.F. (1975). Images of women in television drama: 1974. *Journal of Broadcasting, 19*, 273–282.

Senger, J. (1971). Managers' perceptions of subordinates' competence as a function of personal value orientations. *Academy of Management Journal, 14*, 415–423.

Severy, L.J., Forsyth, D.R., and Wagner, P.J. (1980). A multimethod assessment of personal space development in female and male, black and white children. *Journal of Nonverbal Behavior, 4*, 68–86.

Sgan, M.L., and Pickert, S.M. (1980). Cross sex and same-sex assertive bids in a cooperative group task. *Child Development, 51*, 928–931.

Shapiro, E.C., Haseltine, F.P., and Rowe, M.P. (1978). Moving up: Role models, mentors, and the patron system. *Sloan Management Review, 19*(3), 51–58.

Sherman, J., Koufacos, C., and Kenworthy, J.A. (1978). Therapists: Their attitudes and information about women. *Psychology of Women Quarterly, 2*, 299-313.

Sherman, M.A., and Haas,A. (1984, June). Man to man, woman to woman. *Psychology Today*, pp. 72–73.

Shockley, P.S., and Staley, C.M. (1980). Women in management training programs: What they think about key issues. *Public Personnel Management Journal, 9*, 214–224.

Silverman, D. (1976–77). Sexual harassment: Working women's dilemma. *Quest, 3*(3), 15–24.

Silverman, T.L., Sprafkin, J.N., and Rubenstein, E.A. (1979). Physical contact and sexual behavior on prime-time TV. *Journal of Communication, 29*(1), 33–43.

Simmons, B., and Whitfield, E. (1979). Are boys victims of sex-role stereotyping? *Childhood Education, 56*(2), 75–79.

Skelly, G.U., and Lundstrom, W. (1981). Male sex roles in magazine advertising, 1959–1979. *Journal of Communication, 31*(4), 52–57.

Slocum, W.L., and Nye, F.I. (1976). "Provider and housekeeper roles." In *Role structure and analysis of the family,* ed. F.I. Nye, 81–99. Beverly Hills, CA: Sage.

Smith, C.B. (1979). Influence of internal opportunity structure and sex of worker on turnover patterns. *Administrative Science Quarterly, 24,* 362–381.

Smith, P.K., and Daglish, L. (1977). Sex differences in parent and infant behavior in the home. *Child Development, 48,* 1250–1254.

Sommer, R. (1959). Studies in personal space. *Sociometry, 22,* 247–260.

Sorrels, B.D. (1983). *The nonsexist communicator: Solving the problems of gender and awkwardness in modern English.* Englewood Cliffs, NJ: Prentice-Hall.

Spender, D. (1985). *Man man language,* 2nd ed. London: Routledge & Kegan Paul.

Spender, D., and Sarah, E. (1980). *Learning to lose: Sexism and education.* London: Women's Press.

Spender, L. (1983). The politics of publishing: Selection and rejection of women's words in print. *Women's Studies International Forum, 6,* 469–473.

Sprafkin, J.N., and Liebert, R.M. (1978). "Sex-typing and children's television preferences." In *Hearth and home: Images of women in the mass media,* ed. G. Tuchman, A.K. Daniels and J. Benet, 228–239. New York: Oxford University Press.

Sprague, J. (1975). The reduction of sexism in speech communication education. *Speech Teacher, 24,* 37–45.

St. Peter, S. (1979). Jack went up the hill . . . but where was Jill? *Psychology of Women Quarterly,* 4, 256–260.

Staffieri, J.R. (1967). A study of social stereotype of body image in children. *Journal of Personality and Social Psychology, 7,* 101–104.

Staffieri, J.R. (1972). Body build and behavioral expectancies in young females. *Developmental Psychology, 6,* 125–127.

Stake, J.E., and Katz, J.F. (1982). Teacher-pupil relationships in the elementary school classroom: Teacher-gender and pupil-gender differences. *American Educational Research Journal, 19,* 465–471.

Stake, J.E., and Levitz, E. (1979). Career goals of college women and men and perceived achievement-related encouragement. *Psychology of Women Quarterly, 4,* 151–159.

Stanworth, M. (1981). *Gender and schooling: A study of sexual divisions in the classroom.* London: Women's Research and Resources Centre.

Steinkamp, M.W., and Maehr, M.L. (1984). Gender differences in motivational orientations toward achievement in school science: A quantitative synthesis. *American Educational Research Journal, 21,* 39–59.

Stern, C.S. (1983). Parties as reflectors of the feminine sensibility: Woolf's *Mrs. Dalloway* counters James's *The Wings of the Dove. Communication Quarterly, 31,* 167–173.

Sternglanz, S.H., and Lyberger-Ficek, S. (1977). Sex differences in student-teacher interactions in the college classroom. *Sex Roles, 3,* 345–352.

Sternglanz, S.H., and Serbin, L.A. (1974). Sex role stereotyping in children's television programs. *Developmental Psychology, 10,* 710–715.

Stewart, L.P., and Gudykunst, W.B. (1982). Differential factors influencing the hierarchical level and number of promotions of males and females within an organization. *Academy of Management Journal, 25,* 586–597.

Stockard J., and Johnson, M.M. (1980). *Sex roles: Sex inequality and sex role development.* Englewood Cliffs, NJ: Prentice-Hall.

Stockard, J., Schmuck, P., Kempner, P., Williams, P., Edson, S., and Smith, M.A. (Eds.). (1980). *Sex equity in education.* New York: Academic Press.

Stoppard, J.M., and Kalin, R. (1983). Gender typing and social desirability of personality in person evaluation. *Psychology of Women Quarterly, 7,* 209–218.

Strauss-Noll, M. (1984). An illustration of sex bias in English. *Women's Studies Quarterly, 12,* 36–37.

Streicher, H.W. (1974). The girls in the cartoons. *Journal of Communication, 24*(2), 125–129.

Sussman, L., Pickett, T.A., Berzinski, I.A., and Pearce, F.W. (1980). Sex and sycophancy: Communication strategies for ascendance in same-sex and mixed-sex superior-subordinate dyads. *Sex Roles, 6,* 113–127.

Swacker, M. (1975). "The sex of the speaker as a sociolinguistic variable." In *Language and sex: Difference and dominance,* ed. B. Thorne and N. Henley, 76–83. Rowley, MA: Newbury House.

Tan, A.S. (1982). Television use and social stereotypes. *Journalism Quarterly, 59,* 119–122.

Tauber, M.A. (1979). Sex differences in parent-child interaction styles during a free-play session. *Child Development, 50,* 981–988.

Taylor, M.S., and Ilgen, D.R. (1981). Sex discrimination against women in initial placement decisions: A laboratory investigation. *Academy of Management Journal, 24,* 859–865.

Tedesco, N.S. (1974). Patterns in prime time. *Journal of Communication, 24,* 119–124.

Terborg, J.R. (1977). Women in management: A research review. *Journal of Applied Psychology, 62,* 647–664.

Thaler, B. (1983, October). Gender stereotyping in the comic strips. Paper presented at the Sixth Annual Communication, Language, and Gender Conference, New Brunswick, NJ.

Thomas, A.H., and Stewart, N.R. (1971). Counselor response to female clients with deviate and conforming career goals. *Journal of Counseling Psychology, 18,* 352–357.

Thompson, E.G., Hatchett, P., and Phillips, J.L. (1981). Sex differences in the judgment of interpersonal verbs. *Psychology of Women Quarterly, 5,* 523–531.

Thompson, S.K. (1975). Gender labels and early sex role development. *Child Development, 46,* 339–347.

Thorne, B. (1979). Claiming verbal space: Women, speech and language in college classrooms. Paper presented at the Research Conference on Educational Environments and the Undergraduate Woman, Wellesley College, Wellesley, MA.

Thornton, A., and Freedman, D. (1983). The changing American family. *Population Bulletin, 38,* 3–42.

Tibbetts, S.L. (1976, Fall). Elementary schools: Do they stereotype or feminize? *Journal of the National Association for Women Deans, Administrators and Counselors, 40,* 27–33.

Todd-Mancillas, W.R. (1981). Masculine generics = sexist language: A review of literature and implications for speech communication professionals. *Communication Quarterly, 29,* 107–115.

Todd-Mancillas, W.R. (1984). Evaluating alternatives to exclusive he. *Communication Research Reports,* 1, 38–41.

Toohey, J.V. (1982). Popular music and social values. *Journal of School Health, 52,* 582–585.

Trecker, J.L. (1971). Women in U.S. history high school textbooks. *Social Education, 35,* 249–260.

Trecker, J.L. (1973). Sex stereotyping in the secondary school curriculum. *Phi Delta Kappan, 55,* 110–112.

Treichler, P.A., and Kramarae, C. (1983). Women's talk in the ivory tower. *Communication Quarterly, 31,* 118–132.

Trotter, R.J. (1983, August). Baby face. *Psychology Today,* pp. 14–20.

Tuchman, G., Daniels, A.K., and Benet, J. (eds.). (1978). *Hearth and home: Images of women in the mass media.* New York: Oxford University Press.

Turow, J. (1974). Advising and ordering: Daytime, prime-time. *Journal of Communication, 24*(2), 138–141.

Up the ladder, finally. (1975, November 24). *Business Week,* pp. 58–68.

U.S. Commission on Civil Rights. (1979). Window dressing on the set: Women and minorities in television. Washington, DC: U.S. Government Printing Office.

U.S. Commission on Civil Rights. (1979). Window dressing on the set: An update. Washington, DC: U.S. Government Printing Office.

U.S. Department of Education, National Center for Educational Statistics. (1981).

U.S. Department of Health, Education, and Welfare. (1978). *Taking sexism out of education.* New York: The National Project on Women in Education. (HEW Publication No. 0E77-01017)

U.S. Merit Systems Protection Board. (1981). *Sexual harassment in the federal workplace: Is it a problem?* Washington, DC: Office of Merit Systems Review and Studies.

Veiga, J.F. (1977). Women in management: An endangered species? *MSU Business Topics, 25*(3), 31–35.

Verna, M.E. (1975). The female image in children's TV commercials. *Journal of Broadcasting, 19,* 301–309.

Vetter, L. (1975). Sex stereotyping in illustrations in career materials. Paper presented at the meeting of the American Psychological Association, Chicago.

Vincent, J.P., Friedman, L.C., Nugent, J., and Messerly, L. (1979). Demand characteristics in observations of marital interaction. *Journal of Consulting and Clinical Psychology, 47,* 557–566.

Ware, N., and Steckler, N. (1983). Choosing a science major: The experience of women and men. *Women's Studies Quarterly, 11,* 12–15.

Warren, D. (1978). Commercial liberation. *Journal of Communication, 28*(1), 169–173.

Wasserman, G.A., and Stern, D.H. (1978). An early manifestation of differential behavior toward children of the same and opposite sex. *Journal of Genetic Psychology, 133,* 129–137.

Weitzman, L.J., Eifler, D., Hokada, E., and Ross, C. (1972). Sex role socialization in picture books for preschool children. *American Journal of Sociology, 77,* 1125–1150.

Weitzman, L.J., and Rizzo, D. (1975). Sex bias in textbooks. *Today's Education, 64*(1), 49–52.

Welch, M.S. (1980). *Networking: The great new way for women to get ahead.* New York: Harcourt Brace Jovanovich.

Welch, R.L., Huston-Stein, A., Wright, J.C., and Plenhal, R. (1979). Subtle sex-role cues in children's commercials. *Journal of Communication, 29*(3), 202–209.

West, C. (1978). *The passionate perils of publishing.* San Francisco: Booklegger Press.

West, C., and Zimmerman, D.H. (1977). Women's place in everyday talk: Reflections on parent-child interaction. *Social Problems, 24,* 521–528.

West, C., and Zimmerman, D.H. (1983). "Small insults: A study of interruptions in cross-sex conversations between unacquainted persons." In *Language, gender and society,* ed. B. Thorne, C. Kramarae, and N. Henley, 102–117. Rowley, MA: Newbury House.

Whalen, C.K., Flowers, J.V., Fuller, M.J., and Jernigan, T. (1975). Behavioral studies of personal space during early adolescence. *Man Environment Systems, 5,* 289–297.

Wheeless, L.R., and Grotz, J. (1976). Conceptualization and measurement of reported self-disclosure. *Human Communication Research, 2,* 338–346.

Wheeless, V.E. (1984). A test of the theory of speech accommodation using language and gender orientation. *Women's Studies in Communication, 7,* 13–22.

Wheeless, V.E., and Berryman-Fink, C. (1985). Perceptions of women managers and their communicator competencies. *Communication Quarterly, 33,* 137–148.

Wheeless, V.E., Berryman-Fink, C., and Serafini, D. (1982). The use of gender-specific pronouns in the 1980's. *The Encoder, 9*(3–4), 35–46.

Wigutoff, S. (1982). Junior fiction: A feminist critique. *Top of the News, 38,* 113–124.

Wiley, M.G., and Eskilson, A. (1983). Gender expectations: Slippery rungs on the corporate ladder. *Sociological Focus, 16,* 99–106.

Will, J.A., Self, P., and Datan, N. (1976). Maternal behavior and perceived sex of infant. *American Journal of Orthopsychiatry, 46,* 135–139.

Willis, F.N., and Hofmann, G.E. (1975). Development of tactile patterns in relation to age, sex and race. *Developmental Psychology, 11,* 866.

Wilmot, W.W. (1980). *Dyadic communication,* 2nd ed. New York: Random House.

Wilson, K.L., and Shin, E.H. (1983). Reassessing the discrimination against women in higher education. *American Educational Research Journal, 20,* 529–551.

Wolpe, A.M. (1977). *Some processes in sexist education.* London: Women's Research and Resources Centre.

Women on Words and Images. (1972). *Dick and Jayne as victims: Sex stereotyping in children's readers: An analysis.* Princeton, NJ: Women on Words and Images.

Women on Words and Images. (1975). *Channeling children: Sex stereotypes in prime-time TV: An analysis.* Princeton, NJ: Women on Words and Images.

Wood, M.M. (1966). The influence of sex and knowledge of communication effectiveness on spontaneous speech. *Word, 22,* 112–137.

Woods, M.M. (1975). What does it take for a woman to make it in management? *Personnel Journal, 54,* 38–41, 66.

Worell, J. (1980). New directions in counseling women. *Personnel and Guidance Journal, 58,* 477–484.

Yerby, J. (1975). Attitude, task, and sex composition as variables affecting female leadership in small problem-solving groups. *Speech Monographs, 42,* 160–168.

Young, J.W. (1978). The subordinate's exposure of organizational vulnerability to the superior: Sex and organizational effects. *Academy of Management Journal, 21*, 113–122.

Zaleznik, A. (1970). Power and politics in organizational life. *Harvard Business Review, 48*(3), 47–60.

Zimmerman, D.H., and West, C. (1975). "Sex roles, interruptions and silences in conversation." In *Language and sex: Difference and dominance*, ed. B. Thorne and N. Henley, 105–129. Rowley, MA: Newbury House.

Zucker, K.J., and Corter, C.M. (1980). Sex-stereotyping in adult-interaction: Some negative evidence. *American Journal of Orthopsychiatry, 50*, 160–164.

Index